LONDON'S CONTEMPORARY ARCHITECTURE +

A Visitor's Guide

Ken Allinson

Third Edition

Architectural Press

AMSTERDAM   BOSTON   LONDON   HEIDELBERG   OXFORD   NEW YORK
PARIS   SAN DIEGO   SAN FRANCISCO   SINGAPORE   SYDNEY   TOKYO

London's Contemporary Architecture +

Dedicated to:

Monica Pidgeon: as friend, mentor and, above all, a huge model of unflagging enthusiasm for architecture and its practice.

Thanks to the following for all their invaluable and unselfish assistance in putting this book together:

Jean Fisker

Martin Hartmann

Jeni Hoskin

Leonora Robinson

Nicolette Spera

Victoria Thornton

And also to the building owners, architects and members of their offices who have provided material used in this book.

Credits:

Book design by Ken Allinson.

All drawings, diagrams, sketches and photos by Ken Allinson except as noted below.

Other images are courtesy of the following:

Cover courtesy of Allies and Morrison (The place; photo Denis Gilbert)

Allford Hall Monoghan Morris: p167 (CAD drawing R.D.)

Allies and Morrison: p190 (CAD drawings); 167 (int. photo)

Brian Avery: p72 (RADA); 104 (Imax)

Richard Baker: 119; 125 (top rt.)

Bennetts Associates: p154 (H.T.)

Branson Coates: p164 (stair)

Buschow Henley: p72 (Talkback)

Dixon Jones: p76 (top and bottom photos - Denis Gilbert); 77 (axo); 103 (fountains at night)

Bill Dunster Architects: p182

Eldridge Smerin: p155 (Lawn House)

Tony Fretton / Helene Binet: p184

Foster and Partners: p46 (No.1 London Wall); p66 (section and plans); p67 (old conditions); 68 (work on roof); 180 (studio; Albion)

Guy Greenfield: 189 (H.G.P.)

Nicholas Hare Architects: p153 CAD image

Martin Hartmann: p9; 56/57 (except 9NT top right and top left; 91/92/93; 114 (Fashion House), 140, 180 (security cameras)

Haworth Tompkins: p105 (close ups, interior court)

Inskip and Jenkins: p103 (aerial of S.H.)

Katsuhisa Kida: p24 (top, boottom and interior shot)

Laban Centre: p116 (by Merlin Hendy - Photoshop processed by KA); 137(two at bottom + dancers)

Lady Susan Lasdun: p99 (interior photo, NT 1976, by Donald Cooper)

Lifschutz Davidson: p102 (section)

John McAslan: p136 (T.C.M.); 152 (R.A.M.)

David Marks & Julia Barfield: capsule drawing

Mile End Park: p167 (Ecology building)

John Miller: p96 photos of Tate Britain

Richard Rogers Partnership: p28 (Board Room); p188 photo (C.B.P.)

Ian Ritchie Architects: 180 (middle photo of C.P.B.)

Paddington Basin: p143

Patel and Taylor: p130 (all except bottom right); p131 (plan)

Terry Pawson: p181 (P.H.)

Quay 3: p179

Sarah Wigglesworth: p157 (S.H.)

Julia Wright (Wapping Project): p123

Wright and Wright: p166 (all except top photo)

Maps based on MIM and the author's own material.

Who is the guide for?

This guide suggests what is good, contemporary and accessible, but it also lists other examples of good architecture when they are nearby, regardless of historic period. It is a guide for those of you who enjoy experiencing architecture, whether you are a Londoner or a visitor with a limited amount of time to see what the city has to offer.

How to use the guide

Buildings have been listed geographically, into the areas and neighbourhoods you might want to visit. They are divided between contemporary buildings of primary interest and other buildings that are 'nearby' – a description including both other modern and historical buildings (at the bottom of the pages).

Buildings are located on maps at the beginning of each section.

If there is something in particular you want to get to, or a particular architect whose work you are interested in, we have provided a full index.

About the author

Ken Allinson is a practising consultant architect and teacher, and founding Trustee of London Open House. He lives in London.

About this Third Edition

• We have increased the guide to 200 pages and many new buildings have been added.
• We have added a 'Riverside' section because this has suddenly become a major dimension of the central London experience.
• The 'Inbetweens' section has now been merged into the 'West End & Whitehall' section.

Architectural Press
An imprint of Elsevier
Linacre House, Jordan Hill, Oxford OX2 8DP
200 Wheeler Road, Burlington, MA 01803

First published 1994 (Ken Allinson and VictoriaThornton)
Second edition 2000 (Ken Allinson and VictoriaThornton)
Third edition   2003 (Ken Allinson)

British Library Cataloguing in Publication Data
A catalogue record for this book is available from the British Library

ISBN 0 7506 5848 7

Printed and bound in Italy

For information on all Architectural Press publications
visit our website at www.architecturalpress.com

Contents

Earth has not anything to show more fair:
Dull would he be of soul who could pass by
A sight so touching in its majesty:
The City now doth, like a garment, wear
The beauty of the morning; silent, bare,
Ships, towers, domes, theatres, and temples
lie
Open unto the fields, and to the sky;
All bright and glittering in the smokeless air.
Never did sun more beautifully steep
In his first splendour, valley, rock, or hill:
Ne'er saw I, never felt, a calm so deep!
The river glideth at his own sweet will:
Dear God! the very houses seem asleep;
And all that mighty heart is lying still!

Composed Upon Westminster Bridge,
William Wordsworth, 1802.

Meetings With Buildings

Architecture is commonly presented as an orderly, linear narrative. But for those of you keen to *experience* it rather than read about it, architecture is a more complex mix that simultaneously comes to you from many directions, both literally and metaphorically. This is especially true in London, where the enthusiast has to be prepared to have a cacophony of historical periods, tastes, values, constructions, and scales thrust upon them all at once.

You have to cope. You will have to piece together a puzzle when the individual parts are mixed up, when some are damaged, altered, added to or otherwise disguised, when some are missing and others don't fit. You have to juggle and juxtapose, making your own order, constructing your own meanings and forming your own architectural geography.

Curiously, one frequently discovers these ornaments of the metropolis to be somewhat mute, revealing little about themselves, especially how they came to be what they are. In this sense it is true to say that architecture - like other cultural phenomena - has two dimensions to its narrative content. One is formal, evidence-based, and ostensibly rational and objective - the stuff of history books and the delight of adademics. Those involved in the making of architecture will also know another, parallel truth: one that is subjective, probably distorted and gossip-laden. These written and oral traditions develop in parallel and both are real. However, attention to either the chat or the accepted academic history is but a complement to an experience of the thing itself. In the final analysis, these peculiar constructs we call architecture make little sense as other than I aesthetic experience of the body, even if they might be keenly attended by the mind.

In pursuit of architectural experience you are likely to become more eclectic and stretch your values, to become as excited by the parts as wholes, as fascinated by the 'almost all right' as the acknowledged icons, as intrigued by the implicit struggles and challenges that materiality bears witness to as you are by the actual thing in itself. Rather than reach any conclusion, your explorations are likely to deepen and become more complex.

It is with this in mind that we offer you this guide to London's contemporary architecture.

What is contemporary? The recent, the current, the modish, of course: the voices of those currently engaged in renewing the city's fabric. However an experience-oriented guide that blinkers itself into denial of the notable historic neighbour or the adjacent architectural curiosity would be narrow-minded and unreal - in the final analysis our subject is the metropolis as a living architectural fabric whose contemporaneity inevitably manifests many kinds of continuity. Hence the '+' sign after the title.

Whilst this courts the danger of falling between two stools, we remain convinced that any guide is, by its nature, edited and our choices are based upon years of guiding people around London and many other cities. The text selects what we consider to be significant and seeks to get at what is essential and important about a building. Where warranted, we sometimes treat a single building in more depth. Occasionally, a building you know of might not be listed. This is almost surely to be because it is entirely inaccessible or the owner has deferred publicity, etc. Similarly, shops and cafes, etc., can be very short-lived and any reference to such comes with that warning.

You will always find a full address and a map location. If you have Web access, you can use the full postal code for detailed map information through 'Multimap' or someone similar.

In the final analysis the guide cannot be the thing itself. Enjoy the book, but enjoy the buildings themselves even more.

Ken Allinson

The City

Charles Birch's griffin, poised upon a pillar designed by Horace Jones, sits in the Strand opposite George Street's Royal Courts of Justice (1872–84) and marks the western-most boundary of a part of London rich in architectural interest, perhaps more so than any similarly sized area in the metropolis. It is a place where contemporary developments have been insinuated into an ancient fabric whose street pattern is saturated with historical reference. In its efforts to stay modern, no other part of London changes so rapidly, and yet is so bound by tradition.

For a significant part of its history, the City of London has functioned as a social club whose limitations were circumscribed by a walk of ten minutes from its functional and symbolic heart at the Bank of England. Histories of the place (such as the superb quartet by David Kynaston) suggest that this was almost as true in the 1970's as it had been in the 1920's or even fifty years before that. However, the City did began to significantly change after WWII, even if there was little significant rebuilding until about 1960. (In 1957, Pevsner's survey of the City deplored what he termed 'the shockingly lifeless and reactionary' new building work), but 1959 saw new regulations that prompted what has been described as 'an orgy of new building'.

After that time - particularly after the so called 'Big Bang' of mid-'80's deregulation - the City not only became socially more open, but broke its traditional geographical boundaries, spread and engendered satellites. In these years the financial district spread east into the heart of the former Docklands, particularly to Canary Wharf. It spread west across the geographical boundary of Farringdon Road (beneath which the Fleet River still runs), into the Fleet Street properties left vacant by the newspapers who had also moved east. It has even crossed south of the river, in Southwark.

Whilst the City remains substantially mono-functional, it would be true to say that it has evolved from a small, inward-looking place to an amorphous beast with a strong centre of gravity but without the readily perceptible historic boundaries it once enjoyed - boundaries that have been, in effect, those of Roman and medieval London. And the inverse of this coin is that inhabitants have started to colonise City areas, replacing banks with bars, coffee houses and even apartments.

If there is an outstanding architectural debate in the City, it has to be the issue of scale and tall buildings. Older tall buildings such as the NatWest Tower (Tower 42) have been remodelled and rebranded; newer ones such as Fosters 'erotic gherkin' have literally given the City a new profile. Meanwhile, smaller sites continue to aggregate into larger ones while the dynamics of urban renewal once again provide London with the privatised streets we thought had long vanished.

But there's more to the City than the current service of global capitalism, especially for an architectural enthusiast. Explore a small area such as Wood Street and you will discover contemporary buildings by Farrell, Rogers, Foster and Grimshaw (all Lords and Knights) insinuated between older ones by Wren, Jones, Gilbert-Scott, McMorran, Powell and Moya, and Chamberlin Powell & Bon. You will also come across the remnants of Roman and medieval walls, streets that are a memory of the Roman fort once on this site, churches and old graveyards from a less secular age, the almost forgotten enthusiasms of optimistic 1950's planners who over-built the ruins and wild flowers of war-time damage, and the polished brass plaques of older institutions (sometimes literally) tucked in among the new buildings.

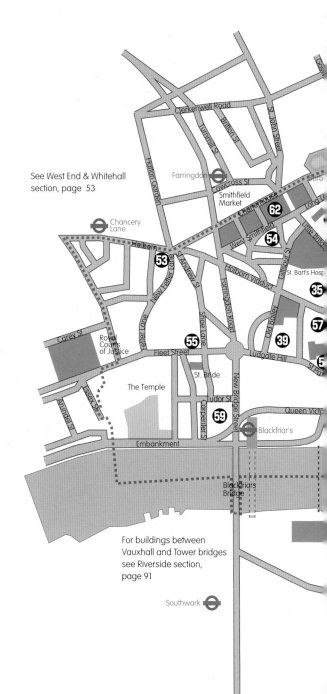

See West End & Whitehall
section, page 53

For buildings between
Vauxhall and Tower bridges
see Riverside section,
page 91

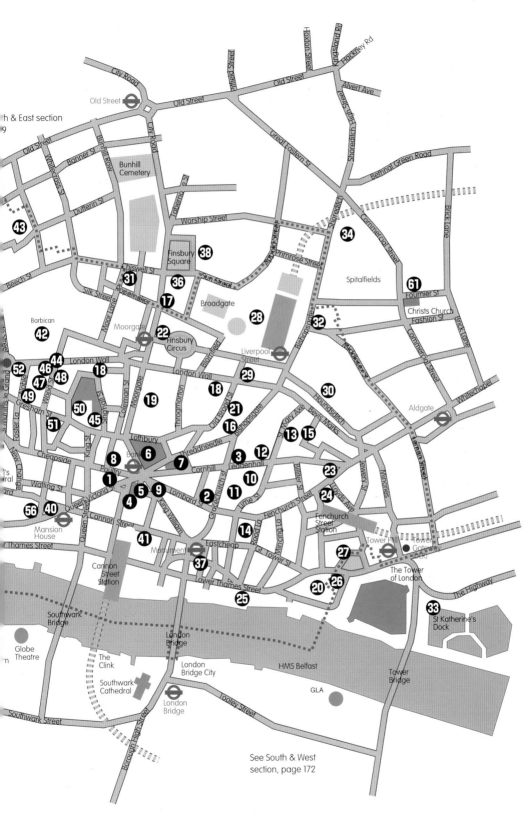

See South & West
section, page 172

Recent City Architecture

The City has undergone three major periods of dramatic change in its history: during and after the great fire of 1666, when two-thirds of the buildings burnt down; during the bombing of WWII, when a third was destroyed or damaged; and during two recent periods of commercial reconstruction that straddle the early 1990's recession. In the first of these, between 1985–93, approximately one half of the floor space was replaced or renewed. The same thing has been happening again during the post-recession boom of the 1990s. The most impressive buildings in the latter period have come from the same architects who dominated the former one: Rogers and Foster, now both Lords of the realm. The Rogers office has given the City 88 Wood Street and Lloyds' Register. The Foster office has given many more, but it is their Swiss Re building that literally and metaphorically stands out.

Many developments (such as Merrill Lynch, More London and Tower Place, apart from older ones such as Broadgate and that satellite of the City, Canary Wharf) continue to serve the demand for large floor plates, resulting in a coarsening of the urban grain and profoundly ambiguous spaces that are ostensibly public but actually private spheres where one's right of way is closely scrutinised and a camera is likely to produce distressed security guards who politely (but 'firmly') point out that photography is not allowed. Private initiatives are hardly new and historians frequently point out that it is private capital that has always fuelled London's development, additionally noting that private landlords are usually more scrupulous in maintaining their properties than municipalities. Perhaps, but there is something profoundly disturbing in finding that one hundred years or more since private gates to London squares were removed by Act of Parliament we are experiencing new and subtle forms of 'gating' that effectively curtail freedom in the streets. Whether the drivers of this pattern truly concern insecurity, or are compounded by growing inequalities in English society that feed upon our traditional cultural propensity toward class distinctions, is beyond the scope of this guide, but it would fit with traditions in the City.

Principal City Areas:

A, central Conservation Area
B. Ludgate, around St. Paul's, to Farringdon Road
C. Barbican
D. Northern expansion, to Old Street
E. Eastern fringe, including Spiltalfield

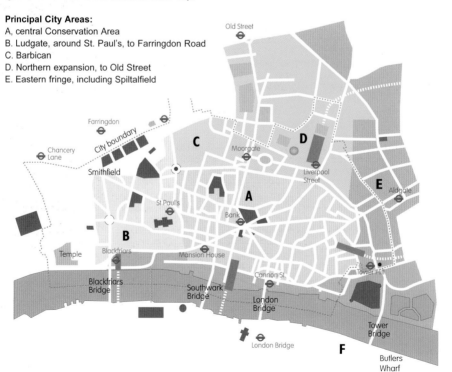

S tand outside Tower Hill tube station and you see around you almost 2000 years of London history. In front there are the remains of a Roman wall built sometime around AD50 and now embedded in later medieval additions. Beyond that wall is the moat and walls of the Tower of London, built during the C11 by William the Conqueror as alterations to the Roman fort formerly on this site.

To the right, overlooking Trinity Square, sits the baroque pile designed by Sir Edwin Cooper (1912–22) for the Port of London Authority (PLA), an organisation which attempted to govern activities within a complex spreading eastward from 'the Pool' beneath London Bridge, one serving trade from what was the world's first global empire and a facility plagued by pilfering and managerial problems. Beside it is Trinity House, designed by Samuel Wyatt in 1792 for those who were guardians of coastal shipping traffic and governors of the light-houses of England and Wales. In front of it (now insurance offices with interiors refurbished by Michael Hopkins) sits a memorial garden and a small edifice designed by Edwin Lutyens and dedicated to the many sailors who died in WWI.

Across the road, dug into the ground, lies a late-1980's, Post-Modern, rustic shed by Terry Farrell, for many years housing a McDonalds hamburger restaurant for tourists who visit the Tower. To the left, is the entrance to the Docklands Light Railway – access to the former Docklands area, for a long time one of the largest areas of urban renewal in Europe. On the eastern side of Tower Bridge (built to a design by the architect Horace Jones and the engineer John Wolfe-Barry, 1886–94) you will see the smallest, newest, and most expensive of the upstream London docks: Thomas Telford's St. Katherine's Dock, opened in 1828 and now a marina. Across the bridge is Southwark Cathedral (C12, but heavily 'restored' in the C19) and Butlers Wharf – a compact area of docklands renewed in the last decade, but remaining one of the more coherent parts of the former docks. And beyond Tower Bridge, over on the southern side of the Thames, you will be able to see More Place - a huge development of speculative buildings by Foster (again), together with the 'strawberry' of the development - London's newest symbol of civic pride: City Hall, the 'blob' that is home to the Greater London Authority and the Mayor of London.

Turn around and you can walk through the back streets of the City, past Fenchurch Street rail station (opened in 1841 and now joined by Richard Rogers' Lloyd's Register building), toward the Bank junction – the heart of the City of London. Here, you will be at the centre of a metropolitan area that can no longer afford rigid planning policies, which must always be ready to adapt its physical fabric in order to provide the buildings corporations consider to be most appropriate to global financial trading. Examples of change are likely to be all around. And sometimes this dynamic of renewal forms fascinating groupings overlaid upon a historical context that insists upon manifesting itself.

T he best of these groups is probably around Wood Street - once the central north-south street that ran through the Roman fort of Londinium, terminating at Cripplegate, where St Giles Church now stands within the Barbican. Terry Farrell's post-modern exercise straddling the realigned Roman Wall bravely attempts to reinvent this gate as Alban Gate and provide a new gateway up to the Barbican deck designed by Chamberlin Powell & Bon. To Farrell's right sits once of the best of post-war office buildings in the UK: Richard Rogers' 88 Wood Street. Its neighbour is 100, Wood Street, another office building, this time by Foster. Opposite it is one of the literally 'strangest' of London buildings: the Wood Street Police Station, continuing the long tradition of prisons and police stations in this area. Behind that is the Guildhall complex, dominated by its history and the Gilbert Scott family's architectural contributions. At the opposite end of Wood Street to Farrell is yet another Foster building - this time neo-Miesian, eschewing all forms of 'blobism'. Opposite that is a Gresham Street building by Farrell's former partner, Nicholas Grimshaw. And behind that yet another Foster design (No.1 London Wall). And in the inbetween spaces all around the area are remains of the old medieval wall, churches with towers but no body, churches left to us as foundations, and churches as former graveyards now used as summer places to eat sandwiches, and even two complete churches: Wren's St Lawrence Jewry and his St Anne and Agnes. All of this in what is effectively the scale of one, small urban block. That's how architecturally rich the City is.

1.

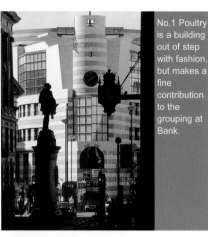

No.1 Poultry is a building out of step with fashion, but makes a fine contribution to the grouping at Bank.

View inside the tiled rotunda - up to the roof restaurant and roof garden landscaped by Arabella Lennox-Boyd.

No. 1 Poultry
le coq on Poultry

The design of this building (begun in 1985) was, by its completion in 1998, stylistically anachronistic: a strident post-modern building that might have been more appropriately completed ten years earlier.

The building's developer, Lord Palumbo, is also a major figure in arts funding. His father began considering redevelopment of this difficult triangular site and its 1890, neo-Gothic buildings designed by John Belcher, with a scheme drawn up by the late Mies van der Rohe in the mid-1960s (Mies died in 1969). The initiative proposed demolishing the existing set of rather small and well-formed buildings, aggregating the sites and replacing them with a large piazza and shoe-box tower (a common City development patter, apart from issues such as the criticism from Prince Charles that the proposed building was a 'glass stump'). Controversy followed, alternatives were put forward (notably by conservative interests and Terry Farrell), and Palumbo jnr. turned to Stirling and Wilford for another proposal – a stunning design that eventually won planning permission (this took place just after Stirling and Wilford's Staatsgalerie had opened in Stuttgart).

No. 1 Poultry is deliberately designed as a symmetrical, axial scheme whose flamboyant mannerisms are argued to contexturally relate to its neighbours (Lutyens, Soane, Hawksmoor, Tite, Wren). Shops are on the ground floor and a mall at basement level links through to Bank station. The top level houses a Terence Conran terrace restaurant (*Coq d'Argent*) with terrace landscaping by Arabella Lennox-Boyd. In between are five floors of speculative office space. All this is organised around a central, open court (formally massed as a rotunda) which also allows the public to pass through the heart of the building and down to a lower level concourse connected to the Underground.

The prominent corner turret looking toward Bank is a satisfyingly strong piece of architectural gamesmanship formally reminiscent of what was there before, but if we can never remember what was there before, the gesture loses its meaning (although some critics argue it to be a roguish quotation of a celebratory Roman rostral column!). In any case, such theatricality is a reminder of how, in other hands, a marriage between the developer's vanity and '80's Post-Modernism could produce some peculiar designs. The building also appears to lack those elements of surprise and invention that made his work so intriguing, as well as the deftness and humour one associates with Stirling – the witty irreverence that lifted his work above the mainstream.

The building joins the company of Lutyens' Midland Bank, Soane's Bank of England screen wall, Dance's Mansion House, Wren's St Stephen Walbrook and Hawksmoor's rusticated facade of St Mary Woolnoth as a notable architectural exercise at this most significant corner of the City. However, No. 1 suffered the difficulty of completion after the recession of 1990 to 1994, an interlude engendering a massive redefinition of architectural fashions whose most notable feature was the termination of 15 years of architectural Post-Modernism and its overnight replacement by a revived, less baroque and theatrical Modernism, more likely to be inspired by work in Barcelona than Chicago (although, ironically, Mies is back in fashion!). Many people feel that they *should* love this building. Bemusement at its outmoded idiosyncrasity is more likely. The media even reported that the building was designed in a spirit of derivative homage by a Stirling associate rather than the man himself (it was, in any case, completed posthumously by Michael Wilford & Associates, now also a closed practice). Such is the secret history of buildings, a clouded oral narrative which buildings themselves do little to elucidate. However, times change and in a few years this strong design might become respected for what it is rather than disparaged for being merely outmoded.

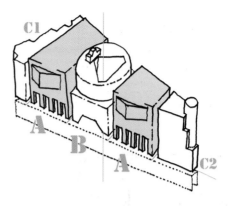

1.

The current design bears within it the memory of both what was on the site previously and the original ideas of 1986, which sliced the site into four disparate parts, including the retention of the John Belcher corner building. This evolved into an A-B-A rhythm flanked by a western service end and a new eastern prow bearing elements of Belcher's design (including the clock and a salvaged terracotta frieze of 1875 by Joseph Kremer on the Poultry side). One difficulty with such architectural games is that they are front-end biased (toward the sensitivities of planners) and the experience depends entirely upon memory - and who can remember a building once it has been demolished?

2. ***Barclays Bank HQ,*** *GMW, 1994. This has to be one of the least distinguished buildings in the City - a Post-Modern design completed in 1994 when everyone (including developers) had gone somewhere else. But it's interesting and is by GMW, who have so many buildings in the City. The peculiarities of this headquarter building for Barclays Bank includes references to Stirling (the neo-Egyptian cornice, from his Stuttgart Gallery), to Otto Wagner (the late C19 Viennese gold decorations on the cornice), and to Rogers (the Lloyd's atrium top. But see it in context, not just with the other buildings in the adjacent alleys, but in terms of GMW's City output that includes the former Banque Belge, the Commercial Union and the ground level lobby of Tower 42.*

3. *The former **Banque Belge**, GMW, 1975 is on the corner of Bishopsgate and Leadenhall, EC. It is a very elegant attempt to make the bottom / middle / top equation work in the Georgian manner: almost entirely with well considered geometrical proportions. The problem is that it should be much taller – in which case it might have put the Commercial Union to shame. Compare it with that building, the rather bizarre, neo-Gothic Minster Court, and the Barclays Bank HQ on the corner of Lombard and Gracechurch (1994) and the base of Tower 42 - all of them by GMW. The entrance canopy on Leadenhall is a later addition of about 1999.*

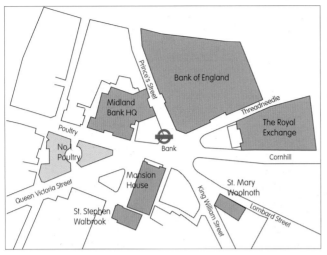

Bank is a place where something like seven roads crush together at a single focal point like jobbers onto a good deal. This is the geographical and symbolic heart of British capitalism, at the centre of a City Conservation Area (that now covers over one third of the City) and a wonderful group of buildings by architects of significance. Whilst the most dominant and prestigious building is now the Bank of England, the design product of John Soane and two of Britain's best known inter-war architects, Edwin Lutyens and Herbert Baker. But it is the Royal Exchange that best establishes the principle of historical continuity and was for a long time one of the most important buildings in the City.

4. *St Stephen Walbrook, 1672-80, is among the better Wren churches in the City, on the south east side of Bank) - a centrally organised church damaged in wartime bombing and now*

fully restored with a modern altar by Henry Moore (1972), sitting at the heart of an interior with distinctly 'Scandinavian blonde' overtones set against the dark browns of Wren's late C17 aesthetic (which still includes the pulpit). Worth a visit. Foster is building a large office building to the south.

5. *The Mansion House, with its squashed portico facing onto the Bank junction, is the official residence of the Lord Mayor of the City of London. It was designed by George Dance the Elder in 1739–52, originally having two tall additions above the pediment line – lopped off (as if in some Freudian gesture) by his son, George Dance the Younger. The pediment sculptures depict the City defeating Envy and Bringing Plenty.*

6. *The **Bank of England** is the most significant building at Bank. It is monolithic and fills the entire urban block, but should be read as two buildings: Sir John Soane's original work dating from 1788–1808, and Sir Herbert Baker's work which rises above the perimeter walls, from 1922–39. The former is a superbly articulated fortress, an original 'ground-scraper', filling the block, with few external openings in its expertly articulated perimeter wall. Behind it was a masterful complex inspired by the buildings of Ancient Rome, drawing daylight from above into rooms where clerks made up their books by lamp-light. By Baker's time, the architect could throw a power switch and achieve the same effect and his architecture removes Soane's work and rises up proudly in its place from behind the old walls. Quite rightly, Baker has been vilified for obliterating Soane's masterpiece, but even his work has features to enjoy (especially if the Bank is open for London Open House - an occasion when you can make comparisons with the similar grand interiors of Edwin Cooper's former Port of London Authority building at Tower Hill.) However, Soane's (mostly blank) walls are, in themselves, an architectural delight.*

7. Like Lloyd's of London, another significant building at Bank – the **Royal Exchange** – was, until recently, another exercise in cultural continuity masking architectural differences. The first Royal Exchange was founded as a place of international commerce and built 1566. It burned down in the Great Fire of 1666 and then rebuilt, only to be burned down again in the 1830's. Each architectural exercise provided the same fundamental configuration of accommodation around a central court where people could meet. The original building had an arcaded court and the present building of 1841-44, by Sir William Tite has a central court that was covered over when the building was refurbished by Fitzroy Robinson in 1990. It was then converted again (2002) into a smart, European style court of expensive shops - in a sense returning the space back to its original intentions as a trading place (even if this is at a rather less strategic and more frivolous level!). .

8. Edwin Lutyens was one of Britain's most acclaimed architects up to his death in 1944. This bank HQ he designed for **Midland Bank** (1924-39) and is a good example of the old man cheerfully fronting (literally and metaphorically) a design executed (millennium style) by others. Somehow, an irascible character comes through: look at the detailing and the Lutyens-designed little boy with goose. Try entering the bank hall from the side and leaving through the opposite side, attempting to deny the latterday tat that promotes financial services and the like the old hall and all its pretensions is still there, not yet a cafe or bar.

9. **St Mary Woolnoth** (1716–27), at Bank, is especially noteworthy among the works of a man (Nicholas Hawksmoor) who served for a long time under Wren and finally came into his own relatively late in life. Despite its difficult site, the architectural elements are almost abstractly simple, underscoring the symbolic geometries that once had so much significance and embodying the C18 sense of the Sublime as something at once wonderful, awesome and terrible. It seems appropriate that this building should sit near to Stirling's No.1 Poultry. One of six churches by this architect: also see St George Bloomsbury (just south of the British Museum); St George-in-the-East, Wapping; St. Alphege, Greenwich; St. Anne, Limehouse; and Christ Church, Spitalfields.

10.

Lloyd's of London, Lime Street, EC3
Richard Rogers Partnership, 1978–86
Tube: Bank

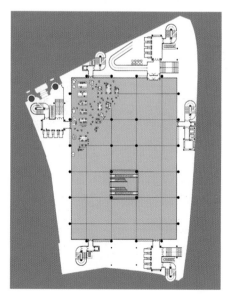

The Lloyd's 1986 Building
an exercise in continuity

The 47,000 sqm Lloyd's 1986 Building is established as a Modernist icon and has become an accepted part of the City fabric, even if it is now overtaken in the glamour stakes by newer neighbours such as Foster's St Mary Axe building, Rogers' own Lloyd's Register around the corner, and suffering a degree of internal abuse.

But the building makes little sense located outside the context of the client's status and history: one of the most prestigious, respectable, and long-established institutions within the secretive world of the Square Mile, an insurance market so-called 'Names' gamble their wealth against the possible misfortune of others through the medium of insurance underwriters and brokers. It was after one of the worst periods of such misfortune and the beginning of a new mass market for insurance that Lloyd's found itself needing and able to move itself from premises in the Royal Exchange to a new, custom-designed building in Leadenhall Street. That was in 1923 and the completed '1928 Building' was designed by Sir Edwin Cooper. The fundamental organisation of this building was followed through in each of the subsequent buildings Lloyd's constructed, including the Rogers design.

The 'grand manner' Portland stone entrance portico in Cornhill is now all that remains of the 1928 Building. From its entrance vestibule a passage led to a palatial, square, double-height hall, 1500 sq.m. in size, lit by a central roof light and huge, suspended light fittings, and dressed in Subiaco marble. At its centre was the 'caller's rostrum' and the famous Lutine Bell: rung, by tradition, whenever a ship was sunk. A secondary underwriter's entrance in Lime Street served as a kind of rear door to the Room (as the market hall was called).

Within eight years of moving into the 1928 Building Lloyd's was expanding into an adjacent building and, after WWII, business had grown to such an extent that a gallery was considered for the Room. However, this proposal was superseded by a scheme to completely rebuild the adjacent building according to the designs of Terence Heysham: what was to become the '58 Building'.

Like its predecessor, the 1958 Building was fundamentally a tall, marbled, top-lit space complete with an array of hanging light fittings; upper floors were for support staff. Lloyds had been able to expand horizontally, stretching the Room into the largest air-conditioned volume in Europe. They were also able to provide a gallery (for the relatively newer, non-marine insurance markets, such as cars and aviation), to bring along the rostrum for the Lutine bell, and also the timber linings and plasterwork of a 1763 country estate dining room designed by Robert Adam – which became the linings of the 'Adam Committee Room' in a new Committee Suite. The underwriting space was now about 4100 sq.m.

By the early 1970s the need for additional accommodation had returned and the Lloyd's Committee

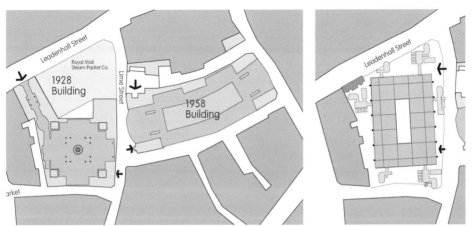

The '86 Building sits on the site of the '28 Building and was designed by Edwin Cooper (1873–1942); he was responsible for the 1932 corner building at Bank, opposite Stirling & Wilford's No.1 Poultry and adjacent to the Midland Bank by Edwin Lutyens; he was also architect of the Port of London Authority building at Tower Hill (1912). The portico of his '28 Building has been retained, both as memory and urban design device lending continuity between the isolated Lloyd's block with the other buildings that stand shoulder to shoulder, lining the street.

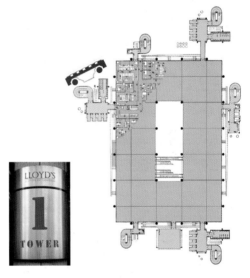

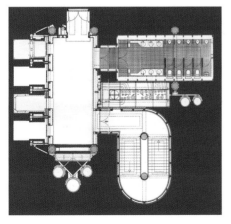

The 'servant towers' of the Lloyd's building have three principal, theoretical roots: the idea of 'served' and 'servant' spaces (as dealt with by Louis Kahn in the USA) the upbeat, Archigram diagrams of the 1960's; and Reyner Banham's celebration and articulation of the idea of an architecture that was more about the service elements than traditional elements of structure and enclosure. The towers - comprising escape stairs, toilets, lifts, lift lobby, and various risers - are almost entirely prefabricated and are intended to be easily replaceable. However, Lloyd's is unlikely to ever again have the funds to test this theoretical possibility. A more important benefit of the strategy was clear internal spaces, particularly within the Room, where only the escalators interrupt the market place.

10.

Escalators originally swept underwriters and brokers up to multiple galleries, above which was a public gallery. The latter was soon removed and the former shrunk back as Lloyds faced difficulties after opening.

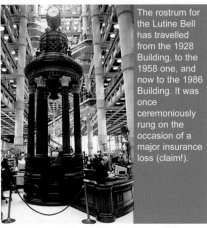

The rostrum for the Lutine Bell has travelled from the 1928 Building, to the 1958 one, and now to the 1986 Building. It was once ceremoniously rung on the occasion of a major insurance loss (claim!).

initiated a search for architects who might design a building to last, not 25 years again, but 125 years! The outcome was a Richard Rogers Partnership design for the site of Cooper's building, a scheme which allowed Lloyd's to retain the 1958 Building for support staff (later converted by DEGW, who added two large and separate basement food courts - for the underwriters and the Lloyd's staff. By late 2002 this building was scheduled for demolition).

Like its predecessors, the1986 Building – as it became known – is all about the Room. Recreating it on the 1928 Building's site meant that expansion had to be vertical rather than horizontal. The single gallery

Heysham designed now became five galleries of insurance market. The rooflights of the 1928 and 1958 Buildings now became a cathedral-like atrium. The marble was reinvented as high specification concrete and the circular, hanging light fittings as sophisticated, specialist-designed, fittings ubiquitously provided for all interior spaces: Room, galleries, offices and even the Chairman's suite on the upper floor. In the latter, the Adam Room was recreated in all its wonderous and incongruous glory as a classical building accommodated within the Roger's edifice – an odd Post-Modern note in an otherwise radically Hi-tech design.

The most controversial aspect of the architecture is undoubtedly the decision to locate all services on the exterior. This daring rationale ostensibly derived from the need to keep the market floors entirely clear of intrusions and has been hailed as both romantic (akin to Gothic cathedrals) and truly modern (one of the most advanced technological edifices in the western world). However, debate concerned with the merits and demerits of oil rig aesthetics has carried another sub-text. The cultural values of Lloyd's, as a rapacious, capitalist City institution with deeply conservative instincts (after moving into the 1986 Building they retained the basement of the 1958 Building as a practice shooting range), proved, in the long run, to be profoundly at odds with those of its left-wing, egalitarian architects fresh from completion of a *grand projet* in Paris. The project's history saw an apparent exemplar of designer–client relations become an adversarial battle between modernist architects and their more reactionary, public school clients – particularly when it got down to who sat (more advantageously) where and on what within the stacked trading galleries. Discontent became rife, focusing on all kinds of design issues.

Problems included a bright blue carpet which was replaced by a biscuit-coloured pattern worthy of a tawdry provincial office; a special design (by Eva Jiricna) for the 'boxes' at which the underwriters sat – diluted to accord with demands they should be just like the old, teak and uncomfortable boxes of the 1958 Building; window 'sails' designed by Jiricna for the Captain's Dining Room (the Underwriter's formal dining space) – unceremoniously removed whilst her granite floor was covered by more tawdry carpet.

In the background were political and financial difficulties threatening the future of the market and paralleling the last years of building completion. These continued and, by 1994, the building had been sold to a German developer – an act soon to be followed by a massive financial claim against the Rogers Partnership for problems with the external pipework and the sale of the '58 building (now being redeveloped). A common denominator between designer and client, one concerning a love of risk, daring and an ambition to make public statements had not overcome cultural disparities and the misfortunes of fate. Will the building last or slowly deteriorate, possibly to be replaced by something more economic?

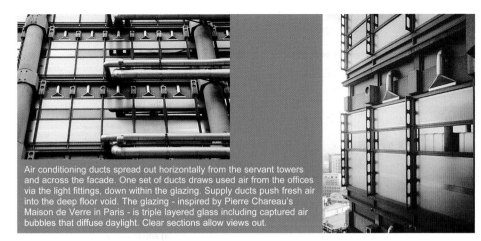

10.

Air conditioning ducts spread out horizontally from the servant towers and across the facade. One set of ducts draws used air from the offices via the light fittings, down within the glazing. Supply ducts push fresh air into the deep floor void. The glazing - inspired by Pierre Chareau's Maison de Verre in Paris - is triple layered glass including captured air bubbles that diffuse daylight. Clear sections allow views out.

11. **Leadenhall Market** (Horace Jones, 1881), on the east side of Lloyd's, is the masterful reinvention of a poultry market which has been here since the C14. Jones exhibits fine architectural gamesmanship. For example, the ostensible formal geometry of the scheme is anything but that in reality and Jones cleverly insinuates his big idea into the surrounding fabric with a series of local and contingent moves. Examine the manner in which he extends southward from the central crossing, pushing the facade concept as far as it will go - even where there is no building behind because of 'rights of light' issues - in an effort to reach out to the surrounding streets that define the urban block. There is an urbanity here that merely awaits the economic

conditions that will bring the market back to life outside of a narrowly defined lunch-time trade to City workers. Remove the parking and get a farmer's market in here! Come on City: wake up! As an example of good backlands utilisation, Leadenhall and similar places (such as Bow Lane) implicitly offers a severe criticism of City redevelopment patterns that pool sites in favour of ever larger buildings and denude formerly rich backland places of their vibrancy. For example, you can walk from here westward through a series of alleys to Bank, passing bland walls of white ceramic brickwork (to reflect daylight) and circular plaques that remind one there was once a pub or coffee house on this site. However, on the way you will also touch upon areas such as that behind St Peter's church, where this same vibrancy and a mix of building scales is still (just) maintained, indicating what is still possible. Such examples are certainly the most severe criticism of the Planner's '50's and '60's enthusiasm for decks and bridges (as at the Barbican).

12. The **Commercial Union** building (GMW 1969, is a classic example of the post-war, North American tower-and-piazza equation that makes a comparison with a later generation's values across the road at Lloyd's as well as with the likes of (less well designed) 1960's City towers that lined London Wall. It's an elegant building that was sympathetically but entirely reclad after the IRA bomb that went off at the nearby Baltic Exchange in the early April 1993 (the bomb that prompted a rebuilding resulting in Foster's 'erotic gherkin'). The major criticism is the usual one for such an architectural equation: the piazza is not entirely unpleasant, but remains a rather inhospitable place.

Like its contemporary neighbour (the lower, former **P&O Building** to the immediate west, now sporting a cheerful 1998 piazza entrance canopy lit by fibre-optics) the CU once had one of those 1st floor decks ('pedways') beloved of the LCC's '50's and '60's planners, waiting to link into a spreading City network that, in 1965 was planned to be 35m in extent. Go around the corner to Leadenhall St. and you will see this dream literally come to an abrupt halt up against a 1929 **Midland Bank** by Lutyens, manifesting the presumption that the bridge would naturally leap from the former P&O building across the gap and that Lutyens' 'grand manner' bank would, in time, fall down before its utterly inevitable progress.

13.

9 St Mary Axe, EC3
Foster and Partners, 2003
Tube: Monument, Bank

St Mary Axe
size matters

In 2003 the City finally got the building to outpace Lloyds' '86 building: Foster's 'erotic gherkin' - opposite Lloyds and adjacent to GMW's elegant Commercial Union building (120m), counterpointing Seifert's Tower 42 a few blocks away (183m; formerly the NatWest Tower, the building that has dominated the City skyline since 1981).

Whilst the overwhelming reality of the 180m high, 40 storey building (76,400 sq.m.) is its dramatic sculptural form and its dominance of the skyline, a key feature of the building's internal organisation is its spiralling lightwells that wind around the building and cut across the simple, circular plan providing a perimeter of office 'fingers' around a central core - visible from afar as a wrapping, tonal banding to the building's triangular glazing pattern. The Buckminster-inspired form enjoys all kinds of instrumental rationalisation: it is described as 'environmentally progressive', the lightwells allowing light to penetrate and they can ventilate the offices thus reducing air conditioning loads (all assisted by an aerodynamic form that sets up appropriate pressure differentials); the stiff diagrid skin eliminates the conventional bracing function of the central core; the glass skin is ventilated; the glazing allows full perimeter views; the tapering geometry reduces reflections and wind disturbance at ground level - which also benefits from an otherwise enlarged public space on a comparatively tight

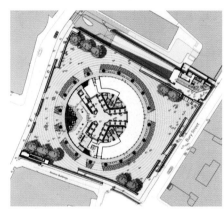

site (as at the Ark). Like the best of Foster's work, the design has a self-evident clarity about it. Unfortunately, the diagrid is heavily encased with fire protection and the internal lining is on an orthogonal grid (perhaps, in part, explaining the dark glass).

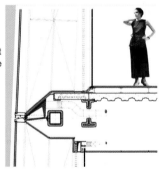

The magic of the building is its spiralling lightwells. These generate 'fingers' of office space radiating from the central core.

Minster Court

The three buildings of this 59,000 sq.m. complex form a 'groundscraper': low and flat, filling the urban block and respecting street lines. Targeted at the insurance market (Lloyd's is around the corner), it's also an idiosyncratic re-creation of those C19 battles between the Classical and Gothic traditions – this time complete with neo-Gothic entry court pillars straight off the CAD screen ('wireframe' representations that will surely date the building precisely to any future archaeologist) and three horses of the Apocalypse straight from the early 1980s London exhibition of the horses from St Mark's Square in Venice. The forecourt with its large glazed roof and inbetween spaces are described as 'public'. They're not, and are gated off at weekends. Beyond them are bars and restaurants. One's principal complaint has to be that the theatre doesn't go far enough. The piers and arches, for example, are disturbingly non-structural and one longs for a Michael Hopkins version of the same game (it would be real!). However, behind the facade games, the three blocks of offices conform to what has been the accepted convention for office design for some time: access floors, suspended ceilings, 1.5 m. planning grids, etc.. The facade itself conforms to another convention of the 1980s: granite cladding, a symbol of robustness and durability, superceded in the 1990s by a softer fashion for limestone.

The building is worth comparing with other GMW City architecture over the years: the elegant Commercial Union building opposite Lloyd's, the former Banque Belge building (the low block on the corner), the Barclays Bank HQ on Gracechurch Street (a most peculiar, bombastic mix of Otto Wagner, Terry Farrell and Jim Stirling), and the new lobby to the Nat West Tower. These buildings provide a unique record of changing architectural fashions within one practice.

14.

Minster Court is three buildings as one, offering a large forecourt area pretending to be public. Like many similar developments this is a lie (canary, broadgate, etc.) This is private space.

15. *Just north of Lloyd's, through an alley off St. Mary Axe, in Bury Street, EC3, sits a remarkable building, **National Employer's House** designed by the Dutch architect H.P. Berlage in 1914, after a US visit (engendering a Sullivan inspiration). This is a building designed for tight City streets and has to be seen obliquely, when the green glazed facade mullions (spaced at 1.3 m. centres and sat upon a brick base) read as a solid wall of tiling. Then move along and watch the windows reveal themselves. The mullions decrease in size, ostensibly manifesting the decreased loads being carried. The small lobby is about all that exists of the original interiors. Go around the corner where the building pops out again and see the wonderful corner sculpture by Joseph Mendes de Costa.*

16. ***Gibson Hall** (1864-5), by John Gibson, on the corner of Bishopsgate and Threadneedle, is a fine example of Victorian, neo-classical banking architecture designed as the HQ of a bank that replaced a neo-Palladian mansion formerly on the site. Externally, the hall is a fine, single-storey screen of large arched windows and giant order columns topped by allegorical statuary (worth comparing with the Bank of England). Inside, there is a large banking hall whose counters were not removed until 1982, after which time the place became an assembly hall and rentable venue. The adjacent Threadneedle Street has many 'grand manner' bank buildings from 1850-1920, now becoming death masks as their insides are hollowed out and rebuilt.*

17.

1 South Place, EC2
Sheppard Robson, 1996
Tube: Moorgate

Helicon

This confident 22,000 sq.m. speculative office building is of interest because it was one of the first significant buildings built after the early 1990s recession and because it helped to define re-established, Modernist fashions. It also manifests current enthusiasms for glass as well as a concern with energy conservation and the control of solar gain as a functional basis for architectural articulation. For example, some facades are triple glazed, incorporating a 900 mm gap with aluminium louvres and acting as a thermal flue that can be opened at the top in summer and closed in winter. The plan has four service cores on the perimeter, whilst floor spaces are arranged around a central atrium beginning at level three, above a retail element at the lower levels.

18.

Deutsche Bank is given a thin, refined aesthetic which plays off the shear scale of the building and its facade as it runs along the street.

Deutsche Bank, London Wall, EC2
Swanke Hayden Connell Architects, 1999
Tube: Liverpool Street.

Winchester House

The sleek London home of the largest bank in the universe (Deutsche Bank) is a speculative office building designed by the American firm Swanke Hayden Connell and fitted out by Pringle Brandon, offering the tenants accommodation that includes three open floor plates of 4,600 sq.m., each with 650 people (described as a dealing factory). On London Wall it streams along the street as a huge, gentle wave with delicately detailed aluminium windows that curve around the corner and punctuate the wall of Lussac limestone cladding. On entry into the grand lobby and between deals the building users can gaze upon expensive art work (including work by Anish Kapoor, Rachel Whiteread and James Rosenquist) that, no doubt, reassures them they are not Philistines, even in the workplace.

19. *The **Institute of Chartered Accountants** is a building to be read in three stages. The first was a much-praised building designed by John Belcher (1889–83), in Great Swan Alley, EC2, north of Bank. Forty years later and in another era his ageing partner, Joass, added an eastern extension – exactly like Belcher's earlier work. Another 35 years later William Whitfield (master planner of Paternoster Square) came along to make major additions. Rather incongruously, he again extended the Belcher and Joass facade in the original manner, turned a corner and added a lively baroque door feature which appears to say: "There you are Mr. Belcher: I can also do it as well as you, in your language." And then, in the same breath, he switches to the current 'served & servant' Modernism of the late 1960s: expressed functional elements differentiated from the office floors, brutalist concrete, large areas of glass, etc. Few buildings exhibit such a skilful architectural gamesmanship (but see Horace Jones at Leadenhall). It's a rare and artful, old fashioned skill (quite unlike the self-conscious display of mannered gamesmanship exercised by Venturi at the Sainsbury Wing) that can be a source of joy to practice and experience.*

Tower Place

Foster publicity for this rather elegant 42,000 sq.m. office building claims it as a reinvention of the famous, early '70's Wills Faber design replacing taller and 'insensitive' 1960's designs, and the medieval grain of small buildings and streets. Two triangular plan buildings are linked by a large atrium to be used as a ventilated (as Hays Galleria) sheltered 'public plaza'. With its fine views, "the stone and glass facades . . . allow maximum daylight penetration, while blade-like aluminium louvres provide solar shading and add a shifting textural layer to the facades." Their claim that what was once *avant garde* is now mainstream misses the point that it is the demand for large floor plates and not the design that is mainstream. And coarsening the grain remains no more desirable now than Ian Nairn found it to be in the 1960's.

20.

Tower Place, Tower of London, EC3
Foster and Partners, 2003
Tube: Tower Hill

21. *'Colonel' Seifert's* **Tower 42** *(completed between 1970-81), at 25 Old Broad Street, EC2, has been - until recently - one of the City's least missable buildings and once the headquarters of the NatWest Bank*

(called the NatWest Tower). The building towers 183 m high and cantilevers its floors from a massive concrete core – so massive that its builders argued it to be as much steel reinforcing as concrete. Consquently, the plan offers a thin periphery of offices (similar to the Smithson's Economist Building). However, the intelligent London pigeon will notice that the plan is that of the NatWest Bank's logo (although no one is any longer quite sure which came first).

After the IRA bombing of 1993 which prompted much rebuilding and refurbishment in this area, the ground floor area (free of columns because all loads come to ground via the core) was given a large glazed lobby, designed by GMW and the entire building was rebranded, reclad and internally refurbished rather than demolished (too difficult and expensive). The transatlantic rebranding is no doubt aimed toward the presence of many US organisations in the City since deregulation in the mid-1980's. Internally, Fletcher Priest did the upper level restaurant and cafes - but they aren't accessible unless a tenant takes you there!

22. **Brittanic House** *(1921-5), in Moorgate (and Finsbury Circus) is another Edwin Lutyens design, unfairly criticised by Pevsner for the 'Americanism' of columniated upper floors. It's enjoyed superb modifications to the interiors by Inskip & Jenkins (1987-9).*

23. *It is on a triangular site at the east end of* **Fenchurch Street**, *EC3, confronting car drivers arriving into the City from the east, that Terry Farrell offers us a solution to the corner problem to be read as a set of interpenetrating bodies, a kind of architectural 'hinge' (1987). Compare it with Stirling & Wilford's later design at Bank). The building is an avowedly Post-modern composition, together with a strong, implied classical arrangement of base, giant order, cornice and attic storey. The cramped entrance lobby around the side, on Leadenhall Street, struggles to offer us an impressive experience but, overall, the building is so much better than other, contemporaneous offerings from the Po-Mo lobby.*

24.

71 Fenchurch Street, EC3
Richard Rogers Partnership, 2000
Tube: Bank

Lloyd's Register
jam in the do-nut

At a plot ratio of 8:1 overall and 11:1 (build area to site area) for the new build parts, the Lloyd's Register of Shipping building is a dense piece of development, squeezed into he site of existing premises like jam injected into a the heart of a do-nut. The building is large and the design is clever: a professional achievement that simultaneously satisfies the requirements of City planners, the client and the passer-by in the street. Lloyd's wanted lots of space. The planners wanted old buildings and facades retained. And, as passers-by, we all want something to engage and enjoy. This design certainly does that. Old and new are married together in a complex manner that - as with all good design - appears effortless and, as a solution, self-evident. Which, of course, it isn't. As at Wood Street (same Director in charge) the conservative street experience belies a much more robust and bloody-minded reality deeper within the site. But the architects have achieved this magnitude of building and high density with a sensitivity to scale. This is especially evident in the entry court - a former churchyard: tight, cramped, over-powered by soaring glass lifts that silently glide up the side of the building . . . and yet is comfortable and pleasant.

Lloyd's Register goes back to 1689, sharing common roots with Lloyd's insurers (for who, Rogers did the '86 building). However, the Register established its own identity in the late C18 and by 1901 it had its own building, designed by T E Collcutt (described as 'arts & crafts baroque'). Lloyd's later expanded into nearby buildings and, in the 1920's acquired and demolished the church of St Katherine Coleman, building more accommodation. And they kept on growing.

In 1993 Lloyd's intended to move its 1300 staff out of the City, but this failed to come to fruition and it was decided to remain in the City, rebuilding on the existing site with a brief for a 24,000 sq.m. (net area) building, a minimum net/gross ratio of 70% (actually quite generous, but reflecting the site difficulties), a high plot ratio (which, as built, is 8:1 overall and 11:1 for the new parts), and the potential for a significant amount of sub-

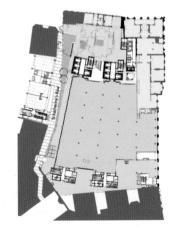

letting (which has turned out to be about 50%). To which the Rogers team added an energy-efficient element.

The Collcutt building is the one that sits on the corner of Fenchurch Street and Lloyd's Avenue, and which has been so cleverly integrated into the new facilities designed by a team led by Graham Stirk (as for 88 Wood Street) so that the better parts of the old building have been retained.

Apart from integrating new and old in this manner, the design strategy is similar to that of the Lloyd's '86 building and 88 Wood Street: an 80:20 equation as managers say, in which most of the accommodation is simple and rational, whilst the remaining part is complex. ('You can solve 80% of the problem in 20% of the time; the other 20% of the problems takes 80% of the time'; a rule of thumb derived from economic theory). The 80% part is the central part that has been described as a series of 'wedges', two of which rise to 14 stories. The 20% is the remainder - refurbishing the old buildings and knitting the old and new together (and adding another storey to be as Listed Collcutt building). On Fenchurch Street, between the East India Arms on one corner and the Collcutt building on the other, sits a building that the architects and their client intended to demolish and replace with a glass pavilion. But the planners refused. And they were right, because it is the contrasts that make this overall configuration work so well.

The 'jam in the do-nut' - the new, central block of office accommodation - comprises a series of 'wedges' nominally 9m wide (but tapered) with atria inbetween. However these intermediate atria are not consistent divisions and the planning results in some very deep floor plates at the lower levels. The key point to be made is that these structures attempt to be as rational and consistent as possible, whilst finding discreet points at which they knit together with existing buildings and similar site constraints.

The structure is mostly precast concrete with some elements poured on site to form a composite structure. Wherever possible, this is exposed so that it can play a role in providing thermal inertia. This allows night-time cooling and so reduces the peak heat gain /

cooling issue during office hours (when computers and lights are heating the place up). These spaces are serviced by a deep plenum computer floor - into which fresh air is pumped - and by a ceiling level light beam / chilled beam fitting that obviates the need for the dreaded suspended ceiling. It also means the architects could provide a coved section to the ceiling soffit (to reflect light).

As with 88 Wood Street the new parts have floor to ceiling glazing, providing excellent views and lots of daylight obviated when necessary by external, motorised louvres. (Although the incompatibility between the energy conservation of lots of daylight and the issue of glare on computer screens remains as ambiguous as ever.) Each cladding element is 3m x 3.250m; there is an inner sheet of laminated glass plus an outer one of solar protective glass; the assembly is shaded by motorised, perforated aluminium louvres. These louvres are tracked, so they can be slid sideways to clean the window glass.

The external lift cores are supported on steel frames and clad in glass - and it is these features that enliven and articulate the building.

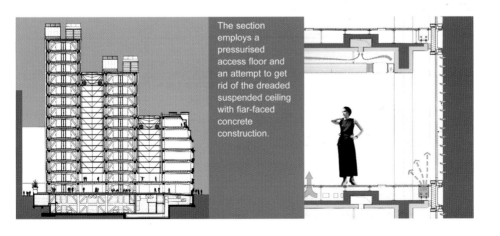

The section employs a pressurised access floor and an attempt to get rid of the dreaded suspended ceiling with flar-faced concrete construction.

25.

Lower Thames Street, EC3
Richard Rogers Partnership, 1988
Tube: Tower Hill

Steel mezzanine floors hang from the original columns. Much of the accommodation is below ground in former storage vaults.

The view from Hays Galleria, with the Barclays Bank HQ (GMW, 1994) in the background. The total floor area is 11,200 sq.m. and the dealing floor was the largest in the City when built.

Billingsgate
one that got away

When the fish market moved out of Billingsgate, they left a building designed by Horace Jones in 1875 and considered to be ripe for redevelopment into deep trading spaces (this was the booming, deregulated City of the mid-1980s). And then the prospective tenant – who was going to ferry staff from here to other offices across the river in London Bridge City – pulled out. What to do? The Rogers team handling the conversion had artfully created mezzanines hanging from the existing structure, brought in diffused daylight via prismatic lenses, created habitable space within deep underground vaulting and, in the process, struggled against a melting permafrost which the stored, frozen fish of generations had formed in the mud beneath the Thames' waters. It was exasperating. Then came IRA bombs and the need for emergency City space, persuading needy tenants that these peculiar spaces had potential. Abortive project work is always painful for those involved and it was good that the building was finally used in a similar way to that intended. But that period ended and, at the end of 2002, Billingsgate's splendid spaces were being used for City parties.
      So what's wrong? The lower floors are literally cavernous; they'd make a great club. The ground floor with its mezzanines suspended from the original columns is spacious, but the City now has more choice. It would make a great . . . market . . . but it's on the wrong side of an urban race-track called Lower Thames Street. Hope lies in a revitalisation of the limited public walkway along the river frontage - surely an opportunity to reinvigorate this fine building?

26. *This half-sunken building on the west side of the Tower of London (Tower Hill Terrace) is both physically and architecturally discreet. Designed by Terry Farrell, its theme is a return to constructional fundamentals of a neo-classical sort, a kind of rustic, 'primitive hut' to house tourist conveniences. The presence of MacDonald's lends the building the kind of populist 'decorated shed' qualities that Robert Venturi (once Farrell's teacher and architect of the Sainsbury Wing) would probably admire. The building keeps company with Sir Edwin Lutyens' similarly scaled war memorial across the road and might well have been an*

acknowledgement of his worthy temple in homage of the maritime dead of WW1.

27. *The **Port of London Authority** at 10 Trinity Square, EC3 was designed by Sir Edwin Cooper (1912, architect of the first Lloyd's building). His baroque wedding cake, designed as the managerial home of the PLA, stands high and proud, looking over the former, busy but troubled dock areas, as if its imperialist bombast might bear upon the workers even as its massing proudly welcomed ships into the Pool of London beneath the Tower of London. Neptune looks down upon the scene from his niche on high and the street level offers 'grand manner' gestures that are attractively urbane in scale.*

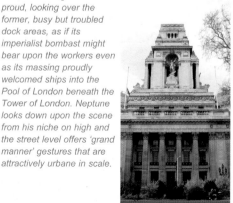

Broadgate
a battle of giants

The story of Broadgate embraces issues of urban change (on a large scale), architectural politics (a battle between modernist traditions and post-modernist sentiments), and a common ground probably unacknowledged by either of the main protagonists. The narrative begins with No. 1 Finsbury Avenue, on Wilson Street, one of the first developments to be targeted at a specific market (financial trading), designed by Arup Associates and their first adventure designing speculative office buildings. Finished in 1984, No. 1 was the 'foundation stone' of a scheme put together by two of London's then most prominent developers (Lipton and Bradman) and British Rail. In brief, the master plan demolished a small station (Broad Street) and amalgamated its services into an adjacent one (Liverpool Street), in the process unlocking the potential to develop a large tract of land on the edge of the City of London. (The contrast with adjacent areas to the north is striking.)

 The masterplan was put together by Arup Associates under Peter Foggo, but only the first half of the building programme was designed by them. The developer laid down stringent requirements and basically told his professionals how they were to design the buildings. Foggo reached a point where design constraints and the pace of development imposed upon him prompted a resignation and he left to set up his own practice (tragically dying of a brain tumour not long afterwards, in 1993). Meanwhile, in stepped SOM (Skidmore Owings and Merrill), an American firm simultaneously working on the Canary Wharf development in Docklands. Whilst Foggo was a part of that tradition concerned with honesty of construction, design integrity and those kinds of design values reaching back through the Arts and Crafts movement to Morris, Ruskin and Pugin in the last century, SOM's loyalties were to the historically-oriented eclecticism of an architectural Post-Modernism borne in the USA in the 1970s.

The Broadgate development totals about 325,000 sq.m. of lettable space, plus another 50,000 sq.m. lettable within the three Finsbury Ave. buildings. It all looks public but is, in fact, a private realm.

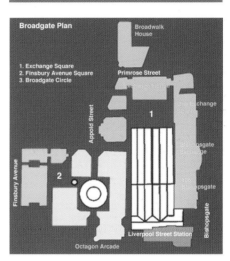

Broadgate Plan

1. Exchange Square
2. Finsbury Avenue Square
3. Broadgate Circle

Broadwalk House
Primrose Street
Appold Street
Finsbury Avenue
Exchange
...sgate
...sgate
Liverpool Street Station
Octagon Arcade
Bishopsgate

28.

Broadgate/Eldon Street EC2
Arup Assoc. & SOM, British Rail Architects 1984–92
Tube: Liverpool Street

Below: the arcade on Bishopsgate, the Liverpool Street entry into the station, and the 'neo-Guimard' Bishopsgate entry enclosure to the station.

28.

The designs of these two firms demonstrate a disparity of values guaranteed to cause one another severe discomfort. The common denominator was the developer, Stuart Lipton, who imposed his own standards upon the design and construction teams, insisting the buildings were clad in granite and that the interiors – whatever the external styling – conformed to a well-researched set of ideas concerning the modern office building of the mid-1980s. However, whilst Arup used the granite as a self-evident form of decoration, with open joints indicating that the stone is in no way load-bearing and getting rid of it as soon as possible (reverting to a picturesque skyline of aluminium cladding), SOM attempt to make the granite appear load-bearing, as it might have been used 100 years ago.

Arup's masterplan is rooted in the tradition of the West End squares of the later C18. There are three of them. The first – where we find No. 1 Finsbury Ave. – is characteristically British in character, moody and informally planted, now with moss growing between the dank cobblestones (which the management periodically attempts to eradicate with doses of chemical). The buildings around this square are all by Arup, although the entirely brown ones on two sides are technically a part of the earlier development and do not have the ubiquitous granite overlay.

The last square constructed is formal and axial, deriving inspiration from the *beaux arts* traditions in which American practice has its roots (and to which Post-Modernism returned, turning its back on the Bauhaus influences of the immediate post-war period). The detailing is 'big' and redolent of the Chicago from where it emanated, although there are distinct hints of H.H. Richardson's work in the rusticated sandstone of the landscaping. Broadgate Exchange – the building flanking the northern boundary – has to straddle the rail tracks and is made up of deep floor-plates carried by four huge parabolic arches, two of which plough through the centre building, whilst the other two articulate the exterior.

Winter skaters in the Arena. The greenery around the Arena is slowly being replaced by buildings in order to supplement the low retail content of the original scheme.

Between these two squares sits a third, the Arena, designed by Arup but with an American influence (Rockefeller Center). Like Exchange Square, it offers lunch-time events to entertain the Broadgate workers. In winter it becomes an outdoor ice-skating rink, complete with brightly attired kids and thumping music. However, underlying this C20 reference are other, historical inspirations. This is a columnated Roman ruin, the kind of ivy-covered, banked amphitheatre architects such as Palladio, Piranesi, Gibbs and many others would visit in order to draw inspiration from the Ancients and to rekindle what we always interpret as lost knowledge. This is the ruins of monasteries destroyed in the Reformation, now overgrown and profoundly romantic. From this perspective, Arup and SOM meet together, even if they do come from entirely different directions.

In between these two poles sits the design of the redeveloped Liverpool Street Station, by the former British Rail Architects Group. It is at once old and new, old rebuilt to be new and new dressed up to appear old. The entrance on Bishopsgate is a self-conscious attempt to recreate Guimard's Metro entrances in Paris, now with cast-steel joints and glass covering. The old roof of the station has been extended in the manner of the original construction. Old-looking brick towers are new concrete ones clad in stick-on brick. Part of the old hotel (now a McDonald's) looks too new to be true; in fact, it was taken apart and rebuilt brick by brick. The forecourt was styled with four large light fittings straight out of the then-influential public works in Barcelona. It's a well executed, if heady mix of values.

Left: No.1 Finsbury Ave. (1982-4) and the more 'English' landscaping of this square. This building was effectively the first of the complex (see aerial view on left). It has two major cores and a central atrium. Unlike the other buildings (esp. by SOM) it enjoys being over-planted.

28.

Above. The Arena and Exchange Square serve as entertainment venues and places to relax between and after work hours. Sadly, the Arena structure - once redolent with romantic associations (Roman and monastic ruins, etc.) is slowly becoming a building ('again' as it were).

Below. The circular building in Finsbury Avenue Square is the management block. The central photo is Bishopsgate Exchange, seen from the entrance on Appold Street. The photo on the right is the same building from Spitalfields.

An heroic external arch at Broadgate Exchange appears to be similar to an earlier US building (the Federal Reserve Bank. Minneapolis), now reversed.

28. Broadgate has made significant efforts to offer public art in the form of artists such as Richard Serra, George Segal, Fernando Botero, Barry Flanagan, Jaques Lipchitz, Jim Dine, Xavier Corbero, Stephen Cox, Bruce Mclean, Partrick Caulfield and Alan Evans, who all brave Philip Johnson's condemnation of such exercises as 'turds in the plaza': a cosmetic palliative on the instrumentlal face of capitalism. It's worthy stuff but argued by art curators to be an outmoded approach. At Canary Wharf they are into the 'entertainment economy' and public art there strives to be as much temporary and ephemeral as permanent.

29. *85 London Wall, EC2 is designed by the Casson Conder Partnership, 1990. It is a pleasant, rather small building (5,085 sq.m. gross) and sits at the opposite end of the spectrum to the size and 'footprint' of buildings such as Minster Court, those at Broadgate, or Foster's 'gherkin'. It is for the smaller organisation and professional user and was executed in an unfashionably anachronistic manner, employing pre-cast stone and concrete panels in order to achieve a rather collegiate look for this conservation area, as if it really belonged in Oxford or Cambridge. The stone is Portland and Juane limestone. The building is worth comparing with William Whitfield's work at Richmond House or Powell & Moya's QEII Conference Centre.*

30. *The spaces between the old warehouses and the new, rather ordinary modernist office buildings at **Cutlers Garden**, E1, just to the east of Liverpool Street Station, are the key to the pleasures of this complex on the edge of the City. In an understated way, the development manages to achieve more than similar schemes. Here is the virtue of comparative reticence and the care with which quiet and calm urban spaces have been reinvented from former industrial warehousing. Unfortunately, they're semi-private and the security guards sometimes let you know it. Have a look, but beware of questions about your camera. The architects were John Seifert Architects.*

Milton Gate

Like the National Theatre, Milton Gate betrays Denys Lasdun's fascination with diagonals and castles, as well as a peculiar lack of interest in entrances. Milton Gate is a block-filling, 20,000sq.m office building, cut by a diagonal route leading into an inner atrium, the exterior being entirely clad in green, double-walled glazing. It might be an intriguing technical and aesthetic exercise with both literal and metaphorical 'green' ambitions, but the design fails to appreciate the message it sends out: corporate defensiveness easily engenders a consequent sense of alienation. In this sense the building is, like his IBM office building adjacent to the National Theatre, less than a huge successful. However it is by an architect who could produce some stunning work and - we admit - many people love it.

31. 1 Moor Lane, EC2
Sir Denys Lasdun, Peter Softley & Partners, 1991
Tube: Barbican

Spitalfield

The redevelopment of the former Spitalfield market area should have overlapped the adjacent Broadgate development, but the early 1990s recession arrived. This EPR-designed office building of nearly 26,000 sq.m. is the first of the post-recession redevelopment and is in marked contrast to Broadgate, revealing the change in developer's tastes in the intervening period. The shape reflects planning constraints that allowed height on Bishopsgate and required low mass on the Spitalfield side. The next phase includes a 100,000 sq.m. Foster development called 1 and 10 Bishop's Square, E1, just to the east. The market buildings are to be refurbished for retail and related uses.
In 2000 Foggo Associates completed an 18,550 sq.m. office building called 280 Bishopsgate, north of the EPR building.

32. Offices, Bishopsgate, EC2/Commercial Street, E1
EPR, 1999
Tube: Liverpool Street

33. *When closed in 1968, the splendid warehouses of* **St. Katherine's Dock***, St Katherine's Way, E1, by Thomas Telford and Philip Hardwick, suffered mysterious fires. Eighty percent of what remains are modern versions that the planners insisted look vaguely like the originals. However, a few of the older warehouses remain from when the docks opened in 1828 and there are the pleasures of the marina, the Historic Ship Collection, and the spaces inbetween the buildings, making this an interesting example of reinvention and urban design. In 1999, Lord Rogers was commencing construction on the Europe House office building at St. Katherine's.*

34. *There was a time when London was proud of its welfare housing programme, begun with schemes like the Arts & Crafts* **Boundary Estate** *(1897–1900), at Arnold Circus E2, just north of Broadgate, an estate of 5,500 people at a density of 200 per acre, designed by LCC Architects. The programme ran right through to the 1970's and, even though the Boundary estate is now a sadly neglected and decrepit example, it still speaks of values to be proud of. Laid out as a series of apartment blocks radiating from a central, landscaped roundabout, it is comparable with the better preserved Millbank estate of the same date, behind the Tate Gallery.*

35.

Merrill Lynch & GlaxoSmith Global HQ, 2 King Edward St, EC1
Swanke Hayden Connell Architects, 2001
Tube: St Paul's

Merrill Lynch
Newgate spin

As the City renews itself it manifests a tendency to gobble up smaller buildings and reinvent them as large complexes with gigantic floor plates. Disguising such bulk is one issue. Integrating it into the urban fabric is parallel issue. In this instance the architects (the American firm, Swanke Hayden Connell) have done much to provide an office building almost as good as any in the City, but a visit to the 'public' spaces is likely to result in all kinds confusing experiences and run-ins with security guards who politely (but firmly) inform you that 'photos ain't allowed around 'ere, *sir*, and 'you jus' crossed an invisible boundary between the street and private territory, *sir . . .*' Like Broadgate and Canary, this is a private realm pretending it is public.

Despite all that, this is a good design that fragments its bulk into a number of parts with satisfying inbetween spaces. The 80,000sqm building serves ML with its requirement for very large floor plates (two of which are 6,200sqm) and even includes reclaiming Wren's bombed-out Christ Church as a garden. Adjacent to it, the frontage and main hall of the former post office on the site has been retained and refurbished (underneath the building are former PO tunnels). 3,500 people work here and the buildings have a 4,200 capacity. The overall aesthetic, in keeping with the client's requirement and the architect's sentiments, aimed for 'solidity, a sense of stability and of timelessness' and not the 'lightness and movement of the High-tech tradition' (David Walker, SHCA). He's a man who sees cities in terms of buildings, streets, squares and other spaces and not people and their movements. Which brings us back to where we started and the shame that some pleasant spaces inside this complex are not really a part of a public sphere. The notion that, as the Architect's Journal said, this building has civic qualities is at once true, yet pure spin.

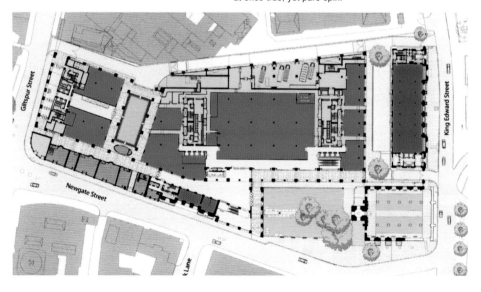

Bloomberg's

36.

Citygate House, 39-45 Finsbury Square, EC2
Foster and Partners / Julian Powell-Tuck, 2001
Tube: Moorgate

This is really a building to see on the inside, but you can get into the building's public art gallery and gain views through to the inner workings. On the outside this is two buildings: a 'grand manner' building from the 1920's adjacent to a new 17,000sqm commercial office building from Foster's studio (posing as SOM circa 1960), unified by Julian Powell-Tuck's interior work. The drama of these interiors stems from Bloomberg's expressive culture: as if the market leader (Reuters) woke up one morning to find it was an ad agency on something pharmaceutical. Bloomberg's actually a sophisticated number crunching shop and information service for financial institutions, but it's all high--energy stuff where staff are well paid, well served and given environments complete with swanky training facilities, a rolling art programme, large exotic aquaria on each floor, a lobby that doubles as a free cafeteria and more monitor screens than people. In fact Bloomberg TV is everywhere - and we mean everywhere, including the toilets and the cafeteria benches. Take it away and the energy level would drop dramatically. And much of the production takes place in Bloomberg's basement studios whose informality and economy is guaranteed to send shock waves through some media visitors.

What strikes one about Tuck's work is that he has managed to realise something authentic: a one-to-one match between culture and design. It might not be the BBC, Reuters or any ad agency one can think of, and it might not be a culture or design to your liking, but the authenticity sings through and demands one's respect. And the more one thinks about that point, the more one becomes curious about what 'good' design really is. Without good styling, the realised design won't command respect; but the presence of good styling alone will not achieve this - something more is needed.

37. *The **Monument** on King William Street, EC3 commemorates the Great Fire of London, 1666, and is designed by Christopher Wren and Robert Hooke (1671-6). We no longer create such monumental civic*

obelisks inspired by the example of the Ancients in order to commemorate important events and one half expects to find a sponsor's plaque at the base. The column used to greet visitors from the south until London Bridge was realigned and is worth a visit in order to experience its peculiarity and scale at ground level, and to enjoy the view of the City from the top.

38. *Eric Parry has completed an office on the east side of Finsbury Square, **30 Finsbury Square** that includes an unusual attempt at a west-facing office facade - worth examining.*

39.

SOM's work is nothing if not eclectic, happily mixing all kinds of style in the cause of entertainment architecture. Which is not to say they aren't good at it.

Ludgate Hill, EC4
Skidmore, Owings & Merrill, 1992
Tube: Blackfriars, St. Paul's

Ludgate Hill

This collection of buildings from the south side of Ludgate Hill, up Limeburner Lane to Fleet Place and Holborn Viaduct are all designed by SOM and completed in the heady days of the late 1980s 'bubble economy'. Forming a coherent grouping that totals some 50,000 sq.m. mounted on anti-vibration foundations and stretching some 1.5 km over realigned railway tracks going into Blackfriars station, they are designed as disparate buildings with varied inbetween spaces that are not without interest. However, the development betrays what the New York journalist, Neil Postman, described as a contemporary urge to amuse ourselves to death (the entertainment economy) – on this occasion in the form of SOM's notion of contemporary Modernism as a mix that includes the vaguely medieval black granite and stainless steel of 10 Fleet Place, sitting side by side with a mock *beaux arts* exercise of Santander House on the corner with Ludgate Hill.

Behind the facades is a similar workplace equation, making outside appearances a skilfully executed chocolate box wrapping (which, to be fair, is hardly unusual these days). This form of professionally dictated entertainment can be disturbingly inauthentic; it is skilful, but with little humour or joy; the surface dressing of an expertise seeking only to serve the client's underlying, instrumental purposes and always in danger of serving as a palliative for our sensibilities.

It's worth comparing this development with Broadgate (where a battle of styles can be seen; the same developer was behind the scheme), or Richmond Riverside, by Quinlan Terry (a more historically theatrical wrapping exercise).

40. *This five-storey 1973-7 office building designed by Whinney Son & Austen Hall sits opposite Bracken House (on the east side, 30 Cannon Street) and is in marked contrast to it. The building sits on the site of a Wren church bombed in WWII and is distinctly unfashionable and now curiously Germanic. Some architects argue that the building's raked, prefabricated glass-reinforced cement facade is a lot more interesting than*

Bracken could ever be! However, whilst the construction was innovative at the time, it mimics '60's load-bearing facades of the type constructed by Seifert and its literally hollow theatricality is the stuff, one suspects, of Hopkins' nightmares.

41. *Bush Lane House, at 80 Cannon St., EC4, designed by Arup Associates in 1972-6, is a idiosyncratic office building whose external, load-bearing stainless steel structure is water-filled as fire protection and the structure straddles the underground (originally, there was to be a station at the ground level). We await the boiling kettle experience. Meanwhile, one can enjoy the strong architectural imagery (a kind of 'branding') which is more typical of the 1990s than the 1970s.*

Wood Street Group
haunted modernism

It's commonplace to note that what was once radical becomes, with hindsight, considerably less so and more deeply embedded in history than we had initially thought. For example, the '86 Lloyd's building, when looked at closely, becomes an exercise in continuity; history and context assert themselves. It's a theme Peter Ackroyd takes up in what at first appears a rather fanciful manner in his excellent *Biography of London*: the notion that the city has a living character that surreptitiously asserts itself and affects what is done within its domain. Take the Wood Street area for example. Currently, it is a fascinating grouping of buildings, many of them very recent and including designs from Fosters, Rogers, Farrell, and Grimshaw. These buildings can all be seen to be accommodating themselves to historical memory, traditions and the detritus history has left as a proliferation of churches, their towers, former graveyards, pieces of Roman and medieval defensive wall, and streets that have their historical roots in Roman and later Medieval times. For example, the Wood Street area of London was once a Roman fort; its principal north-south axis is now Wood Street and at its northern end was a gateway that became known as Cripplegate (adjacent to St Giles Church, which still stands, now within the Barbican).

The physical manifestation of this rich history was badly damaged (and in many instances obliterated) in the Blitz of World War II. Christopher Wren's church of St Alban's, for example, survived only as a tower - the one that now stands in the centre of a widened street - and one has to imagine a scene that for many years took on a curiously romantic character as nature populated the ruins of what had become a garment area of large Victorian warehouses with grasses and pretty wild flowers. David Kynaston describes the Barbican area as 'virtually a wild heath, littered with the remnants of a commercial civilisation'. But the LCC planners saw it all as a massive opportunity to march optimistically into the future, taking the relaxed building controls of the mid-'50's as an opportunity to offer the City a realigned London Wall ('Route Eleven', the making of which unearthed hundreds of human skulls) and the Barbican.

And yet, in the 60 years since the Blitz and its devastation, the area has increasingly settled back into a manifest history. The Barbican - as an unconscious reinvention of the Roman fort - carefully knit its way around old Roman walls like an elephant avoiding eggshells; the Guildhall reconstructed its ruinously damaged halls and demarcated the line of a recently discovered Roman amphitheatre in the paving of its piazza; McMorran's police station reinvented the prisons of the street; Alban Gate attempted to recreate Cripplegate; and modern temples to Mammon from Fosters, Grimshaw and Rogers nestle up against preserved former churchyards.

1. Alban Gate (Terry Farrell)
2. 88 Wood St. (Rogers)
3. 100 Wood St. (Foster)
4. Police Station (McMorran) + St Albans Tower (Wren)
5. 25 Gresham St. (Grimshaw)
6. Guildhall (Giles G. Scott)
7. 10 Gresham St. (Foster)
8. St Ann & St Agnes (Wren)
9. St Lawrence Jewery (Wren)
10. St Giles
11. Barbican (Chamberlin Powell & Bon)
12. N0.1 London Wall (Foster)

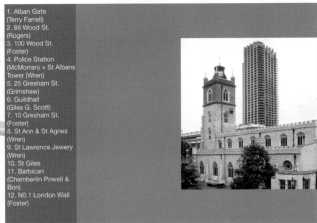

42.   Barbican

The **Barbican**, Silk Street, EC1 by Chamberlin Powel & Bon, is a classic 1950's dream of regeneration, replacing an area that was heavily bombed during WWII. A key planning concept at the time concerned enthusiasms for elevated pedestrian walkways and decks. When debated in 1959, one City Deputy suggested that, 'opposition to elevated walkways was based on prejudice' and that ' once people were up on the walkways there was no need for them to come down at all - until they wanted to go home'. The notion developed into plans for a thirty mile City network, only abandoned after the early 1970's property boom collapsed and alarmed conservationist sentiments were reversing the lack of perceived value in anything Victorian or the City's medieval street pattern, significant parts of it obliterated by highway widening schemes that accompanied the pedway scheme. The concept was meant to slowly insinuate its way across the City as buildings were replaced and remnants can still be found in unlikely locations, e.g. opposite the north side of Lloyds, waiting for Lutyens' Midland Bank building to be demolished. It was a planning concept that entirely missed the opportunity to develop the network of City back streets and alleys (as at Leadenhall Market or Bow Lane), allowing pedestrians a choice: either to tackle the traffic and fumes, or wind one's way through back streets alive with the kinds of activities developers deny and frequently replace by blue plaques noting the former location of a coffee house or some such.

The Barbican development itself (1957-79) is one large, 'gated' deck serving private apartments, an arts centre and schools, at the heart of which is a central landscaped area complete with lake, ornamental medieval church (St Giles) and what the Pevsner guide now describes as a 'thrillingly vertiginous crossing' slung at high level between gigantic concrete columns (visitors no doubt following the painted yellow lines on the paving so they don't get lost whilst seeking the arts centre). The composition comprises tower blocks and terraces, all of it monolithic and 'brutalist', providing an experience that mixes exhilaration with hesitation. No one says so, but its success owes, one suspects, as much to a sustained middle-class content as any design feature.

The Barbican's **Waterside Cafe** was refurbished in 2002 by Allford Hall Monoghan Morris. The same architects are also responsible for a current masterplan for the arts centre.

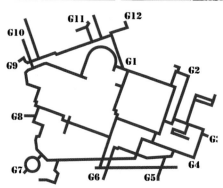

43.   Golden Lane, EC1, immediately north of the
Barbican and preceding it in design, is a classic post-war example belonging to an era when few self-respecting architects would dream of working for a 'commercial' (i.e. private) practice and most wore a left-wing, humanist bias on their sleeve. It is designed by Chamberlin, Powell & Bon (1952–62) as something distinctly urbane, without garden suburb association. The principal block has a remarkable roof-line which lifts the less expressive architecture of the lower parts. Ignored or derided for years, the development - like many similar '50's and '60's schemes - is now prime home-hunting territory for young architects.

The Barbican is a gated city within a city, accessed via a high-level pedway system that was once planned to network across the City and separate pedestrians from cars. Alban Gate attempts to cope with the gating and access issue along London wall (formerly Route Eleven).

Alban Gate

The developer for Alban Gate argued that replacing a 1960s shoe-box office tower (Lee House) was not feasible unless the new building could be much larger. Farrell's idea was to acrobatically use air-rights over London Wall and provide two linked towers totalling 35,000 sq.m. of office space for multiple lettings, all within the planner's height constraints. The Post-Modern outcome is no longer in fashion and Farrell's compositional concerns have commanded respect but not affection. However, the towers themselves - the parts up there - are only one half of what was going on and what Farrell was attempting to achieve.

Always an urbanist, Farrell brought his own agenda to the project and attempted to design the building as a new gateway up onto the Barbican deck - a reivention of the medieval Cripplegate that had been located slightly north, adjacent to St Giles Church in the heart of the Barbican development. His intention was that the planners should be persuaded to pedestrianise Wood Street and he could then provide a sweep of stairs up to the deck level and partially heal the divorce between the Barbican and the rest of the City. It never happened and the resulting difficulties at the lower levels are an uncomfortable compromise. Where is the front door? At ground level (it is, around the rear in Monkwell Square) or up on the deck level? It simply doesn't work, but Farrell might have pulled it off and he should be praised for having had the vision and commitment to attempt to redress the legacy that 1960's planners had left to the City.

The building belongs to the same era as others by Farrell especially Embankment Place (1991; p98) and MI6 Building (1992; p97) and what the architect sees as the building's principal merit - its then fashionable, neo-Michael Graves compositional play with step-backs, granite and glass – is what many others dislike about the scheme. But in this concern he is hardly different to the best Modernists, men such as Lubetkin, who were profoundly concerned that Modernist ideology neglected compositional issues. The problem is that his designs are read as bombastic and over-worked - a kind of shoulder-padded 'Gucci architecture' strutting its stuff and ironically, given his genuine concern with populist themes, unloved. As a champion of Post-Modernist architectural values during the 1980's Farrell was among the best. But this building (1991) is the gravestone of a set of stylistic values that vanished overnight with the recession then swallowing the construction industry. When it emerged a few years later (around 1995) the Post-Modern themes that had dominated architectural debate from about 1975 (very much a North American import) had been dismissed and forgotten, apparently never to be spoken of again (even by developers). Everyone had become Modernist a new kind of post-modern Modernism, minus the appetite for 'ironically' mining history for themes and features. The obvious comparison is with the building's neighbour, 88 Wood Street - a building Farrell condemns as 'non-contextural'.- and with the Gresham Street building by Farrell's former partner, Nicholas Grimshaw.

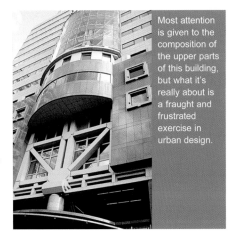

Most attention is given to the composition of the upper parts of this building, but what it's really about is a fraught and frustrated exercise in urban design.

44. London Wall/Wood Street, EC2
Terry Farrell & Partners, 1991
Tube: Moorgate

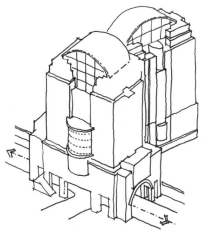

45. *The **Guildhall Art Gallery** that sits on the eastern side of the piazza in front of the old Guildhall frontage is a bizarre post-modern building designed by Richard Gilbert Scott (the grandson of Giles), thus continuing a peculiar line of patronage. The original was destroyed in WWII and the new one is as much reception facility as art gallery and has a link on its northern end into the old parts of the Guildhall. The City runs a marketing suite on the gallery's south-east corner which includes a wonderful model of the City area, used for marketing purposes and therefore only accessible by arrangement.*

46.

88 Wood Street, EC2
Richard Rogers Partnership, 2000
Tube: Moorgate, St. Paul's, Barbican

88 Wood Street

How does an architectural firm upstage its own acknowledged masterpiece (the 1986 Lloyd's building)? For one thing, lots has changed since then. The partners who brought Lloyd's to realisation are the mature men of the practice, with Rogers himself as a Lord of the Realm more involved with political and strategic issues than the details of buildings. The simple answer is that one doesn't try: a younger generation in the office is encouraged to take over the firm's values and make the pitch (in this case, Graham Stirk). And, at 88 Wood Street, the outcome is a building that many people consider to be one of the best office buildings in London. Devoid of the demand that, like Farrell's building, it should play an urban design role as a gateway into the Barbican, No.88 is left to cleverly accommodate itself to its difficult site with disarming ease (with a strategy, it might be noted, that is fundamentally similar to the Lloyd's building).

The design was begun in the heady 'bubble' years of the late 1980's with Japanese client (Diawa) and planning permission was granted in 1992 for 18,000 sq.m. of lettable office space. But the building only got as far as foundations (locked into an existing telephone exchange that was, for a time, listed) before the early '90's recession hit.

When the client returned it was with a brief for a building of 24,000 sq.m. lettable space within the same building geometry. Four extra floors were cleverly insinuated by means of reducing the floor thickness and partly by moving air conditioning plant to the basement.

Construction began again in 1995 with Diawa taking nine of the floors and now requiring a large service pavilion to be provided on the south side of the building - a 'blind' building that subsequently had to be glazed and converted when Diawa decided not to move in after all.

When completed at the end of 1999, no..88 Wood Street comprised three terrace blocks rising in steps from 8 to18 storeys, arranged to fit a difficult site geometry and serviced by six perimeter access cores.

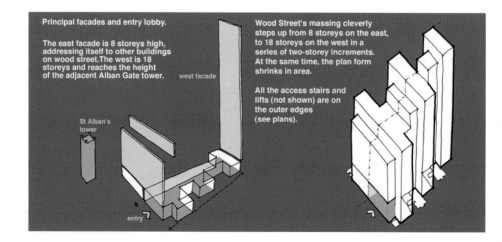

Principal facades and entry lobby.

The east facade is 8 storeys high, addressing itself to other buildings on wood street.The west is 18 storeys and reaches the height of the adjacent Alban Gate tower.

west facade

St Alban's tower

entry

Wood Street's massing cleverly steps up from 8 storeys on the east, to 18 storeys on the west in a series of two-storey increments. At the same time, the plan form shrinks in area.

All the access stairs and lifts (not shown) are on the outer edges (see plans).

These also have toilets, provide primary services distribution, fire escapes, etc., and in this sense are very similar to the Lloyds building. The strategy is the same: offer a regular and rational, usable geometry of space within the peculiar shape of the site, and to design the service cores in the left-over spaces around the perimeter.

Despite Terry Farrell's contention that the building is 'non-contextural', it is distinctly so on the Wood Street frontage, where the height is kept down to something like the general height of frontages along the street. The building then cleverly and systematically rises up in two-storey increments to 18 storeys on the western frontage - a height that more or less matches the bulk of Farrell's adjacent building. This was allowable so near to St Paul's Cathedral because the building effectively sits with the visual 'shadow' of Farrell's building. (Other noteworthy neighbours - such as Foster's 100 Wood Street and the Sheppard Robson building opposite that - did not have this advantage.)

A major characteristic of the design is its extensive glazed perimeter. This is partially shaded by the cores on the south side and by the restricted frontage on the west but is, in any case, obviated by triple-glazing and an air extract system that draw the air heating up between the panes of glass before it enters the building. The pure, white glass then allows spectacular views all around - off-setting the depth of the floor plate at some points. The only irony is that these two factors - daylight and aspect - can be at odds with one another in a modern office building loaded with computer screens.

The lobby area is another of the building's dramatic features, stretching from the east through to the west facade, looking out on to London Wall along the building's northern flank. Its long internal wall is of polished plaster.

The 33,000 sq.m. gross building is on a 1.5m grid, its structure alternating 15 x 6m bays with 10 x 6m bays of in-situ, post-tensioned concrete. External bracing - articulated on the north and south ends - stabilises the building. The service cores (normally what stabilises a building) are themselves stabilsed by the building frame.

46.

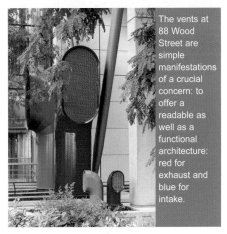

The vents at 88 Wood Street are simple manifestations of a crucial concern: to offer a readable as well as a functional architecture: red for exhaust and blue for intake.

Floor 7
(lower floors similar, but without street terrace)

47.

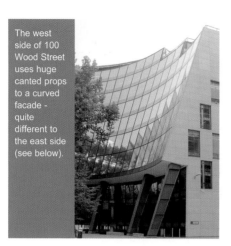

The west side of 100 Wood Street uses huge canted props to a curved facade - quite different to the east side (see below).

100 Wood Street

Foster and Partners' eleven storey, 20,405 sq.m. contribution to the grouping in Wood Street is a sandwich of offices inbetween two entirely different facades, addressing two different urban demands. Venturi would approve.

The east facade (on Wood Street) is an exercise in good manners, encouraged by the City Planners who insisted upon Portland stone, a height restriction and cutbacks at the upper level - the latter being interpreted by the Foster team as a major opportunity to get away from the offset of glass and stone on the facade and indulge in what they love best: a curved and trianglated construction that vaults over to the west side of the building. But if you were to quickly dart through the retained medieval alley to see what was happening on the St Mary Staining side, you get a surprise: the vaulting has disappeared and an entirely different game is going on seeks to respect anther planning demand - this time to allow daylight onto the former churchyard. The facade becomes a dramatic curved and raked exercise ostensibly propped by large cast columns akin to the 'giant order' of an arcade.(One can't but help remember an early Jim Stirling scheme that involved a leaning facade.)

Here, too, the building has to cope with some significant neighbours: the rear ends of Rogers' 88 Wood Street, a Sheppard Robson building in Noble Street, and Nicholas Grimshaw's 25 Gresham Street - not to mention fragments of Roman and medieval wall that are just opposite. They all jostle together around the focal point of the green grass and tree of the churchyard.

48. *Directly opposite 88 Wood Street sits the **Police Station** designed by McMorran and Bird. This is pure architectural Mannerism, but of a refined and cool pre-Venturi genre. As constructed, the station was intended to serve that central one third of the city so badly Blitzed in 1941. As a part of the 1960's rebuilding that included the adjacent Route Eleven and Barbican, it belonged to a promised future. As a design, the station belonged to the 1930's rather than the 1960's. And as an institution strongly imbued with pride, ceremony and the hierarchical mores of a City Police force with a long history, it was the swansong of an era: fifteen years later it had been reinvented as a specialist support facility to the other stations in the Square Mile and its police talk nostalgically about the old days. The design was idiosyncratic even in 1966. At a time when capitalist interests in the City were breaking new ground by embracing post-war Modernism, McMorran was offering the Police an Italian Renaissance villa (simultaneously conforming to the accepted development convention of a*

tower and podium). The latter was the courted villa, including stables for 16 and 18 hand police horses, and prominent vents disguised as chimneys; the tower was a tall block whose upper half was given over to residential accommodation for unmarried officers (separate sexes, of course). On the outside it's Portland stone, while the inner court is faced in London stock bricks. However, the detailing - African hardwood doors and sash windows, for example - is always well considered and as sturdy as the structure is deliberately Cold War bomb-proof. The lobby even includes stonework from Roman walls found during construction. (McMorran also designed the Old Bailey extension and a building on the west side of the Reform Club in Pall Mall. Sadly, he committed suicide just as the station was completed and the large hall on the station's piano nobile (the tall windows on Wood Street), was named after him - only to be renamed some years later.)

25 Gresham Street

Nicholas Grimshaw's simple exercise at the west end of Gresham Street is his first City building and a well-designed and interesting building made somewhat idiosyncratic by the employment of green slate cladding panels held by a multiplicity of stainless steel holding devices that are distinctly decorative (the planners insisted upon stone).

The plan (1000 sq.m.) is straight-forward but most of the 'architecture' is focused upon the south (front) facade, where a sunken 'memorial garden' (once a church, St John Zachary) is offset against a rising wall of suspended vegetation (apparently far less so than originally intended). The front of the building hovers above this garden - Grimshaw has to get acrobatics in there somewhere. But it works.

25 Gresham Street, EC2
Nicholas Grimshaw & Partners, 2002
Tube: St Paul's, Bank, Barbican, Moorgate

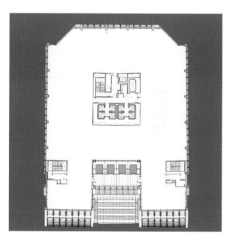

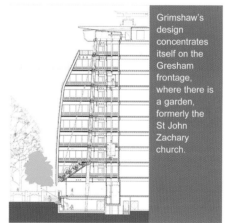

Grimshaw's design concentrates itself on the Gresham frontage, where there is a garden, formerly the St John Zachary church.

50. *The Guildhall*, *Guildhall Yard, EC2, is the town hall of the City, home of the Corporation of London and a layered architectural history dating back to 1411. These older parts were badly damaged during WWII and carefully restored. At that time they were also extensively added to with additions by Sir Giles Gilbert Scott, Son & Partner (1880–1960). The comparatively provincial looking 1955–58 north block bears comparison with his Bankside power station (now the new Tate Gallery); the detailing is very similar. The long block on the west side, undertaken after Scott's death, is a mere eight years later (1966–69), and designed by the same practice now, apparently, led by an opportunistic younger generation in the office with different ideas to the old man. The result is classic, high quality 1960s: lots of prefabricated concrete that steps out at the upper levels, nodding toward medieval traditions. This wing helps to form the piazza in front of George Dance's C18 Gothic / Indian facade. On the opposite side sits a recent (2000) replacement for the bombed City Art Gallery (see p41), now both gallery and reception centre for Guildhall functions. It's what used to be called 'a well appointed' building, but it is also a bizarre post-modern design. And guess who was the architect? Giles Gilbert Scott's grandson, of course! Within this building on the the south east corner is a City marketing suite that houses a large and very up to date model of the City, used to sell its benefits and opportunities to developers, their clients and possible tenants. During the construction of the gallery, Roman foundations were uncovered that demonstrated this was where they had an amphitheatre. This has become the prompt for an occasional fancy dress celebration of this City heritage within the piazza.*

St Lawrence Jewry and St Agnes and St Anne's are two fine Wren churches on Gresham Street, the former adjacent to the Guildhall, the latter to the west.

51.

10 Gresham Street, EC2
Foster and Partners, 2003
Tube: St Paul's, Bank, Barbican, Moorgate

10 Gresham Street

We were all awaiting a reaction to computer-generated curves and a nostalgia for the more brutal constructional verities of Mies van der Rohe to return to fashion. And here it is - from the Foster team, where Wood Street meets Gresham. This 27,000 sq.m. office building has comparatively narrow 18m deep floor plates clad in a ventilated facade with *wood* Venetian blinds and a PR blurb that says lots about natural materials and turns the planner's constraints into positive architectural features. There is even something Miesian about the scale of the fenestration, although the chamfered corners and attic stories (for planning reasons) hark back to a different theme in '60's design. The building on the west is the Wax Chandler Hall, now a discrete building with a public way between it and 10 Gresham.

52.

No 1 London Wall, EC2
Foster and Partners, 2003
Tube: St Paul's, Bank, Barbican, Moorgate

No. 1 London Wall

Squatting above and around new premises for the Worshipful Company of Plaisterers (entry on the Noble St. side; the remainder of the grd. floor is service areas) are the flowing curves of this 19,308 sq.m. office building that makes quite a contrast with its neighbour, 88 Wood Street. It's small entry lobby is on London Wall, from where escalators take users up to the office floors (1900-1300 sq.m. net). Reception is on the 1st floor, where there is a central lift core serving the remainder of the building (and also a bridge link across to the Barbican). It's interesting that facility managers aren't scared of curves these days (unlike when Erskine's Ark was built).
Powell & Moya's Museum of London is across the road - currently being worked on by Wilkinson Eyre.

53. *The **Sainsbury Business Centre** (41,000 sq.m.) is a Foster replacement for a '60's block once occupied by the Daily Mirror (designed by Sir Own Williams). All the usual competences are there, including a large atrium entrance backed by large office floors behind vast areas of glass. The ground floor has its glazing faced with limestone louvres, lending a base to the building and a different scale and character at pavement level. The building is much better in the evening, when the facade slowly becomes transparent (but the real glitter - and an utterly different scale - is across the road in the jewelry shops of Hatton Garden).*

Haberdasher's
exercise in scale

The Guilds remain a curiosity of City culture, many of them lost as well as rooted in their histories and few of them desiring or managing to plausibly reinvent themselves - except for the Worshipful Company of Haberdashers, who have insinuated themselves into the urban fabric of Smithfield, deeply hidden away behind older buildings and within the heart of an urban block - giving its designers the interesting problem of how to cope with a very difficult site (entirely without street frontage) as well as any cultural and symbolic demands.

The contemporary Haberdashers is as much rentable conference venue as club or ancient guild, demanding a balance between these disparate roles. Hopkins deals with such issues and the site by forming a central, 20m cloistered court dominated by the barn-like volume of the main hall that is on axis to arriving visitors - who then turn right and are taken up to the principal accommodation on a *piano nobile* via a spiral stair.

A fundamentally important keynote to the scheme is the handling of scale e.g. the diminutive arches of the cloister, topped by the taller windows of the first floor and, in the case of the hall, capped by a tall, pitched leaded roof with two dominant ventilating chimneys. It's where so many architectures go wrong and hopkins' team have got it right.

Soft red brick, limestone and oak are predominant materials. Get in during London Open House if you can't make it at on any other occasion.

Haberdashers sits deep with an urban block and provides accommodation around a cloistered courtyard. It's all about scale. The oak-panelled, double-cube livery hall with its pitched roof is at first floor level.

A limestone spiral stair leads from the entrance up to the piano nobile, where most of the public spaces are located. Oak is the dominant finish.

55. *The **Daily Express** building in Fleet Street is now no more than a highly impressive frontage with a highly impressive art deco entrance lobby. The former was designed by Owen Williams, 1930-3, and was the first true curtain-walled building in London (black Victrolite glass spandrels in chromed metal framing). The latter was designed by Robert Atkinson and is quite special.*

54.

Haberdasher's Hall, 18 West Smithfield EC1
Michael Hopkins and Partners, 2002
Tube: Farringdon

56.

1 Friday Street, EC4
Michael Hopkins and Partners, 1991
Tube: Mansion House, St. Paul's

Bracken has relatively little cladding and Hopkins makes the most of the budget, delivering a clever design that serves at many levels at once.

Bracken House
declaration of intent

Bracken House is an example of architectural gamesmanship that assures you experts are at work. At the instrumental level there is inventiveness and expertise providing sound, functional office space but, as always, that is not what is interesting about the design, and certainly not where one finds the wit in a design that sent a notice to the profession: here was an architect - formerly a partner of Norman Foster - who was not going to be pigeon-holed into prevailing stylistic categories. Instead, Hopkins effectively made a declaration that he was cutting across the categories and wet and crusty materials as well as industrialised ones in the cause of good architecture and sound construction.

Bracken is a composite of two buildings: the retained wings of the 1959 Financial Times building, looking - as did many City buildings of the period - as if they belonged to 1929, sandwiching the do-nut plan of a central part by Michael Hopkins. The latter replaces the former FT printing hall but cleverly picks up on a variety of features of the retained

Palazzo Carignano
Turin
Guarini, 1679

wings, reinventing them and making an elegant marriage of old and new. It's as if the two parts are engaged in some form of curious, frozen duet with one another.

The original building, of which the north and south wings remain, was completed in 1959 as the home of the eastern-most of the 'Fleet Street' newspapers - the pink broadsheet that is the Financial Times - appropriately located within the City itself. In 1952 the FT's owner, Brendan Bracken, had asked his architect, Professor Albert Richardson, to provide a new building with a curved facade. Richardson obliged by quoting references to a Renaissance palace in Turin (the Palazzo Carignano) and giving Bracken a design comprising a central printing hall and two office wings (on the northern facade of which you can find a zodiac, featuring the head of Sir Winston Churchill, a rather bizarre and amusing homage to the great friendship forged between the Bracken and Churchill during the war). In the mid-1980s the FT moved to a Docklands building designed by Nicholas Grimshaw (from where they have moved on), and the intention was to replace the old building with a new Hopkins design.

Again quoting the geometry of the Turin palazzo, Hopkins (with his fellow-director, John Pringle) proposed retaining the two wings but replacing the less interesting printing hall with a doughnut plan of offices radiating from a tight central atrium (which accommodated the lifts). Many of the key features of this new, central part relate back to the character of the two wings. For example, the attic storey carries through; the gunmetal cladding derives from the use of this alloy on the old windows; the geometry of the cladding bays derives from windows on the wings; and the stone piers

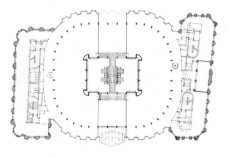

on the ground floor are in the same pink 'Hollington' stone used by Richardson.

Underlying the 26,300 sq.m. design were two other contextural considerations. The first was that the new owners - Japanese bankers - had hoped to build much higher. However, the height restrictions imposed by proximity to St Paul's Cathedral made the development rather expensive and demanded the designers squeeze the floor to floor heights. The second consideration concerned Prince Charles. His influence was everywhere – nowhere more so than around St Paul's, an area ripe for redevelopment and subject to his close scrutiny.

56.

Charles was of the not unreasonable opinion that contemporary facades tended to be thin and two-dimensional: their designers should return to the good days when thick, masonry cladding leaned against the steel frame of the building and carried its loads straight to the ground (rather than hanging the cladding off the steel frame, the modern practice). So Hopkins provided a load-bearing facade, but one that is stunningly contemporary. It's a gesture with wit, inventiveness and even humour, incidentally underscoring the fact that all good architecture is essentially contingent and rooted in time, place and circumstances, locking the mundane and the intellectual together as one voice: architectural design as an action of the moment.

The team set the external columns far back from the facade, so that the cantilevering concrete slab sags under its own load and has to be supported by the gunmetal cladding which takes out the deflection by propping the slabs and carrying the loads to ground. Well, to large cast, cantilevering brackets that 'catch' the loads with a quiet piece of acrobatics. Sat up stone piers (the real thing, of course, not stone facing to concrete) that match the Hollington stone of the '59 building, these brackets reach out to pick up the loads and are counter-balanced by stainless steel tie rods down the back of the piers.

At the heart of the interior sits a top-lit atrium with four lifts structured within large cast steel panels, bringing users out onto bridges studded with glass block - a device used at every level, including the roof, in order to keep the overall level down.

It's all very clever and beautifully designed. Not many architectures are informed and defined by such multi-level gamesmanship.

The Bracken House gunmetal facade (an alloy of zinc, bronze and lead) is a rare example of architectural gamesmanship, at once acrobatic and respectful of its contextural references and inspiration. The cantilevered, concrete floor slab naturally deflects. The cast metal facade takes the weight of this deflection, levelling the floor. Loads from the upper levels pass down to the vertical tubes to the cast brackets at ground level. Being themselves cantilevered from a pivot, the vertical forces are counter-balanced by a steel tension tube on the opposite (rear) side. All the weight is borne by a stone pillar (no concrete is involved, except for the foundation). The entire arrangement neatly confronts the criticisms of Prince Charles in that contemporary facades are too thin and not articulated because they are not load-bearing.

57.

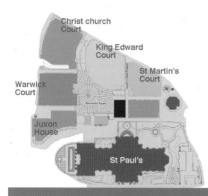

Christ church Court

King Edward Court

St Martin's Court

Warwick Court

Juxon House

St Paul's

Paternoster Square, EC4
Various architects, 2001
Tube: St Paul's

The buildings are from the following practices:

- Christ Church Court - Rolfe Judd
- King Edward Court - Eric Parry
- St Martins Court - Allies and Morrison
- Warwick Court - Richard MacCormac
- Juxon House - William Whitfield

Immediately north of the Cathedral is the Chapter House, home for the commercial side of St Paul's (800,000 visitors generating £3m plus £2m turn-over in the shop!).

Paternoster

The Paternoster Square development has been plagued ever since its post-war birth in an area devastated by the German Blitz of WWII. It had, historically, been an area of book publishers and over 6m books were destroyed in the bombing. The replacement was another of those 'traffic-free precincts' designed over a car park, master-planned between 1955-62 by Lord Holford, and executed by a number of architects, 1964-7. Ideas for an '80's replacement scheme became bogged down by the interventions of Prince Charles and worthy schemes (e.g. by Rogers and Arup Associates) were rejected. Neo-Georgian, neo-Roman and neo-Florentian schemes were sampled, finally resulting in Sir William Whitfield being appointed to reconcile tastes and values (see his mention on the Institute of Chartered Accountants, work done in the mid-1960's). His key contribution was to tighten the spaces between the buildings, his plans also requiring a ground level colonnade and to be no more than 6-7 stories high (in stone). The outcome is an artful framing of views of the cathedral that has been criticised as 'stage scenery', but is no more so than most planning exercises in conservation areas.

A handful of medium-sized office buildings are being completed in 2003 (the term is relative). On the north-west corner is one by Rolfe Judd, next to it are others by Richard MacCormac, Eric Parry, and Allies and Morrison. Whitfield is responsible for Juxon House on the prominent south-west corner.

Thomas Heatherwick has sculpture here, disguising a two cooling towers from an electricity substation.

58. **St Paul's Cathedral** *must be London's principal work of architecture. It's big (155m long, 111m high). It's old (Sir Christopher Wren, 1675-1711). It's an impressive construction, was designed by an English genius of note and has - particularly since its survival during WWII - come to serve as a symbol of all that is English.*

In town planning terms St Paul's dominates central London and has engendered recurring controversy among supporters and detractors of its need for prominence. Viewing corridors from a variety of London vantage points impose constraints upon the development potential for tall buildings and issues of adjacency have been among the more contentious architectural debates since bombing prompted redevelopment of what had been a book district just to the north (the Paternoster development). This controversy became quite heated during Prince Charles' intense interest in the mid 80's redevelopment proposals that are coming to fruition in 2003 (by a group of architects, under the general guidance of Sir William Whitfield).

Does the building merit all this? The design belongs to the tail end of an era when geometry embodied cosmological meaning, when Wren the self-taught architect was deeply conscious of the French concept of 'Natural' and Customary' beauties, when London was changing and Modernism as we understand it in a broad cultural sense was manifesting itself whilst many architects were pretending to a secret, masonic knowledge. It's a building on the cusp. It's also a dry and mechanical design, hardly informed by the emotive content that Wren's assistant, Nicholas Hawksmoor, was able to give his own church designs in the early C17 - buildings whose smaller scale is yet imbued with with more feeling of an awesome 'Sublime'. (Try reading Peter Ackroyd's 'thriller' about Hawksmoor.) In truth, St Paul's is a Gothic church in disguise (as Wren was painfully aware) and was hardly deemed to be architecturally radical, even by its author. It now serves ritualistic bonding ceremonies between City and Monarchy and can't be treated lightly, but has to be subject to a careful interrogation and deconstruction of its meanings.

JP Morgan
transmogrification

This surreal Po-Mo building reinvents the Renaissance palace as a deep-plan financial trading centre, over 66,000 sq.m. gross, with two trading floors of 4,645 sq.m. each and 55% of its volume given over to services: a fortress buzzing with digitised financial trading involving sums one can hardly imagine.

The BDP design grows out of the back of a rather grand Davis & Emmanuel school of 1880 (described by Nicholas Pevsner as 'unscholastic') which JPM use for their Boardroom, etc., as one might expect. The accommodation extends itself up the street, underground and across the road to another block. It's big. The palazzo model is then transmogrified. Classical elements such as the cornice) become carefully proportioned functional features - for example, guttering and a cladding maintenance track - and air conditioning grilles marry themselves into the idea of Baroque rustication.

Knowingly or not, the architects have given us a theatrically phrased monument to their own patronage by the wealth and power of the occupying market-makers: latterday Princes. Its all rather Disney . . . and yet very real and not fantasy at all. Modish and 'structural' themes in architecture ('Customary' beauty and 'Natural' beauty, as the C17 termed it) are the appropriate informants of the scheme - perhaps not quite as someone like Sir Christopher Wren might intend it, but the principles are the same.

59.

John Carpenter Street, EC4
BDP, 1992
Tube: Blackfriars

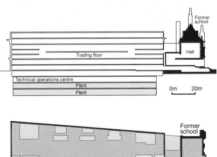

Former school

Trading floor

Hall

Technical operations centre

Plant

Plant

0m   20m

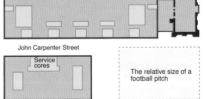

Former school

John Carpenter Street

Service cores

The relative size of a football pitch

60. *St Bartholomew's Church, West Smithfield, EC1, is usually offered to us because it is loaded with history (an Augustian priory, founded in 1123, partly destroyed in the Reformation), restored by various architects, notably Aston Webb, who added to the four bays of the aged choir (1886-98; see, for example, the transepts and west front). Forget all that and simply experience the building as a splendid mix of spaces, textures and other architectural qualities that have been layered, violently edited back, restored, and yet (somehow) have managed to retain architectural coherence. What one experiences is, self-evidently, as much accident as design, but this hardly detracts from the satisfaction of the experience and - one must admit -*

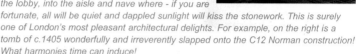

its romantic undertones. The place feels like a cliched oasis midst the raw urbanity of equally large meat market bustling with huge multi-axle trucks loaded with bloody carcasses, an equally large hospital, the frothy life of Farringdon media types who populate the local bars and restaurants, and a background of the Barbican. leave all this; progress down the long path through the graveyard, through the lobby, into the aisle and nave where - if you are fortunate, all will be quiet and dappled sunlight will kiss the stonework. This is surely one of London's most pleasant architectural delights. For example, on the right is a tomb of c.1405 wonderfully and irreverently slapped onto the C12 Norman construction! What harmonies time can induce!

61. *Nicholas Hawksmoor's **Christ Church**, Spitalfields, E1, sits on the eastern edge of the City monumentally towering above the domestic properties that sit beneath it's magnificent tower and steeple. Commissioned as part of the Fifty Churches Act of 1711 that attempted to bring religion to London's masses, it was designed in 1720 and is only now being slowly restored.*

62. *Most of the original Smithfield meat market buildings (**Smithfield Market**, Charterhouse Street EC1) were designed by Horace Jones (the Tower Bridge architect) and completed in 1831. What one now sees is HLM's 1994 renewal of the facilities in order to bring them into line with European Union standards. It didn't come cheap and HLM have taken the opportunity to offer an idiosyncratic mix of stainless steel modernism and a colourful renovation of Jones's sheds. Two new*

floors have been added within the existing frame, providing offices and facilities for the traders. A principal difficulty with the design is the peripheral glazed canopy which proclaims a reinvention of the facilities, but offers little else and clearly presents maintenance problems (it is always dirty), but bike couriers find it convenient.

The West
End &
Whitehall

If the City of London is the oldest and, in some senses, the most modern part of London, the West End represents London's westward expansion, beginning with the establishment of the Church and Court at Westminster, giving London two foci around and between which it might develop – and extending through to latterday Heathrow.

Westminster is where Edward the Confessor founded a royal palace in the C11, adjacent to a Benedictine abbey of obscure origins, already a place where kings were crowned when the Normans conquered England. Later, the royal residence of the Palace of Westminster shifted to Whitehall Palace and the former residence became the place where the Lords and the Commons met. Most of Whitehall Palace was destroyed by fire in 1698, apart from Inigo Jones's Banqueting House. In 1834 the Palace of Westminster was also burned down, prompting a competition for new Houses of Parliament, 'in the Gothic or Elizabethan style'. This resulted in the present design, by Charles Barry and Augustus Pugin – in turn, damaged during WWII, restored by Sir Giles Gilbert Scott, and now supplemented by Portcullis House, designed by Sir Michael Hopkins.

As London expanded westward, the aristocratic estates of the area were speculatively developed into the set of Georgian squares and streets that characterise much of the West End. The first of these included St James' Square, Covent Garden, Lincoln's Inn and Bloomsbury Square, while the grander residential areas around Belgravia tend to be early or later C19. Many of the former buildings have now been converted to offices, but significant areas remain in residential or mixed use and some fine Georgian terraces exist in Bloomsbury (despite inter and post-war enthusiasms for 'comprehensive redevelopment' - visible, for example, around London University and at Brunswick Square).

The private and speculative nature of these urban developments is one of their important features. Even Regent's Street and Park were privately financed and it is only in the later Victorian period and the early years of the C20 that civic-minded 'improvements' cut new streets (such as Shaftesbury Avenue, the Aldwych and Kingsway) through the old fabric and created significant urban features such as the Embankments. One can't imagine such interventions being repeated.

Meanwhile, Whitehall consolidated as an area of government buildings adjacent to the Royal palaces of the Mall and St James', spreading west into the Victoria area (where you can also find the Richard Rogers design for Channel Four). Perhaps the next (inevitable?) stage is this development will be the vacation of the palaces and their conversion into tourist venues (a process that appears to have already begun).

An Architectural Geography

Whilst this guide divides the whole of central London and its architecture into two broadly defined areas that suit our convenience, the underlying reality is somewhat more complex and should be noted. Between the two historic foci of power and influence in London that underly its architectural geography - the City and Westminster - sits an 'inbetween' area that has tended to enjoy a distinct character of its own. This is the original 'west end', a place of escape from the dense overcrowding that once characterised a C17 City having suffered plague and fire. Its heart is an area on the west flank of Farringdon Road (under which lies the old Fleet River), stretching north from the Fleet Street / Strand arterial.

The southern part (the Inns of Court and Temple) is an area where lawyers have congregated since the Middle Ages and where journalists and lawyers would later work, meet and gossip in the coffee houses of a later era enjoying the novel concept of 'publicity' and news journals. Architecturally, many parts of the Temple date back to the Middle Ages (the Middle Temple Hall of 1571, Gateway of 1684; and New Court of 1676; the Inner Temple Gateway of 1611; and halls at Lincoln's Inn, Staple Inn and Gray's Inn of 1492, 1581 and 1560 respectively). It was here, at Covent Garden, in the 1630's, that London saw the first of the 'regular' developments around a square that were to become a dominant feature of urban change in Westminster over the following one hundred and fifty years (later followed by more Inigo Jones designs at Lincoln's Inn Fields, c.1640).

In a future era, when tabloids for the masses were taken for granted and East End docks were closing, the journalists (or rather newspaper owners, such as Murdoch) grabbed the opportunity to move east and provide themselves with new facilities and simultaneously a chance to cope with accumulated restrictive labour practices within their printing works. It happened quickly, leaving the the more robust culture and traditions of lawyers behind and - more to the point - a need to reinvent parts of Fleet Street and its northern hinterland, previously occupied by newspaper support industries. However, it was not until the boom years of the late '80's (pushing West End studio prices up) and recession of the early '90's (pushing incomes down) that this really got under way. Designer types now found the large, relatively inexpensive, 'authentic' and vacant warehouse spaces in the northern parts of the area and Clerkenwell a welcome alternative at a time when computerised journalists were also being attracted to offices within the new Gotham City of Canary Wharf. Both Clerkenwell and Canary enjoyed a new fashionablity. Meanwhile, sites around Fleet Street (e.g. behind the frontages of Daily Telegraph and Daily Express, and the JP Morgan site) were appropriated by City developers able to rebuild on the sites of former printing works and supply a much vaunted need for large floor-plates. An historic cultural pattern that had held for generations was changing, relatively overnight.

From our viewpoint of convenient architectural exploration, the notion of the West End and an 'inbetween' area should also extend south of the river, embracing parts of comparatively unfashionable Lambeth and Southwark, on the southern side of that great divide, the Thames. They have always featured as significant parts of an historic London and are latterly experiencing a novel union with the north, in part because of London's rediscovery of the river and also because of the Jubilee Line extension. It is for this reason that we include buildings such as the Imperial War Museum and Cullinan's Lambeth Health Centre.

The West End has come to be defined as a central area ringed by older 'village' centres such as Knightsbridge, Notting Hill, Marylebone, Angel, etc. - places of quite different architectural character and development opportunity. Even the central heartland is divided between the pretensions of St James', the government quarter of Whitehall, an Oxford Street separated into distinct shopping halves at Oxford Circus, the two entertainment areas of Covent Garden and Soho (which should be similar but are very dissimilar), and the 'inbetween' area (inbetween the West End and the City) of Holborn, bounded on the west by the electronic and furniture offerings of Tottenham Court Road and, on the east, by the utterly different characters of the Temple and the studio warehouses of Farringdon. Seemingly, the only thing unifying such disparities is the fascination proffered by tourists. That, and the fact that this is the historic heart of London mostly developed during a boom period of 'Georgian' expansion.

The architectural interest of the West End is embedded in this history and the place's deep-rooted urban character. For example, it is difficult to appreciate Hopkins' Portcullis without addressing its context: Scotland Yard and the Palace of Westminster. Somerset House means more if one appreciates it as a riverside palace supplanting an earlier palace and at odds with a competing work of architecture (the Aldelphi) just upstream. (Similarly, Farrell's Embankment Place has less meaning when divorced from this series of large riverside works.)

To the east, buildings in Farringdon have to be dealt with as the reinvention of what was once the backyard of Fleet Street newspapers, just as Fleet Street itself was partly appropriated by the City following the exodus to Docklands. And to the west, Knightsbridge and Notting Hill have become ever stronger bastions of affluence, resistant to significant architectural change.

Almost without exception, important architectural work in the West End appears increasingly contextual and to engage a broad range of issues. The new British Library cannot be divorced from its relations with British Museum and plans that go back to the 1960's. Foster's Great Court at the BM is very much a part of a pattern of expansion and alteration that has always characterised the BM. Venturi's Sainsbury Wing may be loaded with his North American, Post-Modern concerns, but it is literally locked into formal relations with a National Gallery architecture created more than 150 years previously.

This is hardly to claim that the area isn't changing. Even as we write about the West End in these terms, this book already acknowledges how its southern edge - the River Thames - has recently been redefined, at once breaking away whilst simultaneously linking the two banks of the river and thus extending the West End into southern parts from which it has long been divorced. And yet look at any old London map and you will see that this southern area has as much history as the north.

As always in London, most of this West End development is rooted in private monies, even if some of it is routed through government agencies. The Millennium outburst of 'grand projets', for example, was based upon the taxed, speculative gambles of large numbers of private people. Such projects that have been more directly dependent upon government sources - such as the British Library or Channel rail links, both at St Pancras - have been fraught with difficulty.

While 'improvement' in the ambitious Victorian sense has evolved into a tinkering with traffic schemes, from the Mayor's ambitious decongestion charging to the more local reclamation of Trafalgar Square, a myriad of comparatively short-lived designs in the form of new retail outlets such as cafes, restaurants, shops and art galleries continue to inform the bigger picture and lend a vibrancy to London that it has not experienced in living memory (no, not even in the 'swinging '60's). This is nowhere more evident than in the night life of the West End.

Nothing lasts, but - to date - the joint has been jumping! One's conclusion is that an enjoyment of the West End's contemporary architecture can hardly be divorced from the totality of the area, its urban history and continued reinvention. It's as if - to paraphrase one London historian, Peter Ackroyd - the city has an underlying nature that quietly but adamantly insinuates new development, absorbing it all into a unified character that alters less than we sometimes presume. Whether that rumination is depressing or intriguing we leave to the reader! It is, however, a traditional architectural concept: the notion of 'natural beauty' which an architect should acknowledge (what is fundamental and 'structural') and a 'customary' (or modish) beauty to which they must also conform.

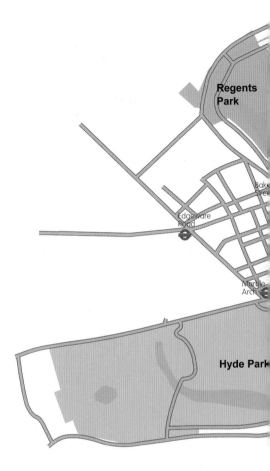

The Southbank area that includes parts of Southwark and Lambeth is included in this section. These parts of London have been developed since the earliest times and are very accessible from north of the river - something that has always divided the area as a whole and has been separated out in this guide as 'London Riverside'.

This overall area - plus the City - coincidentally is the new London congestion charge zone.

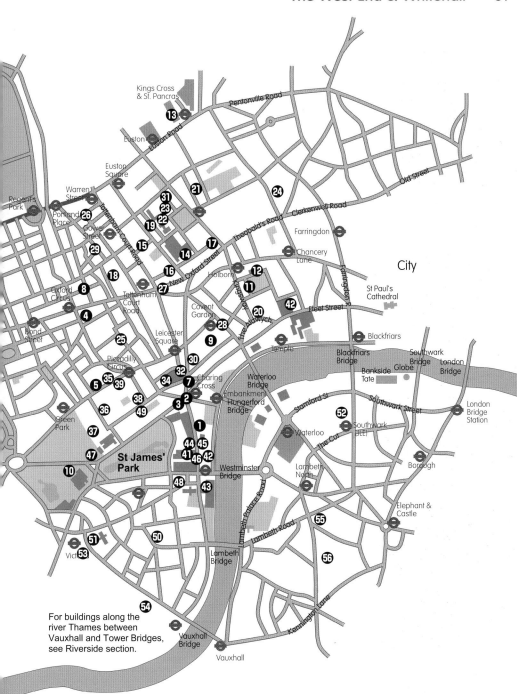

City

St Paul's Cathedral

For buildings along the river Thames between Vauxhall and Tower Bridges, see Riverside section.

1. *In a London of Tudorbethan buildings, Inigo Jones's* **Banqueting House** *(1619) in Whitehall, SW1, must have been horribly modern, foreign, erudite and shocking as well as ultra-fashionable among the debauched aristocrats who held parties there. This alien from foreign parts was a message from on high to the Philistines below, a play-palace for King Charles. Yet it was also a classic example of belief in what was later expressed as 'Customary' and Natural' beauty. The customary (modish) part was the lavish banqueting; the 'natural' beauty was embodied in the geometries of the facade and the double-cube room at its heart which encapsulate the cosmological beliefs of the day in hierarchy, order and proportion: 'Untune the string and hark what discord follows.' No doubt the Banqueting House once experienced its share of untuned strings.*

2. **Nelson's** *statue in Trafalgar Square sits upon a Corinthian column raised in 1843, formally dominating a square that serves as a dividing place between government buildings in Whitehall and the popular shopping and entertainment areas to the north. The column towers above a square that has always attracted political crowds and stirred paranoia in the minds of the establishment, engendering features such as the crowd-disrupting fountains placed there in 1845, later modified by Edwin Lutyens and now a feature of Foster's reclamation of the square (a 'world's square' project that excludes traffic from the northern side).*

3. **Admiralty Arch** *(1911), on the south-west side of Trafalgar Square, WC2, is a triumphal arch straddling the entrance to the Mall, its tapered plan attempting a formal transition designed to reconcile the dissimilar urban geometries comprising the route from Buckingham Palace, through the central Arch, along the Strand and Fleet Street to St Paul's Cathedral in the City. It was designed by Sir Aston Webb who (like Foster now) had, at that time, one of the largest practices in the country.*

4. *Raymond Hood's name – associated with skyscrapers in New York during the 1920s and 1930s – is an unsuspected one for the London scene.* **Palladium House** *was designed in 1928 for the corner of Great Marlborough and Argyll Streets, W1. Compare with the* **HMV** *shop in Oxford St. and the* **Daily Express** *frontage in Fleet St.*

5. *Modelled on Parisian precedents,* **Burlington Arcade,** *Piccadilly, W1 was designed in 1815 by Samuel Ware. It remains one of the more pleasant (if expensive) shopping experiences in London. The less pleasant end facades were added in 1911.*

6. **Selfridge's**, *Oxford Street, W1 is one of the more impressive facades in London. Designed between 1907–28, its 'giant order' columns have a marvellous scale that brings the Chicago of Daniel Burnham to London (others involved included RF Atkinson and Sir John Burnet); 'the motif made history in England', commented Pevsner. In recent years the interior has been reinvented and the store transformed in status into one of London's premier shopping venues.*

7. James Gibbs' **St Martin's-in-the-Fields**, *(1720–26)*, in Trafalgar Square is a much-copied, Roman-inspired design whose symbolism is almost Hollywood Gothic (take a pagan temple, complete with portico, and drive a Christian stake - i.e. the tower - through its heart). The interiors were

amended by Reginald Blomfield, 1887, and there are current plans to make significant extensions. Nearby, at the Aldwych, you will find **St Mary-le-Strand**, another fine church by Gibbs (1717), who was at one time involved at Burlington House (before Palladianism reigned supreme).

8. **All Saints,** Margaret Street, WC1, north of Oxford Street, is a truly amazing design that you'll either love or hate for its 'constructional polychromatic' brickwork and shadowed, incense-laden, high-church interior. Apart from which this, it is an immensely skilful piece of architectural organisation - completely filling a 33 m.sq. site that is surrounded on three sides - whilst still offering an appropriate entry court as well as the church itself, a choir school and a priest's house. Designed by William Butterfield in 1858, it is a masterful work: architectural gamesmanship at its best.

9. **St Paul's** church Covent Garden, WC2 is a committed piece of architectural theatre finished in 1630. Its principal facade (which is, bizarrely, the blank east portico and not the west front) has become a theatrical proscenium and faces into what was once an open square and arcaded piazza - a part of what was an original design novelty in London streets called 'regularity'. The area's developer had to have permission of the King, who foisted the Royal Surveyor, the accomplished virtuoso Inigo Jones, onto the unfortunate man who, asking for 'a mere barn of a building' met the response from Jones that he would have 'the finest barn in England'. The outcome was a fashionable area that slowly degraded as the West End developed, its piazza becoming a market and its arcades apparently becoming the resort of London's more debauched residents. However, much of what you see now is a restoration after a fire of 1795. Other London works by Jones include: the Banqueting House, 1622; the Queen's House, Greenwich, 1615 on; St Mary's church; Lindsey House, Lincoln's Inn Fields, 1640.

The market was established as early as 1670 and the buildings themselves are early Victorian (Charles Fowler Snr., 1828–31) and served as London's main vegetable wholesale market until the early `70's, when a GLC scheme to move the market to a more accessible location and redevelop the area with new buildings, highways, pedways and lots of concrete prompted a popular unrest and effectively ended 'comprehensive redevelopment' in London. The Garden promptly became London's first trendy ad agency / studio precinct before retail values pushed most of them out in the '80's to other warehouses around Farringdon (then being vacated by support sectors to the newspapers of Fleet Street, themselves off to Docklands and new employment practices). Since then Covent Garden has remained a characterful retail and restaurant area focused upon the retained and restored central market buildings.

10. Within the depths of **Buckingham Palace** (1705-1913; Buckingham Gate, SW1, at the end of The Mall, laid out in 1660) are the remains of the original country house, which became the focus of the Prince Regent's attention in the 1820's. John Nash was the architect and neither he nor the Prince Regent came out of the reconstruction without scandal (the latter overspending the budget by some 300% ; the former benefiting privately from the works and being replaced by Edward Blore). Other architects were later engaged, but the present frontage and 'rond point' (including the Victoria Memorial by Sir Thomas Brock, 1911) are by Aston Webb, 1913.

Slowly, parts of the palace are being opened up to the public (such as the 2002 **Royal Collection** galleries by the Prince of Wales' favourite architect, John Simpson) and Terry Farrell has undertaken a scheme take this trend to a more radical conclusion (unlikley to be in the immediate future). Meanwhile, the true significance of the Palace concerns urban design issues rather than its heavily criticised and unloved architectural qualities, i.e. its role as the beginning of an impromptu royal, processional route from here, along the Mall, through Aston Webb's Admiralty Arch, down the old avenues of Strand and Fleet Street and on to St Paul's Cathedral in the City itself.

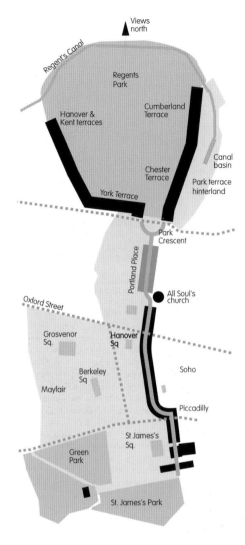

Views north

Regent's Canal

Regents Park

Cumberland Terrace

Hanover & Kent terraces

Canal basin

Chester Terrace

Park terrace hinterland

York Terrace

Park Crescent

Portland Place

Oxford Street

All Soul's church

Grosvenor Sq.

Hanover Sq.

Berkeley Sq

Soho

Mayfair

Piccadilly

St James's Sq.

Green Park

St. James's Park

11. *Lindsey House* on the west side of Lincoln's Inn Fields (Inigo Jones, 1640) was divided in two in 1751 and is without surviving interiors, but the outside gives a good idea of what was happening at the time, when such a facade was a novelty in London. Strip it back and you have the basis of the Georgian London house front embodied in the building regulations of the C18.

Regent's Street (1811–30) was designed as a via triumphalis (a 'royal mile') between Carlton House (on the south side of the Mall), to a speculative development of aristocratic villas and terraces on a crown property to the north (to become Regent's Park). It was never used as such, but its pragmatic, disjointed character says a lot about urban design and large scale development in London, especially during one of the city's most expansive and formative periods.

It also says a lot about the skilled architectural gamesmanship of its architect and planner, John Nash, reputed to be a favourite of the Prince Regent following a convenient marriage to the Prince's mistress (which brought Nash instant career success as well as an instant family). Cleverly, Nash proposed to follow a route along the edge of a rather dense and crowded Soho in order to make the new street a part of Mayfair and differentiate the 'nobility and gentry' from the 'mechanics and trading part of the community'.

In a marvellously pragmatic manner, the street winds its way north from Waterloo Place and the east end of the Mall via a necessary curve which then avoided the better properties of St James's and prompted the idea of grand colonnades (since demolished and replaced by the 'grand manner' buildings we see today). It then sweeps north, through a junction with Oxford Street to another difficulty: Portland Place. This already existed, developed and designed by the Adam Brothers, and aligned so that Langham House (now replaced by the Langham Hotel) could look to the fields due north. At the crucial junction of new and existing, Nash masterfully provided a church (All Souls) with a circular colonnade at its west end to help us round the double bend into Portland Place.

At the north end of this stretch, Nash faced further formal difficulty and provided a crescent to allow for an offset to the park itself. This was followed by a series of splendid terraces within the park (especially on the east side, e.g. Chester Terrace, 1825, and Cumberland Terrace, 1826).

Only five of the intended villas were ever built in the park, served by the Regent's Canal along its northern edge, where there was also a market. In the 1980s, Quinlan Terry was allowed to design three new villas along the Regent's Canal, complementing the original group.

At the north east corner of the development sits Park Village East and West (now split by a Victorian railway that characteristically charged its way through the urban fabric), a delightful group of 'cottages in the city', which set a keynote for future, anti-industrial developments in London (e.g. the villas populating St John's Wood, immediately to the north) whilst continuing a traditional theme in London's building mix.

Within Regent's Street itself, Nash had to struggle to create order among disparate developers. However, none of the original buildings now exist, most of Regent's Street having being redeveloped between about 1913–28 to a scheme involving Norman Shaw, Aston Webb, Ernest Newton, and Sir Reginald Blomfield (all major architects of the day).

An Original Cabinet of Curiousities

12. *Surely no serious architectural enthusiast can visit London without taking in the* **Soane Museum***, Lincoln's Inn, WC2, the remarkable house, office and private museum of Sir John Soane, built between 1731 and 1833 (at which time the houses were left to the nation).*

The Museum is actually three, adjacent Georgian terrace houses (nos. 12, 13 & 14) that the architect secured and carefully developed stage by stage, typically slicing off the rear end of the last of the three to benefit the central house, then selling off the remaining property. The central part that forms the core of the scheme and the present Museum (since extended into the first of the three houses, on the west side, and fitted with a small display room designed by Eva Jiricna) is almost sufficient in itself and filled with architectural delights that marked Soane's aspiration toward urbane living. But behind the horizontal layers of this splendid but otherwise not untypical Georgian house Soane blossoms into another kind of game that exploits the vertical possibilities and links a series of architectural devices together into a (ostensibly) complex enfilade of top-lit spaces.

From the stone and brick arches of the basement, the construction reaches up in lighter construction layers toward the daylight, adorned at every step with plundered classical antiques to delight the architect and educate the staff of the practice. It is difficult to understate the inventiveness and civility of it all, including such delights as the picture room with its layered walls and connecting views.

And there, in the heart of it all, in the vaulted basement, Soane secured a home for an invented, alter ego figure redolent with the romance of the late C18: a monk living amongst Gothic architectural features 'borrowed' from works at Westminster Cathedral. This Monk's Parlour is rather mischievous, perhaps humorous, yet underscored by personal bitterness and even cynicism that reveals Soane as a real person as well as a distant architect of huge ability. Few works of architecture have such a strong voice, dissolving the underlying formalities and concerns of its places and spaces as it speaks to us about making and inhabiting an architecture.

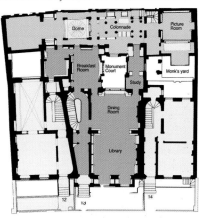

13.

St. Pancras, Euston Road/Melton Street, NW1
Colin St. John Wilson, 1964–98
Tube: Euston, St. Pancras

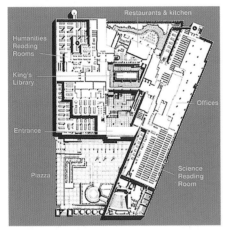

The British Library

The British library project began as a joint venture between 'Sandy' Wilson and Sir Leslie Martin (1908-99), then head of the Cambridge school of architecture and famous as the former head of the LCC architect's department and the key figure in the design of the Royal Festival Hall. At the time, Wilson was a one-man practice and a lecturer at Cambridge when, in 1962, the British Library competition came up. By the late '60's Martin had withdrawn into retirement and Wilson (together with his wife and other partners) was carrying on the project in the face of all kinds of political and sentimental opposition that transformed a job into a career.

Their first design (1962-64) was for a site immediately in front of the Museum, in Bloomsbury, but the brief grew enormously and later designs had to accept that the site was too small. In 1973 another site was found at St Pancras. By 1978 a new design had been completed and the building Wilson & Martin had started together was to be completed in three stages: the basement areas, entry hall (concourse), and Humanities reading rooms; the Science reading rooms; and an extension for a 'bindery' and more reading rooms. Construction was finally completed in stages between 1997-9. It had taken over 35 years.

Both the two early schemes to 1972 were low-rise, high density, mixed use schemes with housing and commercial uses, as well as a new library. (See the nearby Brunswick Centre.) The initial scheme also gave reference to a W.R. Lethaby proposal of 1891 for a 'Sacred Way' from the British Museum down to Waterloo Bridge. It was also at this time that Wilson made a proposal that, when the Library moved out, the Reading Room should be returned to public use and placed upon a north-south route - something Foster was later to return to with his Great Court scheme.

Wilson's original sketches for St Pancras indicate the concept of two major parts to the design concept: an orthogonal part, to which more irregular parts are attached, much as ships at a quay. In reality, the actual designs appear to be more rigid and organised than this. The current plan, for example, clearly has a direct correspondence with the concept sketch (a rigid spine to which more informally arranged parts are connected), but the 'irregular' parts are arguably as formal and orthogonal as the principal spine. Nevertheless, there is a strong 'parti' (a traditional term referring to a scheme's fundamental parts or themes that are configured into an overall architecture) to the scheme.

The section is as organised as the plan. The deepest floors are for book stacks and help to make the building a veritable 'iceberg'. Above this are mechanical plant areas. As we move above ground a key criterion that enters the scene is an aspiration toward daylight and the layers of reading rooms vary in height according to what goes on within them. These upper parts offer a sensuous unfolding of the architecture, particularly within the central 'concourse' area (it would be difficult to call it a foyer or lobby), where the inspiration of Alvar Aalto's public spaces can be clearly read. In Wilson's own

Homage to a Stunning Place
Sandy Wilson's King's Library at the heart of the British Library concourse is a straight homage to Gordon Bunshaft's design (while at SOM) for the Beinecke Rare Books Library in Yale (1963) - but without the 1.25 inch glowing marble panels.

words, there is a lot of 'icing' layered upon the raw, underlying concrete structure, but most of this derives from acoustic and maintenance criteria that insinuated themselves into the design. It is worth comparing the building in these terms with Wilson's mid-'90's design in the East End for St Mary's College, where the finishes of this library are much simpler and owe much to Lewerentz rather than Aalto (Wilson courageously dares to employ Lewerentz-style 'bagged brickwork' - a more ruder and rustic treatment that literally uses a bag to spread the joint mortar).

• *The BL was designed to last 250 years (i.e. more or less the period from its beginnings, projected into the future).* • *It has over 12m books on 340km of shelving* • *The building goes 25m under ground and 48m above ground.* • *The gross floor area of the Library is 112,643 sq.m (1,212,039 sq.ft.)*

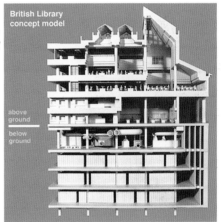

British Library

1972 scheme

13.

Books in 250 years' time?

"Those who would carry on great public schemes must be proof against the most fatiguing delays, the most mortifying disappointments, the most shocking insults and, worst of all the presumptuous judgement of the ignorant upon their designs". Edmund Burke, quoted by CW.

There is something profoundly ironic within Wilson's stamina-loaded achievement of realising the British Library at St Pancras, a building designed to last 250 years. The design was started in 1962 only four years after the integrated circuit was invented by Jack Kilby at Texas Instruments, at a time when the concepts of programming languages and programming software were well established. Perhaps this reality is somewhere in the background to the history of a project that underwent a 37 year gestation period and was finally allowed (by the then Prime Minister, John Major) to be finished in 1999 on the basis that it did not fulfil its ambition to a final phase of

British Library concept model

above ground

below ground

expansion - one of the very reasons it was located where it was. (A finish did not mean completion.) By that time every architectural practice took Computer Aided Design (CAD) for granted; an age of architectural 'blobs' had arrived and Wilson's great inspiration - the work of Alvar Aalto - self-evidently belonged to a previous era.

It had taken a long time and Wilson is fond of quoting the parallel period of gestation taken by St Paul's Cathedral under Sir Christopher Wren ("on half pay for ten years and sacked before completion"). However, whilst we await the fates of books in a digitising era, it is hardly fair to criticise the British Library in terms of fashion. It's ambitions drew upon more profound sentiments. In the architect's mind, "the library and what it houses embodies and protects the freedom and diversity of the human spirit in a way that borders on the sacred". In a way, this notion of the sacredness of knowledge is embodied in Eduardo Paolozzi's piazza sculpture of Sir Isaac Newton, as inspired by William Blake's woodcut done in the 1790's.

The parts of the Library that have been constructed form one of London's major buildings, currently sitting astride St Pancras Station and King's Cross Station: three neighbouring, isolated and autonomous beasts awaiting some form of urban cohesion (which could begin with the transformation of St Pancras into the new arrival station for the EuroStar trains).

14.

Gt Russell Street, WC1

Foster and Partners, 2000

Tube: Tottenham Court Road, Holborn

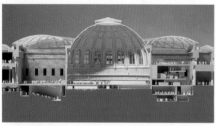

British Museum Great Court

creation, obliteration, and reinvention

The British Museum's Great Court addresses 200 years of the building's history: from the Museum's 1808 scheme for extending the house occupying its site, through a history of rapid change and addition that closed off and built over the original landscaped court designed in 1823, obliterating the original concept of a central, public green space. Driven by the Museum's need for additional accommodation, the three sides of the original court were supplemented by a fourth and, at its centre, a large circular Reading Room was provided for the British Library. In turn, this was to become surrounded by storage rooms filling the interstitial spaces between the Reading Room and the quadrangle. The site was full; the museum continued to expand its collections.

A 1960's plan to move the Library to other accommodation unleashed a new potential, finally enabling the central court to be rediscovered and reinvented – this time paved and covered, conceived as an indoor public space that simultaneously, provided a radical re-organisation of the Museum's circulation. However, none of this would have been possible without the Library moving out to St Pancras (see British Library). By reinventing the Court as a covered, indoor space protected by a unique, domed glass roof, Foster's design returns this central area to public use, provides new facilities, reveals and opens the Reading Room, and entirely reforms the Museum's circulation.

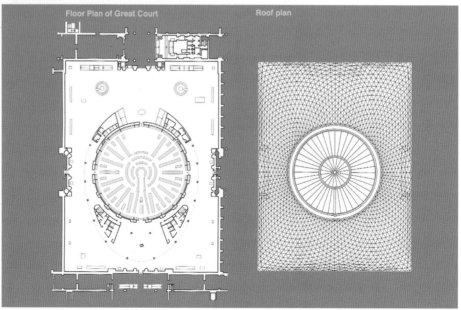

Floor Plan of Great Court

Roof plan

The new roof to the Court, completed in 2001, is a tour de force. Ironically, it may prove to be the celebrated central design feature at the heart of a problematic situation which has the Museum bogged down in financial difficulties and falling attendance numbers (pulled off to London's other attractions, notably the Tate Modern). However, it remains a remarkable architectural achievement.

The Foster scheme is deceptively simple, but also a radical act of imagination that reinvents the quadrangle as a major public space radically changing possible access into the galleries whilst also giving the Museum much-needed extra facilities (such as the education rooms and auditorium in the basement). It was also a major and complex construction task requiring as little disruption as possible to the Museum and considerable restoration work to the earlier construction, the Reading Room and the entry lobby.

The new design has cleared away the areas around the Reading Room, initiated a major renovation of the surrounding quadrangle facades (including a controversial restoration of the south portico), given the Reading Room back to the general public, surrounded it with new shops, a restaurant and an exhibition space accessed by a symmetrical pair of grand stairs that sweep around the Room's curvature, and - above all – provided the Court with a spectacular glazed roof covering a quadrangle that is about 92 x 73m (larger than a football pitch). There are also extensive new facilities beneath the Great Court (galleries, the Clore Education Centre and the Ford Centre for Young Visitors).

Part of Foster's rationale for the scheme was that the new Great Court would offer itself as a covered public space featuring as a crucial component part of a pedestrian route from the new British Library at St Pancras, down through the Great Court, and on to Trafalgar Square - an idea that has a history. 'Sandy' Wilson, architect of the new British Library, had proposed offering the central Reading Room to the public and opening up a north-south route in a report of 1962-4, associated with the first scheme to remove the Library to a site just south of the British Museum. In turn, this referenced a 1891 scheme by W.R. Lethaby to create a 'Sacred Way' between the Museum and the old Waterloo Bridge. Current financial problems (late 2002) at the Museum have rather curtailed this concept, reducing its opening hours in line with the galleries.

14.

The upper level of the central building has a restaurant sheltered by a very refined fabric canopy.

14.

The court as it was.

Demolition work around the Reading Room.

Background

The BM has always occupied this site in Bloomsbury, formerly Montagu House and its gardens, originally built in 1675. It opened there in 1759 and grew rapidly, extending into the former garden in 1808. Robert Smirke came onto the scene in 1816 and again in 1821, suggesting new wings. His scheme was later amended to accommodate the King's library and became what was finally built: an initial stage providing new wings that formed an open,landscaped quadrangle, followed by the demolition and replacement of Montagu House itself. Smirke's splendid and proud neo-Grecian design was begun in 1823 and Montagu House was demolished in the 1840's; however the building had no sooner been completed in 1852 (together with a main entrance portico housing sculptures in its pediment symbolising the progress of civilisation from paganism to the sciences of the day) than further works were implemented to accommodate the expanding stock of the British Library. This was carried out by Robert's younger brother Sydney Smirke, who designed the domed, central reading Room that is larger than that of St Paul's and almost the size of the Pantheon in Rome. The need for additional space continued unabated and the interstitial spaces between the Reading Room and the Museum began to be filled by book stores. The pattern continued, notably in 1904-14, when the Edward VII galleries where added, designed by John Burnet, and then in 1936-8 when

John Markham added mezzanine floors to the buildings along the north side of the quadrangle and also inserted new windows. The outcome of these layers of expansion and change were that the core of the do-nut plan housed the British Library, whilst the surrounding quadrangle of accommodation formed the Museum, accessible to visitors by a perambulatory, up and down route contrasting with a Reader's passage from the main entrance portico, through the entry lobby, into a tight low passage that led into the Reading Room (reserved for academics and researchers). When it was planned that the British Library – always hungry for extra space – would move to Colin St John Wilson's St Pancras, the potential was released for a reinvention of the Reading Room and its relation to the Museum, whose visitor numbers appeared to be climbing toward 6.5m a year. Initially, proposals involved extensive demolitions and rebuilding within the areas around the Reading Room. This was amended in stages, slowly moving toward a more accessible concept. A competition was then held and Foster appointed with a scheme for a roofed central court and new accommodation surrounding the central reading Room, leaving little space around it. However, funding from the Lottery Commission came with the requirement that the Court was open to the public for longer hours than the surrounding Museum, and the transition to the concept of a covered public space was complete.

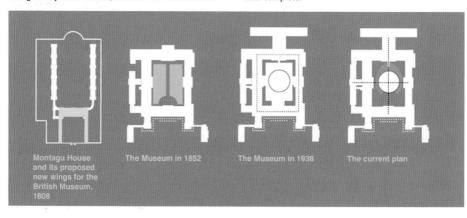
Montagu House and its proposed new wings for the British Museum, 1808

The Museum in 1852

The Museum in 1938

The current plan

The Roof

The 6,700 sq.m. roof of the Great Court would have been impossible to either design, manufacture or construct until the advent of low-cost computing and the appropriate software. Every part of the 800 tonne lattice shell structure is different, designed so that the generalised geometry of the framing will fit to the disparate geometries of the quadrangle walls, the disparate heights of the portico pediments, and the location of the Reading Room (5m off-centre).
• The built design is a highly curved torus, described as a square doughnut with a central hole. Available double glazing sizes determined a grid that has 3,312 panes of glass and 1,800 welded steel nodes (requiring 5,200 members).
• The outer supports are behind the stone parapets of the surrounding quad walls, resting on sliding Teflon bearings on 120mm stub steel columns that, in turn, rest upon a new concrete parapet beam; this allows for 50mm of thermal movement. The edges are actually louvred for natural ventilation.
• The central supports for the roof comprise twenty 457mm steel columns filled with concrete that surround the Reading Room, in turn encased in limestone, so that an in between space can be used for services.
• The roof is 26.3m high above floor level at its

14.

highest point (which disturbed local planners, who argued this was somewhat above the planning permission given!). The tapering steel components were constructed in Vienna and then shipped to Derby and made into 152 prefabricated units totalling 478 tonnes of steel (with another 315 tonnes of double-glazing added to them). Ceramic surface 'fritting' on the glass copes with solar gain and covers 57% of the glass surface, but this is almost invisible to the naked eye.
• The 11kms of roof structure was built to an accuracy of 3mms. Each outer pane of glass in the roof is covered in 50% green ceramic dots ('fritting') to reduce solar gain.

Façade Restorations

The internal facades of the Court have been substantially repaired and restored. In particular, this includes the controversial restoration of the south portico, entirely demolished in 1875. The stone used for the restoration (a French limestone) was revealed to be self-evidently different from the older Portland stone used by Smirke. A lot of people got upset, wanted to know why this sleight of hand had been pulled, leading to calls for demolition and rebuilding. The Museum had to offer the rationale that, like the restoration of an old Greek vase that differentiates between old and new, the restored portico is quite properly different and not a pastiche (an attitude to 'honest restoration' that goes back to the likes of William Morris). This rationale proved difficult to fault and made a lot of sense, especially in the context of the British Museum and even more so when they - rather than the architects or contractors - provided it.
• There are 1000 tonnes of new stone in the great Court scheme. The flooring of the Court is a French limestone called 'Balzac'.

The Reading Room

Based on the impressive results of using prefabricated cast-iron for the Great Exhibition of 1851, the original Reading Room structure was an impressive structure that used 2000 tons of cast-iron. The ribbed dome has a diameter of 42.6m (140 feet), only 61cm less than the Pantheon in Rome. The interior was a thick form of papier mache, 1.27cm thick. Its shrinkage, together with constant movements of the cast-iron and timber framing, resulted in an extensive pattern of cracking. All of this cracking had to be dealt with in the restoration by filling the gaps with wadding and applying a flexible 'bandage'. This was then repainted in a manner matching the original materials, and new gold leaf applied. This restoration work to the internal linings and their decorative scheme was revealed by 'stratigraphic charting', scraping and using solvents to reveal the original decorations.

The Reading Room now houses the Walter and Leonore Annenberg Centre. This is a modern library that combines computer access screens with 25,000 volumes from the Paul Hamlyn collection of books.

15.

25 Store Street, WC1
Ron Herron and Imagination Ltd., 1989
Tube: Goode Street, Tottenham Court Road

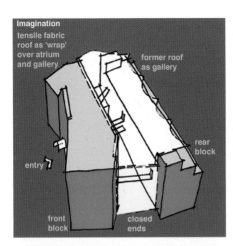

Imagination
tensile fabric
roof as 'wrap'
over atrium
and gallery
former roof
as gallery
rear
block
entry
front
block
closed
ends

Imagination

This is a project by an architect who built little but was highly acclaimed by others who have built lots (such as Richard Rogers and Norman Foster), a building designed as a home for creatives famed for developing 'brand experiences'. This was their very own brand experience. Coincidentally, the building is also a fitting memorial to an architect one might characterise as an East Ender of vision, a man whose work repeatedly came back to themes that overlaid and reinvented the status quo, a man who grew up in a 1950's London enamoured with Pop Art and all things American, including Hollywood movies and the blue Gauloises cigarettes that probably helped kill him at a comparatively early age. His obsession with the idea of 'architectural sets' and private realms behind public facades (possibly an architectural reflection of Herron's private social and political concerns, as well as a homage to a famous 1949 scheme by Lubetkin) is amply demonstrated in this building.

At the heart of the building is a tented, central atrium, designed almost entirely without a defined, instrumental purpose: a "cheerful" space that would suggest uses rather than serve anything specific in a brief, a space with open doors to potential, architecturally branding Imagination as an organisation with attitude. The hardware and the detailing of the atrium are delicious but, in essence, this is a design only superficially focused upon the stuff of things. It is the narratives acted out by people using the spaces that are really significant: this is Herron's own Hollywood set, awaiting its actors. Ironically, its owners have somewhat silted it up with a mix of physical additions and anecdotal myth, and in 2002 they were reported to be searching for new premises – acts of modification, obsolescence and replacement that Herron would probably have acknowledged.

16. *Congress House is the home of the Trades Union Council (1948-57; Great Russell Street, WC1) effectively the HQ of the trades union movement in the UK and dedicated as a grand monument to those trades unionists who died in two world wars - symbol of the power held by some 9 million trade unionists right up to the late 1980's. The post-modernism that brought Thatcherism and Blair's New Left government has placed a question mark over the movement and this institution, but the building David du R. Aberdeen designed for the unionists is a fine work of architectural gamesmanship worthy of attention. Aberdeen won a competition for the building in 1948; it was a grim, dire period in London's history, but among architects it was also a time of great optimism and hope for the future of post-war Britain. One has to imagine this work of bright, transparent Modernism arriving in a tightly urban street midst terraced, Georgian central London: a sooty, polluted place prone to the dense smogs contemporaneously romanticised by the likes of Frank Sinatra many thousands of*

miles away from the reality. By the time the building was completed the country was well on the road to recovery, the Clean Air Act was two years old and Aberdeen's building was a significant social symbol. Rock 'n roll was at the door, a service economy was developing and an 'angry young man' syndrome had arrived upon the arts scene. However, the opening was to coincide with the beginning of a period of wretched union battles with governments of all political persuasion, reaching its finale with Margaret Thatcher's employer and MI5-assisted victory against the miners in the early 1980's. And David du Aberdeen was not to design another significant building.

Herron's design is the adaptation of an H-plan Edwardian building c 1900 into offices for a design and publicity organisation having a powerful reputation as 'head-in-the-clouds, feet-on-the-ground'. The architect's brief was to help find and design a new home for the organisation – a brief that was to engender an 'Imagination City' scheme at Camden Town before the Store Street designs where, ironically, Herron did very little on the interiors, being caught in a classic shell and fit-out split that saw Imagination's own designers addressing the office layouts while the architect got on with the shell conversion, the services and the toilets (pseudo-pods that are well worth a visit, whether you need to go or not). Herron recognised that the light wells of the H-plan held the key to unifying the two wings into one whole. To achieve this he demolished the linking part of the H-plan and conceived of the new space as a unified whole covered with a tensile roof that spilled over the rear half of the plan that was lower than the front, thus creating a new roof-top space covered by the translucent, tent-like roof material (what is now the Imagination Gallery). Enlivening the space, new steel and aluminium bridges would dart across the void in an irregular manner, suggesting a vibrancy of occupancy and interaction. The intention was that the space was a habitable one, but fire regulations required that it was, technically a heated and ventilated outdoor space. The decision to use a fabric rather than a glass roof was based on the combined facts that the fabric would have a life of 15 years, was five times cheaper than glazing and has one sixth of the weight of glass. (The tensile roof was originally intended to stretch to ground level at the ends of the atrium, but the fire regulations prohibited the use of fabric for the side cladding.) The outcome of this (outrageous) design has been a whole series of not entirely expected uses, from parties, to launches, seminars and exhibitions - many of them inviting 'the public' into Imagination, generating all kinds of security pressures that have become a key constraint on the atrium's potential.

15.

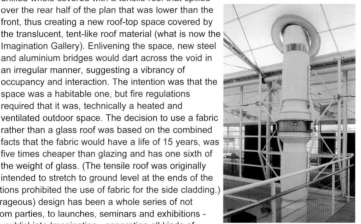

Victoria House

17.

Tube: Holborn

Alsop Architects, 2003

Southampton Row, WC1

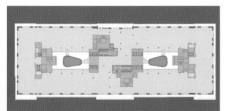

This conversion of a 1922-32 'grand manner' building in Holborn started as a bid proposal to house the GLA (see City Hall). Instead, Alsop was commissioned to strip out its heart and convert the former insurance offices into into 20,000 sq.m. of new office accommodation together with a health club and retail spaces at ground level.

The 'kerb appeal' of it all is hidden away within two new atria of unusual section, inhabited by double storey 'blob' meeting spaces propped on legs like some mini version of herron's *Walking City*. It's Peckham, Mecanoo's Budapest bank, and Gehry in Berlin and . . . quite cheerful, uplifting the dreary architecture of the average office. But to see this kind of thing at its best (admitedly with less fashionable, '80's Scandinavian styling) one still has to look at the interior of Erskine's much under-rated Ark in Hammersmith.

18.

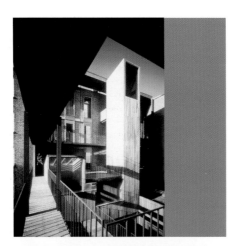

20-21 Newman Street, W1
Buschow Henley, 2001
Tube: Tottenham Court Road

TalkBack

Admin facilities for an independent TV production company that, we admit, are difficult to access. What is hidden behind the old street facade is a superb conversion that articulates the architect's determination to avoid the usual office stereotypes without resorting to gimmickry, i.e. a design informed by an appreciation of urban syntax,l notions of the office as a place with domestic undertones, and self-conscious enthusiasms for a 1950's English architecture. Typologically similar to Ron Herron's Imagination, older inner and outer blocks are reinvented and unified into a new architectural whole by strap-on circulation routes and other devices. But there is an entire absence of intoxication with anything hi-tech - replaced by a joy in natural materials and 'accessible' detailing more likely to come from an Essex timber yard than some remote foreign factory.

19.

62-64 Gower Street, WC1
Avery Associates, 2001
Tube: Goodge Street, Warren Street

RADA

Brian Avery almost always has some inventive quirk to his designs. He has become a skilled theatre architect and here, at the Royal Academy of Dramatic Art, he has cleaned out one half of a long slice of building between Gower Street and Malet Street to provide a new teaching theatre (the Jerwood Vanburgh) of 203 seats, together with production spaces, workshops and the like. The building is ten storeys high, three of them underground, and the fly tower of the new theatre forms the Malet Street frontage. The rear end of the Vanburgh is separated from the John Gielgud studio theatre further along the slot (within the retained Gower Street half of the complex) by a thin, full height space that reaches from the ground level foyer up to a skylight high above.

     The highly adaptable new theatre is intended to teach students at a small scale what they will have to practise at a large scale, and to add to that a variety of conditions and arrangenments they will have to cope with. It has four levels appears tall but the balconies are a mere 2.5m floor to floor, their fronts dissolved into wires so as to extend perceived volume to the outer walls.

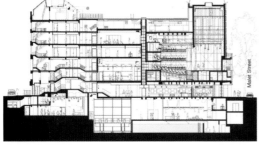

LSE Library

This 20,000 sq.m. library with 1200 study places is the conversion of a former book store (1916) on a site that has been a burial ground, a workhouse and a hospital. It's low budget and the Foster team offers a simple (almost utilitarian) solution that confronts the visitor with a splendid, full height space populated by earnest students and nearly 500 computer workstations. The building is served by a central circulation core (capped by a ventilating roof light and daylight reflector) comprising lifts and a large, spiralling, stepped ramp that feeds onto the gallery book-stacks (50km of shelving and 4m volumes), the 14 group study rooms and two training rooms. Penetrate the narrow banks of the latter and one comes to an almost secret perimeter study space. The 4th floor is the LSE Research Laboratory; the 5th is a new build extension. It's a busy place: each May sees about 5500 swipes through the turnstiles!

The LSE library is a cheap-and-cheerful building whose principal features are its large volume and its circulation core: lifts and a large stepped, spiralling ramp.

20.

10 Portugal Street, WC2
Foster and Partners, 2001
Tube: Holborn, Temple

21. *Plonked down into the heart of Georgian Bloomsbury, Patrick Hodgkinson's **Brunswick Square** project arrived in 1972 like an alien ship: complete, almost fully formed and demanding of its own 'living space'. Conceived by Patrick Hodgkinson with Sir Leslie Martin, 1959–72, the complex was intended to stride further north, to have private tenants, and to have other features such as glazed covering to the pedestrian deck. Intended as a demonstration, high density / low-rise urban block, it is rather flawed, but will always have an important place in London's architecture. Whatever merits it had, they did not include respect for what existed or any attempt to 'knit into' the existing urban fabric. In fact, one is reminded of Hans Hollein's contemporaneous drawing of an aircraft carrier nestled in a hilly landscape. Born in a climate of progressive big thinking by angry young men who preferred buildings to impose their own infrastructure rather than accommodate themselves to an existing one, Brunswick was truly a Modernist manifesto preoccupied with new ways of living as opposed to the hierarchical values believed to be implicit in the Georgian terrace. This was especially true with regard to the most fundamental point that Hodgkinson was attempting to make: that low-rise / high-density could work as an alternative to tower schemes set in a parkland (as occasionally happened) or an urban wilderness (the usual reality). He was also attempting a mixed use/mixed classes scheme that flew in the face of a current planning orthodoxy and its concerns to separate and zone. Unusually, the project started off as a (then) rare example of mixed-use, speculative development. It ended up as another complex of single-class social housing and a not entirely successful project that has posed difficulties and problems to this day. However, the scheme made Hodgkinson's name and he has been respected for it ever since. It's worth comparing with the **Alexander Road** complex at Swiss Cottage (London Borough of Camden Architects, under Neave Brown, 1969–79).*

22.

University of London, Thornaugh Street, WC1
Nicholas Hare, 1995
Tube: Euston, Russell Square

Brunei Gallery

Respectfully knitting in with one's neighbours has become a major architectural game (a legacy of Post-Modernist sentiments, contrasting with Modernism's instrumental penchant for contrast and, sometimes, a rejection of history). The Brunei attempts to relate to the materials, massing, organisation and careful geometry of late C18 neighbours (who employed an *implied* classical order); however, once around the corner, the design quickly changes mode and enjoys a new freedom not given in Russell Square, breaking away into a more free articulation around the entrance, where the brickwork now transforms itself into a veneer. Accommodation includes a cafeteria for students and an Islamic roof garden. The Gallery itself shows Islamic art and is worth your attention.

23.

University of London, Torrington Square, WC1
Stanton Williams, 1998
Tube: Euston Square, Euston

Clore Centre

Stanton Williams' design for the Clore Management Centre, close to the Brunei, adopts a different approach to contexturalism and terminates a Georgian terrace. Similar formal themes are adopted (base, *piano nobile*, attic storey), but their longer facade gives them the opportunity to carry through the geometry of the adjacent 7 m. Georgian structural bay. However, when it comes to the key central section of the facade, they have rejected the windows-in-load-bearing-masonry approach in favour of large areas of hung glazing.

24.

200 Gray's Inn Road, WC1
Foster and Partners, 1989
Tube: Chancery Lane

It's worth looking at the rear of ITN as well as the street and entry side.

200 Gray's Inn (ITN)

Independent Television News is a 10 storey, heavily serviced, 37,000 sq.m.. building, with two of the floors underground. Its architectural interest principally resides in three features: the central atrium; the elegant double-glazed cladding with its 300 mm gap; and the set-back entrance area sporting an extremely tall revolving door once intended to lead to a more lively space, where the public could experience the news broadcasting. Unfortunately the construction timing hit the recession and the possibility of low rental incomes, cutting back the budget. The entrance works well, the atrium has a dramatic hanging mobile by Ben Johnson, and the openness of the building is engaging, but there is a certain blandness about the place.

Broadwick House

This is a deceptively simple piece of architecture: a ground floor of retail units, offices above (used by Ford for its multi-brand design consultancy), and a double height + mezzanine office loft space at the top. But it's put together with panache and - whilst bearing all the Rogers' team hallmarks - neatly fits itself into this corner site in Soho, at the end of Berwick Street market. The entrance lobby leads to lift and services risers, toilets etc. that, as usual, terminate in the manner land-marking church spires once did. (We'll probably be able to scan the city skyline one day and easily spot all the Rogers' buildings!) See it as part of a recent family: C4, Lloyd's Register and 88 Wood Street.

25.

15 Broadwick Street, W1
Richard Rogers Partnership, 2002
Tube: Oxford Circus

26. *The 186m high **British Telecom Tower** in Cleveland Street, WC1, in Fitzrovia, went up in 1964, suffered an IRA attack and then had its public deck and revolving restaurant closed to the public. Since then it has remained as an enigmatic landmark clouded*

in the kind of secrecy that surrounds a major urban microwave communications structure. Together with Centre Point, the new St Mary Axe building, St. Paul's, the former NatWest Tower (Tower 42), and Canary Wharf it helps define the London skyline. Access can be arranged, but it isn't easy.

27. *Colonel Seifert's **Centre Point** building on the corner of Tottenham Court Road and Oxford Street, W1, was in its day, notorious as an example of outrageous speculative greed. The ground level arrangements remain very unsatisfactory and await major urban renewal at this important road junction, but as memories fade and all architects acknowledge they are 'commercial', some have even started to enjoy Seifert's load-bearing building envelope and many of his other London buildings.*

28.

Bow Street, WC2
Dixon Jones BDP, 2000
Tube: Covent Garden, Holborn

Royal Opera House

E.M. Barry's Royal Opera House of 1858, together with the adjacent Floral Hall (also by Barry) have recently undergone a massive, long-winded, expensive and controversial renewal. At the root of the complex is a competition-winning scheme designed by Jeremy Dixon in the early 1980s, carried out in collaboration with BDP and Dixon's latter-day partner, Ed Jones. On the one hand it is an urban design exercise locked into historical and contextural issues concerning Inigo Jones and the original Covent Garden Piazza (hence the recreation of the arcade, extending the one built in 1877 which, in turn, recreated the Inigo Jones scheme of the 1630's). On the other hand, the design is concerned with programmatic issues concerning facilities for opera-lovers, dancers, administrative staff, storage, etc., together with the renovation of Barry's work.

The future of the theatre was ensured by upgrading to three performance spaces. The auditorium was re-raked, re-seated, re-gilded and re-lit whilst retaining its familiar character (now seating 2262 people). Air conditioning was also added and sight-lines improved. The Floral Hall has been restored, reached by escalator and now with a mezzanine level restaurant bar, and serving as the focus of the new foyers. Escalators again take visitors up to the roof-level Amphitheatre Bar and terrace. Behind the scenes (literally and metaphorically) are vast areas of studio space and workshops, a new rehearsal room (underneath which is the new Linbury studio theatre with 446 seats) and four new ballet studios added to the two existing ones. The stage area has been rebuilt (effectively as another ground level across much of the site), given new stage lifts and a new fly-tower three times the height of the proscenium arch. More workshops and offices are in the southern-most wing and the Covent Garden Piazza side is colonnaded for retail units.

Since the building is so large and the parts address different contexts, Dixon Jones have varied the manner in which they are handled - perhaps the most controversial aspect of the project.

To suggest it is a complex project would be an understatement. It required 150,000 documents and 80,000 drawings. The architectural outcome is another scheme which manages to blend old and new together (as with Bracken House, Lloyd's Register and Liverpool Street Station, for example), whilst utterly transforming backstage facilities (increasing the 'productivity' by a potential 50%, enabling three productions per day, instead of two) and giving the public hugely enhanced accommodation – including rooftop loggias overlooking the Covent Garden Piazza.

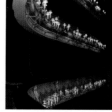

28.

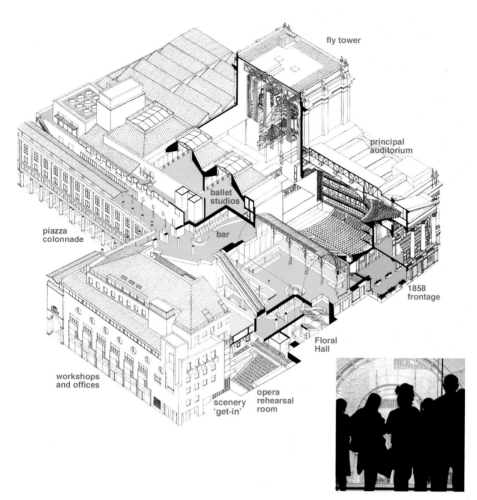

fly tower

principal
auditorium

ballet
studios

piazza
colonnade

bar

1858
frontage

Floral
Hall

workshops
and offices

scenery
'get-in'

opera
rehearsal
room

29 /30. *Sanderson's Hotel (37 Berner Street, W1)
is the conversion of the '58 Sanderson's wall
paper shop into a 'hip hotel', designed by that trendiest
(and talented) French designer, Philippe Starck (2000).
Also see Starck's design for a similar 204 room hotel
conversion (1999) for St Martin's Lane Hotel (38 St
Martin's Lane). Both interiors are good; St. Martin's is
probably the better one. (The developer for both was Ian
Schrager.)*

31. *Two Denys Lasdun buildings are nearby:
SOAS (1973), clad in white precast panels;
and the Institute of Education, 1970, stretching
along Bedford Way (both adjacent to Stanton
Williams' management centre and the Brunei
Gallery).*

32.

St Martin's Place, WC2
Dixon Jones, 2000
Tube: Leicester Square, Charing Cross.

National Portrait Gallery

The National Portrait Gallery sits discreetly behind the National Gallery like some poor relation and, until recently, its lack of presence was exacerbated by access difficulties and a consequent reluctance of visitors to penetrate its depths (including a C20 room of glass screens designed by Piers Gough). But it has its own, splendid collection and the architectural changes implemented by Dixon Jones (the Ondaatje Wing) have entirely reinvented the place and lent the attractiveness it's so desperately needed. Their key strategic move was to see the opportunity for a space swop with theNational that benefited both organisations. This enabled the architects to introduce a new circulation system much in the manner that Foster had done at the Sackler. Visitors still have to penetrate E.M. Barry's older but now short sequence that brings them into a new, tall lobby with a long escalator that sweeps them up to the top floor, thus enabling a simple glide back down through the gallery spaces - or, if they want, they can enjoy the excellent views from the upper level cafe.

It looks easy and has transformed the NPG into a more enjoyable place. But realising the lobby space and its suspended mezzanine floor required some old fashioned acrobatic engineering (that Dixon Jones have discretely hidden away).

Below: photos of the older parts

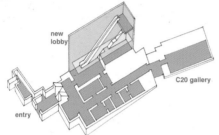

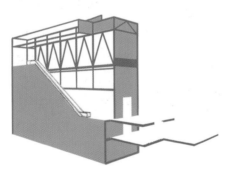

Cross section through the NPG, showing the tall new lobby with escalator and the restaurant at the top.

Wallace Collection

The Wallace Collection was bequested to the nation in 1897 and forms a fine collections of French 18th c. paintings, old masters, furniture and china, including Frans Hal's *Laughing Cavalier*, all housed in a late C19 mansion in central London, formerly being to the Wallaces. Like most galleries, the Wallace was short of space and the kinds of facilities people now expect. But the building was without room for expansion. Mather came up with the idea of excavating the basement in order to create a new lecture theatre, educational facilities and gallery space. In addition he proposed to glaze over the house's central courtyard to create a new, top-lit café. The outcome is not a Sackler or National Portrait Gallery with entirely reinvented circulation patterns, but is nevertheless a very good example of the quiet updating of an important London gallery.

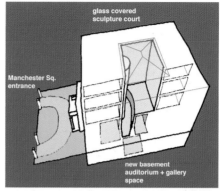

glass covered sculpture court

Manchester Sq. entrance

new basement auditorium + gallery space

33.

Manchester Square, W1
Rick Mather Architects, 2000
Tube: Bond Street, Marble Arch

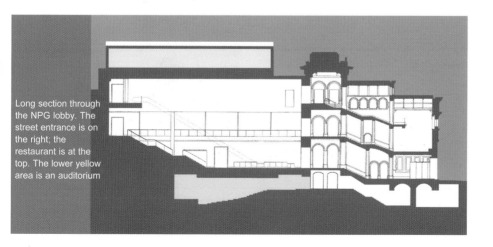

Long section through the NPG lobby. The street entrance is on the right; the restaurant is at the top. The lower yellow area is an auditorium

34.

National Gallery, Trafalgar Square, WC2
Venturi, Rauch, Scott-Brown & Partners, 1991
Tube: Charing Cross, Leicester Square.

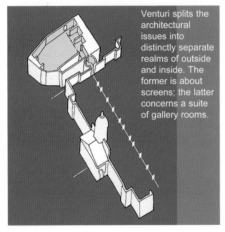

Venturi splits the architectural issues into distinctly separate realms of outside and inside. The former is about screens; the latter concerns a suite of gallery rooms.

The National Gallery has always had an unfortunate relation to Trafalgar Square, now the subject of a redesign by Foster, aimed at re-routing traffic and connecting the NG to the pedestrian areas. This has also prompted a re-examination of access arrangements by Dixon Jones, who have proposed a new, ground level entry that overcomes the problems of steps up to the confined portico.

Sainsbury Wing, National Gallery
Post-modern manners

The controversial history of this project, which began as a commercially funded extension to William Wilkins's building of 1832, began when the competition winners, Ahrends Burton Koralek (ABK), had their scheme denounced by Prince Charles as 'a carbuncle on the face of an old friend' – a somewhat saccharine comment about a rather weak neo-classical building that forms the northern edge of Trafalgar Square and sits as the termination of an axis up Whitehall. Another competition was held (limited, this time, to keep out the riff-raff) and the eventual winner was Venturi, Rauch, Scott-Brown Architects, from the USA (now VSBA). The outcome was a controversial scheme, but one that is rich in intellectual gusto. No doubt you'll either engage and possibly respect that, or - like most of the English architectural profession - turn in disgust from the whole enterprise. (To gauge the tenor of the times look at the opposite, south east corner of Trafalgar Square where there sits a multi-storey office building ostensibly at least 100 years old; it was constructed at the same time as the Sainsbury Wing, replacing an original building that looked exactly like this.)

The VBSA scheme almost literally hangs on a long transverse axis that passes through the main galleries of the Wilkins building, projected out into the new Sainsbury Wing building and terminated within (not by) a perspectival painting set within an arched frame (Cima's *The incredulity of Saint Thomas*). The architects then bring the painting's architectural content out into their own architecture, so that the two blend together in a forced perspectival play with a series of arched openings. This one gesture alone justifies a visit to the building and constitutes a powerful flourish of gamesmanship.

Visitors turn off this armature into a simple series of interlinked room settings with continual plays upon views of the unique and permanent collection of Medieval art, with carefully articulated diagonal views between rooms. Each of these enjoys well-engineered lighting (of which only a tiny proportion is real daylight) and makes reference to John Soane's rooms at the 1826 Dulwich Picture Gallery (England's first public gallery) whilst re-engineering the lantern to mask an upper service void and roof lights.

Outside, VBSA treats each facade as a set of discrete screens fronting a coherent internal suite of rooms, as if the two had little or nothing to do with one another - another move contradicting Modernist orthodoxy. The principal facade plays with the elements of the Wilkins frontage and 'ghosts' them into (out of?) their screening extension along this northern side of Trafalgar Square. The opposite, rear facade plays with neo-Las Vegas billboard themes (it faces toward Leicester Square, to which it reaches out in implicit desperation) and the west side is utilitarian, plain and brick. The area between the new wing and the old building is more complicated: a clever inside / outside game that places the main stair in an ambiguous situation, at once outside (the solid internal walling, stone-faced and similar to the other facade screens) and a large glass screen that protects it from the elements whilst offering a view (a reminder) of the Wilkins building and the bridge link that features as a discrete tower. Because black glass and heavy framing was chosen it doesn't work and Venturi has admitted as much, but it's a game try at something complicated and ambitious.

It adds up to erudite Post-Modernism, continually quoting precedents and employing recurring references (to the original Wilkins building; gives a nod to Finland's great architectural hero, Alvar Aalto on the main stair, and the way a mezzanine landing is used; and even homage to Egyptian sources (small columns, the deeper meaning of which no one has yet uncovered and which Venturi claims is arbitrary). It's a design that exudes competence, is clever, ironic (as Post-Modernists used to say), playful and even witty. For example, the large arches above the grand staircase leading from the entrance lobby up to the gallery spaces enjoys a reverse perspective and are a reference to Bernini's famous Scala Regia at the Vatican. However, in this instance the ceiling arches deliberately float, touching nothing (they're plywood), playing the game and giving it away at the same time, enjoying participation in the history of architecture whilst asserting originality.

Perhaps the English profession is being overly dreary in dismissing all this. Arguably, however, the validity of architecture rests ultimately in its authentic *actions* rather than mind games and a self-conscious architectural mannerism that continually says, 'look at me being clever. . .' Aesthetics, as Terry Eagleton contends, is a discourse of the body, not the mind. In the end one has to ask: does the heart keep pace with the head's respectful applause of VSBA's erudite acrobatics? Is the essential immediacy and emotive quality of the building – fundamentally important to all architectural experience – forced into the background, prompting intuitive discomfort?

Perhaps, in Venturi's own words, the Sainsbury remains 'almost all right' and is worthy of your attention. For, make no mistake: this is a level of architectural gamesmanship far too many architects are hardly capable of. Make a visit, but be prepared to stay awake.

34.

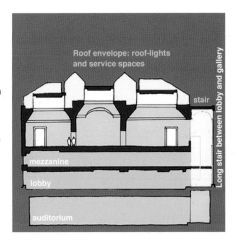

Roof envelope: roof-lights and service spaces

stair

mezzanine

lobby

auditorium

Long stair between lobby and gallery

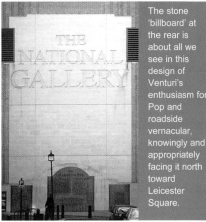

THE NATIONAL GALLERY

The stone 'billboard' at the rear is about all we see in this design of Venturi's enthusiasm for Pop and roadside vernacular, knowingly and appropriately facing it north toward Leicester Square.

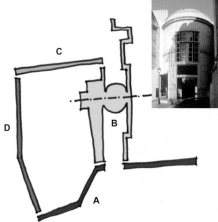

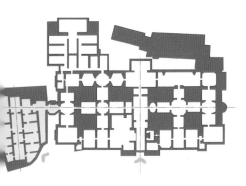

C

D   B

A

The external screening of the Sainsbury Wing divides into four separate architectural constructs that have an implict hierarchical significance (dominated by the Trafalgar Square facade). However, the most complex is 'B' below.

35.

The lobby of the Sackler straddles the full length of Burlington House above the two light wells that lie between the old house and Smirke's Victorian extension. White glass screens off roof-top views; the three gallery spaces are on the right.

Royal Academy, Piccadilly, W1
Foster and Partners, 1991
Tube: Piccadilly, Green Park

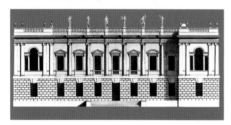

Sackler Gallery
heart surgery

At the core of the present Royal Academy building lies the only surviving mansion from a bygone Piccadilly: Burlington House, designed by Sir John Denham, built in 1664 and, in 1714, inherited by Richard Boyle, third Lord Burlington - a young aristocrat who included architecture among his enthusiasms and was to be described as 'the Apollo of the arts'. Boyle began to develop his estate in 1715 and - together with Colen Campell and the man who was to become his *protégé*, William Kent - he was to transform Burlington House into a showpiece of Italian Palladianism, based upon his experiences of Palladio's work on two Grand Tours and his studies of Palladio's *Quattro Libri*. Initially, however, significant architectural work began with a French-style screened and gated entry forecourt together with a double quadrant arcade, designed by the Italian-trained James Gibbs (later ousted during political machinations) and was later complemented by a host of trend-setting artists-in-residence. Burlington House came to epitomise Good Taste. Perhaps it still does.

One hundred years after Burlington's work, between 1815-19, came more remodelling, this time including Lord George Cavendish's relocation of the main stair to where it can be found now and a new garden facade, this time designed by Samuel Ware. In the meantime, London had changed enormously, the estate having to develop the Burlington shopping Arcade to capitalise upon the potential of a rapidly changing context.

Almost two hundred years after the remodelled house had been originally constructed, the house was purchased by the government for the purposes of making a home for Royal academies - which involved selling the garden to London University, who, between 1866-69, had Sir James Pennethorne design what became The Museum of Mankind. (This is currently the subject of a Michael Hopkins scheme that will extend the RA into these premises.)

Between 1868–74 Charles Barry (son of the architect for the Palace of Westminster) and R.R. Banks were changing the forecourt to what one sees now whilst Sydney Smirke set about providing a bridge from the landing of the old stair landing up to new gallery spaces located to the rear of the original Burlington House. In the process, two light-wells were generated between the old house and the new block. In addition, a third storey was added to the house in order to accommodate what was called the Diploma Galleries and a new facade screen was layered onto Burlington's frontage.

Over the next century, yet more architectural amendments were introduced, including a new stair and restaurant by Norman Shaw (1883), a reworking of the front rooms and hall by Sir T.G. Jackson (1899), a remodelling of the library by Curtis Green (1927), and another reworking of the entrance hall by Raymond Erith (1962). Architectural action was piling upon architectural action. Burlington House was still somewhere in there, but by the late 1980s it had become accepted that the building's arteries were seriously clogged. Strategic change was overdue and an opportunity arose with the need to replace the original, roof level Diploma Galleries. Norman Foster was appointed and his team (led by partner Spencer de Grey) subsequently instituted a remarkable piece of heart surgery to the aged pile, by then 325 years old.

In a dramatic and imaginary manner, the architects cleared out the two light wells, roofed them over and transformed these formerly silted-up, redundant spaces into the most significant features of a new pattern of circulation. This includes a lift to one well and a stair to the other, straddling the old link between the old Burlington House and the Victorian block. These lead to entirely new gallery spaces on the upper level (where the Diploma Galleries had been), complete with their own cool and spacious entry lobby.

The horizontal line of the Smirke's cornice - used as a shelf for classical and neo-classical sculptures - gives a unity to this space and is wrapped by a steel-framed enclosure holding white, translucent glass that admits daylight whilst obscuring the roof clutter outside (the current blinds on this glazing were a later addition). Beam to column joints are carefully sweated over, air conditioning slots are neatly incorporated into the skirting, leading to ducts within hollow walls and artful strips of glass flooring carefully differentiate old from new whilst emphasising a vertical dimension that runs through the scheme and links the lower entry level to this new, easily accessible upper level. Similarly, inside the galleries themselves, the architects offer bald, vaulted and top-lit spaces with the minimum of distracting rhetoric or clutter.

There are, however, difficulties with a tight-fit, poised design which rationally disposes every element of the design into a composition that only the audacious or ignorant might to dare to alter in any part because of a possible compromising and deleterious affect upon the whole. RA issues not anticipated or dealt with at the briefing stage and inevitably arising as needs and circumstances change have featured as a 'silting up': for

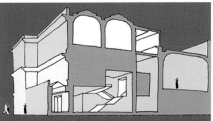

35.

The Sackler is experienced as the penetration of a series of screens and layers that draw the visitor deeper into the RA, beginning with the street screen, followed by the Burlington House frontages and the interior spaces that lead up to the Sackler Gallery lobby, and then into the galleries themselves.

example, the upper gallery lobby is often overloaded with miscellaneous furniture additions and the lower stair lobby sometimes accommodates heavy, Victorian pieces sitting upon the glass floor that contradict one's intuitive sense about its brittleness and load-bearing capacity. Despite such things, the design is still remarkable and it is a rewarding experience to walk an architectural promenade from Piccadilly, through Bank and Barry's gateway, on through Smirke's screen, into Burlington and Ware's hall, to then stand in the two light wells and experience Ware's pretentious garden facade on one side and Smirke's blind, utilitarian facade on the other, to then glide up in the glazed lift and sit in the upper lobby beneath Foster's frosted glazing and enjoy the work of the Ancients set upon the cornice. The architectural ghosts appear to be comfortable; no one being offended by Foster's interventions to keep old Burlington House alive and kicking.

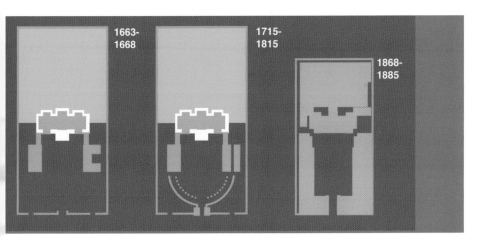

1663-
1668

1715-
1815

1868-
1885

36. *The **Economist** complex in St James's Street, SW1, designed by Peter and Alison Smithson in 1962–64, ranks as a supreme piece of urbanism - in part, the basis on which the Smithsons became architectural heroes. The development comprises three blocks (two offices and one apartment, together with a small window addition to the adjacent Boodles' club) arranged around a small, raised piazza – a mini Acropolis, all of it skilfully*

composed so as to terminate an urban block in the heart of establishment St James'. A textured version of Portland stone infested with fossils lends an almost mannered air to a design born into an era of 'angry young men' and architectural 'brutalism', and more famous for rude, interventionist examples of ostensibly progressive 'comprehensive redevelopment' than anything so polite as this. The design was also coming from a generation looking across the Atlantic for inspiration and there is a neo-Miesian inspiration to.the manner in which the columns are adorned. However, whilst the intention was to be progressive, the offices harked back to a previous era of the professional gentleman's facilities rather than the coming age of large floor-plates and open planning. The corner (former bank) block, with its double height piano nobile, is occasionally reinvented as gallery or expensive bar. SOM have altered the lobby of the offices and added a gratuitous canopy.

37. *Sir Denys Lasdun's **St James's apartment block** at 26 St James's Place, SW1, dates from 1958–60 and comprises split-level units (inspired by his former association with Wells-Coates' and the Tecton group's pre-war work) overlooking the park. It was the first such private block of apartments after WWII and is a fine compositional exercise which helped to establish Lasdun's reputation.*

38. ***New Zealand House***, (*Robert Matthew, Johnson-Marshall,1957-63; Haymarket, SW1) represents a fine example of the podium (with recessed ground floor) + tower (some 70m high) model that was once so fashionable. It was also one of the first buildings in*

London to be fully air-conditioned – a factor encouraging the architects and engineers to rather over-optimistically provide an all-glass facade. This produced so many problems that internal curtains were later added - which only adds to its character. The top level bar (not public) has a terraced perimeter with fine views.

39. *At the east end of Piccadilly sits what was Joseph Emberton's **Simpson** department store building (1935), now Waterstone's bookshop. Enough of the original remains to get a feeling for what it was like (try the upper level bar). Further along, adjacent to Wren's **St James' Church** (1682-84; his only 'green field' church design) sits a small ex-Midland bank by Edwin Lutyens - an enjoyable 'Wrenaissance' piece of 1922.*

Norman Shaw's New Scotland Yard building on Victoria Embankment (access from Parliament Street, SW1, is in two parts. The first and better half was designed and built between 1887–90 and the second between 1901–07. Both served the Metropolitan Police and are described by one historian as the nearest Shaw came to being serious (Baroque and Scottish Baronial). The base is made from granite quarried by convicts at Dartmoor. Above this rises a stout, square block in red brick with Portland stone stripes. The whole is topped by large gables and tall chimneys. At the corners, 'tourelles' are provided which help to give the building a stately castle air of the kind Shaw was familiar with from his Scottish background.

Portcullis House

When Norman Shaw's New Scotland Yard building was opened as a new home of the Metropolitan Police on the Victoria Embankment in 1890, it was popularly known as 'the jam factory' because of its horizontal bands of alternating red brick and Portland stone that were similar to a Crosse & Blackwell Pickle Factory in Charing Cross Road (the tradition continues as the Cockney nickname for a white and red striped police car, known as a 'jam sandwich'). Among its other peculiarities of this 'very constabulary' building, as it has been described, was the fact that the lower granite walls of Shaw's fortified, castle-like edifice were quarried by prisoners at Dartmoor and constructed upon the foundations of an incomplete national opera house. Scotland Yard is square in plan, with a central courtyard; its roof is steep and dominated by huge brick chimneys. It is this building that became one of the principal references for Portcullis House.

After 'the Met' moved out of Scotland Yard to a nearby building (of 1967), the 'Norman Shaw Building', as it became known, became a useful adjunct to the Palace of Westminster, just across the road. In turn, the growing complex of parliamentary accommodation was recently added to with a new building on the corner of the Embankment, known appropriately as Portcullis House, providing additional and much-needed offices and meeting rooms for members of Parliament. However, Michael Hopkins' design does more than pick up on a tradition of medieval and defensive references suggested by the building's name. It also tries hard to architecturally nestle into the historical tradition whilst remaining a contemporary act of design and construction, emulating many of Shaw's major architectural moves, particularly the general plan and roof forms. And make no bones about it: this is also a defensive design. Its cladding as surreptitiously bomb proof against today's terrorists as Shaw's had to be in its day (the original Scotland Yard buildings had been bombed in 1884).

The other contextural reference for Hopkins has been the Palace of Westminster itself. Dominated by the tower of Big Ben, the Charles Barry and Auguste Pugin design (completed in the 1850's) is surprisingly regular, even modulated, and has a strong vertical character that fights against its horizontal massing. It is this regular vertical emphasis that Hopkins picks up on and applies to his own facades. In this way he strongly and positively responds to the two significant works of architecture that define a context for the Portcullis House design.

The outcome has been a contentious building that divides opinion. But as an example of architectural gamesmanship it is remarkable, offering two surprises to its contextural game: an amazing, neo-Piranesian Underground station beneath the building (Westminster station) and a timber-framed courtyard roof that is quite outstanding and a contrast with the rather comparatively dour exterior.

Houses of Parliament, Victoria Embankment, SW1
Michael Hopkins & Partners, 2001
Tube: Westminster

The Design
The design of Portcullis is basically a five-storey do-nut with a 13.2m deep perimeter of offices off a double-loaded corridor, intended to accommodate 210 members of Parliament and linked to Barry's splendid building across the road by an underground tunnel - all designed to a brief that required the building to last 200 years. And be terrorist-proof.

Westminster Underground
At the heart of the Portcullis House do-nut is a central courtyard and at each corner of the building there is a set of lifts and stairs. In principle, it's very simple. However, the building sits upon a massive structural zone that enables the relatively shallow District and Circle Lines to pass beneath it. In turn, this sits upon a deep 'escalator box' that drops down to the deep level of the Jubilee Line tubes. This 'box' is an outstanding experience, redolent with Piranesian references. You must go there.

40.

The central court is a surprising contrast to the exterior. A diagrid aok structure with stainless steel joints and integral ventilation and lighting caps the entire inner area.

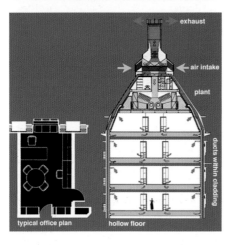

typical office plan   hollow floor

The Court

The ground floor of Portcullis provides shops and an entrance to the underground station on the street side and the building's main entrance along the river side. Internally, it is dealt with as one large room that reaches up two storeys and is covered by an arching laminated oak and glass roof studded with stainless steel fixings and bracing. The central part of this floor is a landscaped court with small trees and pools. On one side is a cafeteria and a waiter-service restaurant on the the other, opposite the main doors. There is also has an escalator that drops down to a tunnel leading under the road and links directly to the Palace of Westminster. A gallery runs around the space at first floor level, serving a series of committee and seminar rooms. This gallery runs behind six huge concrete arches that receive the building loads above and transfer them to pillars that penetrate through the lower structures beneath the building.

That roof and the cladding

The aluminium bronze alloy roof of Portcullis (three storeys high) is a ventilation system. The 'chimneys' draw foul air from the building, pulling it through huge pre-fabricated roof ducts (from secondary ducting built into the façade) up to where it is vented. And the roof form accommodates the machinery that draws the air out and pulls fresh air in (from the base of the chimneys), processing it and pumping it back into the building by means of other ducts in the façade that feed down and into deep floor voids, from where it gently enters the offices – and then leaves via the perimeter façade ducts. 13 chimneys extract and discharge air; the 14th chimney serves a generator and the boiler flues. Water for the air conditioning comes from two deep bore holes. This is fed through heat exchanges and provides cooling, thus obviating the need for refrigeration plant. (The same water is used as 'grey water' in the sanitary systems.) The roof, for example, includes three-storey, 700mm deep spine ducts cast made from welded 6mm aluminium bronze plates assembled off site. Each duct assembly - weighing 3 tonnes and containing insulated air intake and extract ducts - is put together with an arching roof structure of steel and aluminium bronze cladding. It's more like ship-building than normal architecture.

The roof arrangement for housing plant and processing air is merely one part of a complex servicing arrangement that provides the building with a rather sophisticated façade - one that it is virtually bomb proof, making it rather expensive. Between the vertical rhythm of Derbyshire gritstone facings on the outside are pre-fabricated façade elements that comprise the ducting, windows, sun-shading and a 'light shelf'. The windows are triple-glazed, with cavity louvre blinds. The blinds help to heat air that is drawn upward to the air conditioning plant, where heat exchangers draw the heat away and provide it to the fresh air being supplied back to the rooms.

41. *The **Foreign and Commonwealth Office** (1868–73), on the west side of Whitehall, SW1, is the design of Sir George Gilbert Scott, who wanted it to look as St. Pancras does now but was frustrated by the Italianate taste of his government clients and the architect Matthew Digby Wyatt, who did much of the interior (including the Dunbar Court).*
*To enjoy the building's architectural entertainments you have to await each September's **London Open***

House and see the remarkable interiors of this building, especially Dunbar Court and some of the staircases. It's worth it.

*To the south, on the corner of Parliament Square, Foster and DEGW have refurbished the interior of the **Treasury** (nothing to see on the outside).*

42. The **Palace of Westminster** (SW1, 1835–60, below right) is by Charles Barry and his assistant Augustus Pugin. The latter is the dominant figure – a precocious and talented man who was an impassioned convert to Catholicism, three times married and dying in the Bedlam Asylum for the insane by the age of 40 (in 1852). Barry carried on until he was 65, but was said to have died as a man worn out by the battle to realise Westminster Palace. Conditions of the original competition stated that the design had to be in the Gothic style, to harmonise with Westminster Abbey. Barry held that regularity and symmetry were the main principles in design; Pugin, who was responsible for the decoration, commented that the design was, "All Grecian, sir; Tudor details on a classic body". Although tourist images appear to emphasise the Gothic, decorative aspects of the design, it is Barry's regularity which marches across the facades and gives the building its underlying strength.

43. For a thorough neo-Gothic work in central London one would have to look at a building such as William Butterfield's 1849-59 church of **All Saints**, in Margaret Street, W1, (just NE of Oxford Circus; see p61) or George Street's masterful, free-style **Royal Courts of Justice** (left; 1871-82) at the east end of the Strand, opposite Wren's **St Clement's Danes** of 1680-2. Street was a remarkable man, working long hours, scratching out all his own detailed drawings and becoming an inspiration to people within the Arts & Crafts movement, coincidentally dying as the scaffolding of the Law Courts came down. The Courts building is profoundly romantic, with a central hall something like a large church nave.

44. **Downing Street** now has iconic significance: gated (since an IRA mortar bomb attack) and the scene of nightly BBC news broadcasts as well as tourists thronging the gate to the street (which used to be freely accessible). No.10 may look like just another domestic, early Georgian terrace house (originally built around 1680; rebuilt 1723 and then refaced in 1766) but it is actually the facade to a a set of rooms knitted into the Whitehall complex. George Gilbert Scott's Foreign Office sits opposite and the Old Treasury is behind (a building complex that bizarrely includes pieces of Tudor walling set behind glass walls).

45. In this unfashionable striped, stone and brick facade sitting opposite Lutyens' Cenotaph, William Whitfield emphasises verticality against the natural horizontality of **Richmond House** (Parliament Street, SW1, William Whitfield and Partners, 1987) and gives street presence to a large government building behind a set-back facade that is rich in references to the C16 (e.g. the cloth-like, 'folded' quality of wood panelling and facades such as that at Burghley House in Northants) and to Norman Shaw's adjacent New Scotland Yard of 1890 (also the subject of reference by Michael Hopkins in his design for Portcullis House, the nearby facilities for Members of Parliament). Try going down the mews on the south side for a view of all three buildings.

46. The **Cenotaph**, Whitehall, SW1, by Edwin Lutyens, 1919–20, is a small and dignified homage to those who died in the horrors of WWI (and is among many memorials by Lutyens including one at Tower Hill in the City). It remains a major site of ceremony and cultural memory and depends entirely upon its simple form and materiality for impact. Originally, it was intended to burn a gas flame – which would still be a nice touch.

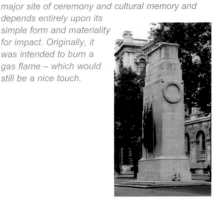

47.

Buckingham Palace, Birdcage Walk, SW1
Michael Hopkins & Partners, 1994
Tube: Green Park

Palace Ticket Office

This demountable building appears in the summer, camouflaged among the trees of Green Park, peeking out at the tourists visiting Buckingham Palace, like some stranded giant slug. Its tensile roof and wooden structure serve to emphasise its temporary, summer nature as a ticket office for visitors to the Palace. Sited anywhere else, it might have aroused more architectural celebration, but one suspects this modest beast is too near royalty and throngs of tourists for most of the architectural profession.

48. *The rationale for the **QEII Conference Centre** (Powell and Moya, 1986, Broad Sanctuary) derives from the context – the glass, lead and stone facades of the neighbours. The most dramatic feature is the employment of deep beams suspending the main conference floor (corresponding to the roofline of adjacent buildings). The stepped-back penthouse levels above hide an inner courtyard, delegates' bars, restaurants, etc., as well as secret parts even the architect is not entirely aware of. The overall aesthetic favoured by P & M is no longer fashionable, but that hardly detracts from the merits of the building.*

49. *The **Traveller's Club** (1829–32) and the **Reform Club** (1841) sit adjacent to one another in Pall Mall, SW1 (the street deriving its name from 'pallo di maglio', a game, and once famous for its coffee houses and clubs). The two buildings are designed by Charles Barry as two Italian palazzo on the Roman model, thus introducing a new thematic note to London buildings. The central atria of both buildings are rather grand, the*

travellers as an open cortile and the reform as a glazed over space. The Reform - the more impressive of the two buildings - has a wide, slow staircase rising to a perimeter gallery (or cloister) and the grand rooms of its piano nobile (esp. the Library). The accommodational arrangement of the normal London house is reversed, with servants in the basement and overnight guest rooms at the top. It's a building worthy of detailed study, especially with regard to its services.

Donald McMorran has a building on the Reform's west side: typically stripped, daunting, but intriguing (also see the Wood Street police station in the City, and his extension to the Old Bailey).

Channel Four

C4 has many of the brand features one has come to expect from the practice, especially a dramatic entrance area, complemented by scenic lifts, air conditioning towers and tall communications masts - features that were later developed in the City at Lloyd's Register and 88 Wood Street. Here, an axial geometry is 'hinged' upon the corner entrance – where 80% of the architectural imagery is strategically focused. A bridge beneath the suspended canopy is another attempt at drama; however, behind this is a curiously constricted lobby whose acrobatic (sharp-intake-of-breath), suspended glazing only just manages to avoid a disastrous conflict of elements (e.g. ties and gallery brackets) - a rewarding experience that, inevitably, does not have the rigour and depth of resolution of Lloyd's. Beyond this again is an open landscaped area shared with a housing development that sits opposite. The two side wings hold offices and the studios are underground, their cladding is similar to that of the Rogers' design for Broadwick House, in Soho.

50.

124 Horseferry Road, SW1
Richard Rogers Partnership, 1994
Tube: St. James's Park.

The entrance forecourt, with office wings to left and right.

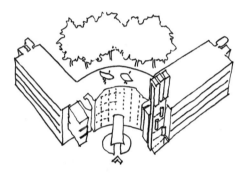

51. Built upon the site of a former penitentiary, John Francis Bentley's **Westminster Cathedral** in Ashley Gardens, SW1, built 1895–1903, is striking enough on the outside (designed to be a different style to Westminster Abbey), but there is a real constructional impact on the inside – the unfinished recreation of an Italian Byzantine church, concrete domes and massive brick vaulting (14 m of them).
The sculptures on the Stations of the Cross are by Eric Gill (1913-18).

52.

Southwark Jubilee Line Station, Stamford Street / Blackfriars Road, SE1
MacCormac Jamieson & Prichard, 1999 /JLE Architects, 1999.

Southwark Station

Another part of Waterloo to explore includes the link from the Waterloo East main line station to the new Jubilee Station further east, at Southwark. Internal area include two ticket halls and two concourses. A tall, naturally lit intermediate concourse is dominated by a blue 'cone wall' (40 m long and 16 m high) designed by MJP and the artist Alexander Beleschenko. It consists of 630 triangular panes of blue enamelled glass held on stainless steel 'spiders' (inspired, it is reported, by Schinkel's set for the Magic Flute!). Externally, the corner entrance refers back to 1930s stations of Charles Holden and his concept of a 'grand corner' leading into a tall, drum-like ticket hall.

Just opposite the station, a Will Alsop designed office building is in construction (due for completion in 2004).

53. *Like Bryan Avery's other buildings there is a distinct quirkiness as well as skill in the design of this tall office building straddling the road on the east side of Victoria Station (**Neathouse Place**). The upgrading of an old 1960s office building is self-assured and the architect has responded with clarity to the different environmental*

demands placed upon the north-east and south-west facades, changing the form of the glazing to suit, from a vertical to a horizontal zig-zag profile. Self-evidently, this is an architect looking for a way to break away from conventions in order to offer an element of reinvention and surprise.

54. *The **Lillington Gardens** estate in Vauxhall Road, SW1, designed by Darbourne and Darke (1961–71), is a much admired piece of comprehensive redevelopment, although subsequent apartment sales have produced a strange crop of neo-Georgian doors and the like. A similar scheme in Islington (Marquess estate, opposite the Future Systems house), has*

undergone radical changes in order to reintegrate its courtyards back into the pattern of surrounding city streets.

*In the midst of Lillington Gardens you will find George Street's equally good church of **St James-the-Less** (1860–61).*

55. *Imperial War Museum (Arup Associates, 1989, DEGW 1999; Kennington Park Road, SE1.) Boys with their horrific toys. Actually, there is also a fine art collection here, all of it housed within a conversion (of what was once the old Bedlam asylum) by Arup Associates. Arup's provided new gallery spaces and a later holocaust exhibition was designed by DEGW. The museum exhibition designs, by Jaspar Jacobs, have been criticised for*

their jolly, sanitised, designer-vision of war but the treatment of the Holocaust is, inevitably, quite disturbing despite a degree of sanitisatation for those into weekend entertainment with the kids.

56. *Lambeth Health Centre (Edward Cullinan Architects, 1984, Monkton Street, SE1, is aging, but worth a visit: an intermediate hospital between the real thing and home care is the nearest anyone in the UK got to the once fashionable work of German 'Deconstructivist' Gunther Behnisch during the 1980's – yet it remains a continuation of Cullinan's earlier rational and humanistic ad-hocism: low on budget, high on the need for lots of client consultation and satisfaction, leaning toward a free-style, arts-and-crafts bias. Characteristically, the street facade features ceramic roundels of healing*

herbs painted by a local artist, but the most important frontage is to the south-facing rear garden rather than the street - not accessible without permission.

London
Riverside

The Thames has always been London's life-blood: a quietly serving, much abused artery that in the Middle Ages provided fresh water and fish, and by the middle of the C19 was a stinking open sewer spurned by all except those river workers - the East End dockers and sailors and the like - to whom it gave a living.

By the1950's the river was still a very sad, grey, cold thing known for its poisonous waters, tides, vicious currents and hot weather smells - a sister to the infamous London fogs. In 1957 only eels could survive in its waters. And then the closure of the docks in the late 1960's quietly co-incided with a period initiating a massive rehabilitation. but hardly any one noticed and most Londoners continued to turn their back upon the Thames.

Then something remarkable happened: around the Millennium, London's citizens rediscovered the Thames and its embankments. It became not only possible but desirable to walk from Vauxhall Bridge all the way to Butlers Wharf and beyond. The riverside - especially the south side - had became a major leisure route. Parisian-style glass topped tourist boats plied the river and offered new prospects and camera opportunities to tourists. Commuter boat services to Canary - an off/on affair at the best of times - were now viable and reliable. London had apparently rediscovered its artery.

Of course, with hindsight, one could see the improvements slowly coming into place. But it is still remarkable how a vast reorientation took place triggered by a few significant events such as the London Eye, the Tate Modern, and the Somerset House terrace. Places that had invariably been accessed from the landside suddenly became features of a new riverside promenade. Older sights such as the Southbank, the Design Museum and the Globe Theatre attained a new significance midst a brotherhood of riverside friends from whom they had previously been divorced. Two new bridges (the wobbly Millennium and the additions to Hungerford) were opened. A new City Hall appeared. Farrell's much criticised MI6 and Embankment Place buildings were suddenly respectable riverside ornaments.

Fishermen watched by tourists now patiently awaited the nibbling attention of live fish whilst older Londoners smiled in bemusement. Web sites on the Thames proliferated. The tourist authority promoted the river experience as a major London event and weekends saw the southern embankment from Westminster to the Tower thick with curious crowds. Even the more disjointed northern embankment enjoyed new attention. And our third edition of this guidebook had to rejig its content.

This section covers buildings along the river, from Vauxhall Bridge to Butlers Wharf, principally on the southern side, especially after Blackfriar's Bridge.

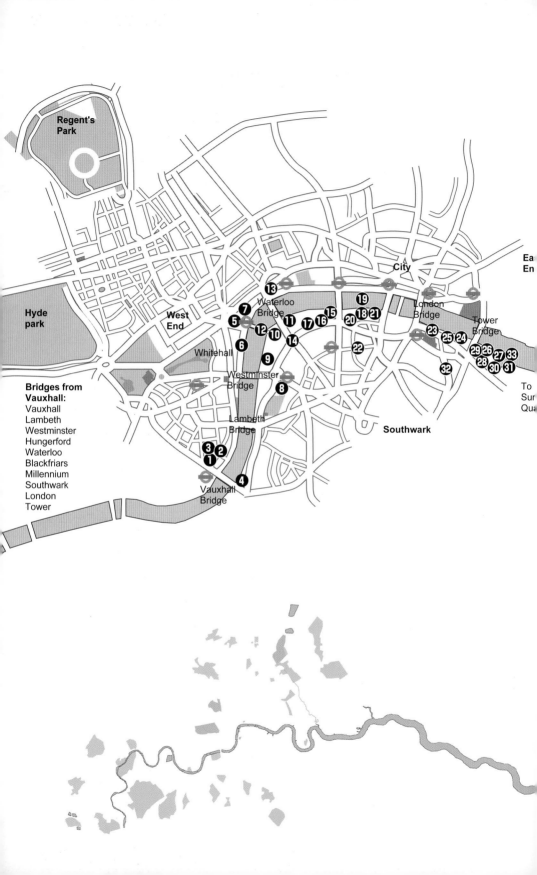

Regent's
Park

Hyde
park

West
End

Whitehall

**Bridges from
Vauxhall:**
Vauxhall
Lambeth
Westminster
Hungerford
Waterloo
Blackfriars
Millennium
Southwark
London
Tower

Waterloo
Bridge

Westminster
Bridge

Lambeth
Bridge

Vauxhall
Bridge

City

London
Bridge

Tower
Bridge

Southwark

Ea
En

To
Sur
Qua

Riverside Notes

The southern embankment of the Thames has become a promenade. Most people are likely to begin using that promenade at Westminster Bridge (using Westminster underground Station) but we begin this section at Vauxhall Bridge, where the Embankment walk logically begins and where the Tate Britain is located (best accessible from Pimlico underground station). You could start here and walk all the way to Tower Bridge and beyond (or vice versa).

At **Vauxhall** you will find (on the south side) Farrell's MI6 building - which has always suffered the fate of huge unfashionability (possibly a good reason to look more closely at it). Your more likely attraction around Vauxhall would be Stirling's Clore Gallery extension to the old Tate and the more recent John Miller work (at Tate Britain, p96-7). You could then find yourself wandering past Lambeth Bridge (perhaps across it to Waterloo) toward Westminster, past the Palace of Westminster, the Abbey and Portcullis House (all on the north side and in the West End section because they are more properly a part of Whitehall; see p85-87). A diversion from this route would be a turn inland at Lambeth Bridge to Rogers' Channel Four building (p89), where the nearby street market makes an interesting lunchtime diversion. You could then walk back toward the Abbey and Westminster Bridge, along Victoria Street.

Starting at **Westminster**, you are likley to come through Hopkins' remarkable Jubilee station (see page 85) and crossing the bridge will provide some fine views that naturally draw you toward the the London Eye. Beyond that is the revamped Hungerford Bridge and the Southbank cultural centre, together with Denys Lasdun's National Theatre and IBM building. The choice here is to go across Hungerford bridge to explore Farrell's Embankment Place and the adjacent Embankment Gardens (with Inigo Jones' riverside gateway). You could then return down the other side of the bridge to the Southbank.

From this point on you are likely to be keeping to the south side all the way to Tower Bridge. This neglects some fine attractions on the northern side such as Somerset House and the Temple, but you could make a diversion across Waterloo Bridge for some of the best views in London.

The southside embankment is particularly pleasant just east of Waterloo and after this it will take you past the Oxo Building, refurbished by Lifschutz Davidson, who also did the recent work at Hungerford Bridge. Another diversion around here is to Coin Street itself, where there is interesting housing by Lifschutz Davidson and Haworth Tompkins.

Winding along the river and under bridges is interesting enough at this point, but your next major attraction is the new Tate Modern, the Millennium (foot) Bridge and the thatched reconstruction of the Globe Theatre (possibly as unfashionable among architects as Farrell's buildings, but well worth a visit if you can stand for a two hour performance!).

As you move east toward London Bridge the attractions become rather touristy (the Clink, Vinopolis, etc.), but scratch the surface and there is genuine historical interest here. But the best attractions are Southwark Cathedral and Borough Market - the latter beginning in the late '90's as a 'farmer's market' and quickly blossoming into a major weekend venue for (delicious but somewhat overpriced) organic foodstuffs. Like a similar 'spontaneous' eruption at Spitalfield, the Borough Market is continually under threat but its success appears to have saved it for the moment (although the 'farming' content becomes increasingly questionable). The Fish restaurant here is an inventive design by Julyan Whickham (no longer in its original ownership).

Walk under London Bridge toward Hays Galleria - a former barge inlet serving warehouses, now infilled and covered. You are now away from the river itself but Hays brings you back to it. On the axis of Hays' central mall are principal City buildings such as Lloyd's of London.

Walking east from here brings you to London's new City Hall, designed by the Foster office (Fosters' testicle as it has been called!).The adjacent office development around City Hall is also by Foster.

Now you are at Tower Bridge (the alternative starting point for this perambulation) and the next attraction is an area that is technically a part of Docklands: Butlers Wharf. You will now walk along Shad Thames - once a street serving the adjacent warehouses that have now been converted (many by Terence Conran) into apartments and restaurants. This leads you past a large Julyan Whickham development redolent with Dutch overtones (his father-in-law is Aldo van Eyck) to the Design Museum and a small building by Hopkins. It's an interesting area, solidly defined, once all warehousing, and worth wandering around.

From here you can cross St. Saviour Dock on a recent footbridge designed by Nicholas Lacey and you can see two buildings designed by Piers Gough (China Wharf and a small housing block, both hanging over the river). However, unless you're feeling adventurous, most of you will now turn back toward Tower Bridge rather than fight your way through to Rotherhithe and beyond (which is not to say this isn't worth doing!). If you do want to go on, you can get to Cherry Garden and Hope (Sufferance) Wharf, where there is a small 'village' including recent work by Hawkins Brown. You can then get to Surrey Quays (which feels like a 'new town'; Canada Water Jubilee Station is here), rapidly changing Deptford (also served by the DLR and where the Laban Centre is located) and on to Greenwich Penninsula (again served by the Jubilee Line).

1.

Millbank, Atterbury Street, SW1
John Miller / Allies and Morrison, 2002
Tube: Pimlico

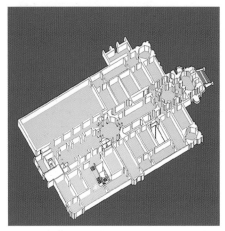

Tate Britain

Since the Tate Modern at Bankside, the old Tate (Sidney Smith, 1897, with the additional 1937 Duveen sculpture galleries by Romaine Walker and John Russell Pope, Llewellyn Davies et al's 1979 galleries, and Stirling's Clore Gallery) has reinvented itself as the Tate Britain and has been provided with new galleries and a new west side entrance designed by John Miller (whilst Allies and Morrison handled the external landscaping).

The Miller design adds about one third to the gallery accommodation (the refurbishment of five galleries and the addition of nine new ones), but this has been seamlessly handled so as to blend in with the old building. The heart of the work is a new, spacious entrance hall with a grand staircase. In all, it's an interesting and finely crafted mix of gallery motifs, taking from Smith, from Stirling and possibly a variety of other sources. Oddly, this almost detracts from the merits, identity and potential uniqueness of Miller's work. Nevertheless, it all adds up to a reinvigorated Millbank Tate that is going to win a lot of converts who hugely favour this building rather than the Herzog & de Meuron building.

2. The **Millbank Estate**, sitting behind the Tate Gallery, was completed by the London County Council (LCC) Architect's Department in 1903, following its very first estate in Shoreditch (the Boundary estate). Further north, in Page and Vincent Streets, SW1, there is a large (and curious) estate designed by Sir Edwin Lutyens (1928–30). It's a curious design, the facades being patterned like a chess-board.

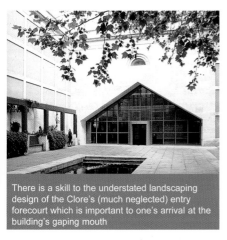

Clore Gallery, Tate

3.

Tate Gallery, Millbank, SW1
Stirling Wilford Associates, 1986
Tube: Pimlico

This a skilled 3,200 sq.m.. addition to Smith's 1897 edifice funded by the sugar magnate, Henry Tate, and designed to house the Gallery's Turner collection. The building sits quietly in a corner of the Tate entrance garden, looking somewhat forlorn and out of fashion – but this does not take away from the interest it holds - much of it based on the fact that Stirling was highly constrained. The budget was tight and the client's brief very specific (room layouts, their sequence, a principal level as the existing galleries, etc.). One feels Stirling searching out room to manoeuvre that could engage his penchant for architectural gamesmanship without encroaching into areas of performative contention - a classic case of the architect reframing a project and posing his own problems. Much of this begins on the pavement as an understated approach through a landscaped forecourt. The facade quietly integrates itself with other buildings on the site by picking up their key formal features (the classical language, red brick and Portland stone), incorporating them and then quickly abstracting and intruding upon their influences. Characteristic Stirling trademarks include notes of irreverence which delight, for example, in using an acid-green he must have known most people dislike. He plays a mild joke with what is ostensibly the structural grid of the facade and then gives the deceit away at the corner and even attempts a joke with corner windows which thinly refer back to 'missing' stonework in his Stuttgart art gallery (1984). The organisation includes an arrival axis at 90 degrees to a series of events (a minor, compressed *architectural promenade*) which includes a brightly coloured, top-lit staircase and a proscenium arch leading into the gallery rooms. Sadly, the latter have now been altered to remove the carpet, change the controversial beige fabric wall colouring and remove a screened seating area formerly overlooking the understated landscaped forecourt.

There is a skill to the understated landscaping design of the Clore's (much neglected) entry forecourt which is important to one's arrival at the building's gaping mouth

MI6

4.

Vauxhall Bridge / Albert Embankment, SE1
Terry Farrell Partnership, 1993
Tube: Pimlico

Once upon a time . . . there was a competition-winning residential scheme (based on the idea of maximising views to the river) which evolved into offices to suit market changes. Such things often happen in architecture. During scheme design, the developer's telephone rang. It was the Prime Minister. She - the lady with the handbag - wanted a large building for a secret service that, one had to understand, didn't exist. And so the design was reinvented as an impenetrable river palace for the mysterious figures of MI6, with the most expensive concrete cladding in Europe and a fit-out costing more than the shell. The architect's design for Big Brother was a sculptural, striking green glass and cream concrete construction, appropriately defying easy interpretation of its inner organisation (the massing derives from origins in a competition-winning design by Farrell for apartments; the idea was that everyone would have a river view). The outer garb was inspired by the New York of the 1920s and 1930s, when Captains of Capitalism wore broad shoulders pads, posed in Moderne guise, and sported stepped-back buildings designed by the likes of Holabird and Root, Raymond Hood, Betram Goodhue and Hugh Ferri. There was even a hint of early Frank Lloyd Wright in Mayan mood in the HVAC housings on the top of the building, and spikey features incongruously reminiscent of the crown on the statue of Liberty. *And James Bond moved in everyone lived happily ever.* You can even walk in front of the building on the riverside walkway and enjoy a close view of where the MI6 spies live.

Charing Cross, WC2
Terry Farrell Partnership, 1991
Tube: Embankment, Charing Cross

5.

Embankment Place

One usually finds a variety of functional, urban and historical themes in Farrell's work. In this instance – one of the few buildings which positively addresses the Thames – they include employing the air rights over the 1863 rail station; external service cores (as at Lloyd's, as Farrell points out); historical references to the large houses and palaces once lining the Thames between the City and Whitehall; references to Ledoux in the water feature of the lobby, to the Moscow Kurskaya station on the station platforms and, near the Embankment, to Otto Wagner's Vienna stations.

   The new work sits upon the old station undercroft of brick vaults (a feature that is comparable with the work of Farrell's ex-partner, Nick Grimshaw, at Waterloo), making it reminiscent of conquering cultures building new temples upon the foundations of the existing ones, literally absorbing history into what is contemporary (and, in this case, simultaneously regurgitating other historical themes). Strong features and contrasts characterise one's experience of the building. For example, there is the massive scale and character of structural acrobatics involved in spanning the rail tracks (best appreciated from the South Bank, from where one can also see how the service towers straddle the sides of the upper offices and the station itself). There is also a (not unsuccessful) contrast between the building's Baroque presence and the scale of older buildings, especially in Villiers Street, on the east side.

*The **Station Hotel** (Strand side,1863–64), is by E.M. Barry, son of Sir Charles, who designed the Houses of Parliament; it is one of the first buildings to use artificial stone. Barry was also involved in work at the Royal Academy and the Royal Opera House.*

6 *The Thames **Embankment** is a tremendous 3.5 mile engineering feat and was constructed in 1868–74, by Sir Joseph Bazalgette. One of its key features, Cleopatra's Needle, is a plundered Egyptian obelisk dating from 1500 BC.*

7. ***York Watergate** (1626), within Embankment Gardens, SW3, is reputed to be designed by Inigo Jones and marks the bank of the Thames before the Victorian Embankments were built. One's imagination might bring back the ghosts of river travellers, mounting steps such as these in order to get to York House and, later, to the streets immediately behind. The latter included Villiers and Buckingham Streets – some of the first speculative developments in London (1670s on), founded on the novel and modern idea of order and regularity, and developed by the notorious speculator, Dr Nicholas Barbon. (Execution usually produced an appealing form of irregularity resulting from the development of individual plots by separate builders.)*

Waterloo Eurostar

8.

Eurostar Terminal, Waterloo
Nichols Grimshaw & Partners, 1993
Tube: Waterloo

NicholasGrimshaw's brand game at Waterloo has been to provide something like the airport experience: arrival, checking-in, waiting areas, restaurants and cafes, etc., offering sleek trains and a sinuous platform covered by an arching roof (which was actually only 10% of the overall budget). Grimshaw has provided a design statement integrated into an existing Victorian station, its structure rooted into the brick vaults supporting the rail lines. The roof structure being the upper, most visible part of what is described as a 'five-layer sandwich' comprising roof, platforms, departure level, arrivals level, and basement car park. It comprises a 400 m long series of three-pin arches with off-set central pins to cope with the eccentricity of five rail tracks and constraints such as underground tunnels. The eastern side is mostly opaque, with an internal structure, reversed on the west side so daylight can be admitted. Standard parts fit the varying, difficult geometry and take the shock-waves generated by long, heavy trains arriving from France (the glazing has to accommodate an 80 mm horizontal movement and a 6 mm vertical movement as the trains impact the station) e.g. all the glazing would normally have been thousands of special cuts, but Grimshaw has used flexible gaskets and standard, rectangular sheets of overlapping glass.

The Eurostar terminal at Waterloo was finished in 1993. Eurostar will soon be going into St Pancras / Kings Cross, when major works are completed there in a few years time (such things take a long time in the UK). Meanwile you can see another Grimshaw rail station exercise at Paddington Station (street side).

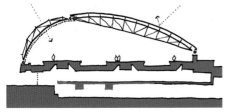

9.

Jubilee Gardens, Belvedere Road, SE1

David Marks & Julia Barfield Architects, 2000

Tube: Waterloo, Embankment

London Eye

The 135 m diameter London Eye was the swan amongst the Millennium ducklings. In itself, this giant rotating bicycle wheel is dramatic and spectacular. But it has also shifted the nature and pattern of tourist attractions in the area, helping to revitalise Westminster Bridge and the South Bank. It was conceived by its architects as a Millennium scheme, in response to the then Conservative government's call for appropriately whacky ideas. They didn't see this (sitting opposite the Palace of Westminster) as a suitable one and, unable to win Lottery funding, the architects resorted to commercial interests. British Airways saw the publicity opportunity and backed the scheme (with part ownership and at an enormous 24% interest rate on the capital loan!). Planning permission was granted - initially a temporary five years - and the Eye's spectacular success had soon won everyone over.

The structure hangs the wheel over the Thames and triangulates and stabilises it where the motors are located. Each glass capsule slowly rotates on bearings as the wheel turns.

The flight (sic) takes about 35 minutes and the views from the 32 capsules of the Eye are superb (on a clear day), but make sure you book before turning up.

10. The **Royal Festival Hall**, SE1, was built as a 'people's palace' for the celebratory Festival of Britain in 1951 and remains its lone survivor (the rest having been demolished by a disgruntled and reactionary Winston Churchill). It was principally designed by Leslie Martin, Peter Moro and Edwin Williams at the LCC Architects Department as an inner 'egg' (the 2,600 seat auditorium) surrounded by foyers and other accommodation, including a remarkable 'flowing' staircase concept and as much transparency as possible. The building is a monument to when post-war architects believed in socialism, progress and the notion that 'art should lead the facts of science' and experts were closely involved from the very beginning in the design of its auditorium. But the constraints of time and budget meant that it was never completed as intended and, by the early '60's, its neo-Scandinavian aesthetics were being dismissed as 'nautical whimsy' (Warren Chalk) and the building overlaid by more robust neo-Corbusian enthusiasms that included extensions, refronting and relocating the main entrances from the side to the river front. By then the building was a firm feature of new masterplans for the Southbank and its lost 'small hall' became the seed for the Queen Elizabeth Hall - added to by the Purcell Room, a gallery idea (now the Hayward) originating with an ICA scheme to move here and the National Film Theatre (a reinvention of the Festival's 'Telekinema'). Much of this became the 'brutalist' concrete buildings and surrounding decks created by London County Council architects (who included the Warren Chalk, Ron Herron, Denis Crompton trio of Archigram). The RFH remains a splendid building, now more easily accessible because of the new Hungerford Bridge. The restaurant was recently refurbished by Allies and Morrison, who are currently architects for a large refurbishment scheme aiming to restore some of the original features.

11. **The National Theatre**, Upper Ground, SE1, designed by Sir Denys Lasdun & Partners (1967–77; petulantly denounced by Prince Charles as something akin to a nuclear power station) makes a superb contrast with the RFH. Where the latter's spaces are open and filled with light, people 'pouring' down its grand staircases, the National offers a different aesthetic agenda more enthused by (a Japanese-like) enthusiasm for shadows and contrasts between dark, light, for huge cantilevering horizontal planes, and embodying an underlying obession with castles (surely the major clue to the whole place?).

The plan configures three halls into a more or less square plan cut across by a diagonal axis that focuses upon the north-west corner, adjacent to Waterloo Bridge, emphasising this entry corner and locating service and support areas to the south and east sides (in different circumstances, the back end of the building). The scheme is simple but the experience is complex and dramatic: insitu concrete finishes, enclosed staircases, views between floors, a plush purple carpet and wonderful views toward St Paul's. Well, it was that way until generations of managers silted up the place in order to provide the layers of before, between, and after performance servicing that theatre-goers now demand. The outcome was late '90's revisions to the lobby area by Stanton Williams that deeply troubled Lasdun and compromised his architecture. Alternatives from the original architect that might have improved access - especially car drop-offs and other vehicular servicing, together with proposals for tented structures populating the rather underused terraces and providing cafes and the like - were rejected, although he did manage to prevent 'pollarding' the terracing and having the SW proposals approved on the basis that everything could be easily reinstated. However, this is a robust building and well worth exploring. Go to the Lyttleton for a performance. But also go some sunny day when the National is empty and quiet, and you can explore its castle-like spaces and search out the ghost of its architect: some little boy probably still excitedly rooting around what he finds to be the most interesting place in the world.

12.

Victoria Embankment, WC2
Lifschutz Davidson. Engineers: WSP Group, 2002
Tube: Embankment, Waterloo

Hungerford Bridge

The proposal for this bridge is rooted in an early '90's consultancy about Waterloo Station, calling for improved access across the river. The problem was that generations of Londoners had suffered a ludicrously uncomfortable pedestrian way strapped onto the northern side of the Hungerford railway bridge - a principal means of getting from Charing Cross to the Southbank cultural centre and to Waterloo. Years later, having dealt with an unexploded WWII bomb, the consequent delays and extra costs involved (requiring Mayor Livingstone to bail out the scheme), Londoners were able to enjoy a hugely improved bridge with two new pedestrian walkways strapped onto the old railway structure.

The architects talk of the suspension structure as 'angel's wings' and such like, but one has little need for this sort of promotional rationale now that the bridge is complete. Structurally, the new work straps itself onto the old like the beast in 'Alien' locked onto the face of an unlucky

astronaut! The white steelwork of the new grabs a hold of the old Hungerford Bridge stanchions and sends tall suspension masts into the air on either side. What the river crossing pedestrian experiences is transformed: what was ugly has become a stroll across a (comparatively broad) river boulevard that comes complete with entrepreneurial street sellers quick to recognise the opportunities that other bridges fail to provide. Meanwhile, commuter trains rattle by. And at night the lighting reveals it as a thing of beauty.

Ironically the project suffered many problems and the architect's idea and design ended as a design & build exercise from which they resigned, leaving all sorts of contention regarding value engineering, details, cross links between the walkways, etc. Sad, but the reality of the thing is sufficient.

Somerset House

13.

Strand, WC2

Dixon Jones / Inskip & Jenkins / Feilden &
Mawson, 2001

Tube: Temple, Embankment, Covent Garden

Somerset House was originally designed by Wiliam Chambers (1766), built to house the learned societies, government offices and the Navy Board. As the reinvention of a former Tudor palace on the site it was effectively London's first major public office building and parelled the quite different Adelphi exercise by the Adam brothers, just upstream, (begun 8 years before). Both schemes straddled a wider River Thames before the Embankments were constructed and enjoyed direct boat access to vaults at the lower level. Access from the Strand was at a much higher level and the difference is still a key part of the experience (e.g. moving from the entry lobby down the flights of stairs to the basement cafe). The building's reinvention in the late '90's cleared out the Inland Revenue and its less-than-imaginative use of the central court as a car park, giving the buildings a long overdue *grands projet* treatment. Dixon Jones were responsible for the excellent fountain court (shades of Parc Citroen in Paris) and the more tentative river terrace (which includes a footbridge link onto Waterloo Bridge). Other parts include the Courtauld Gallery, Hermitage

The river terrace offers a tentative cafe - quite well designed but rather unsure whether it should be there or not.

Rooms, and Gilbert Collection (of decorative arts). However, it is regrettable to see much of it sinking back into a stereotypical English mish-mash of half-resolved gestures, situations, and services. The building fabric was handled by Feilden Mawson. Inskip & Jenkins did the Gilbert.

14.

Waterloo Bridge/Waterloo Station, SE1
Avery Associates, 1999
Tube: Waterloo

IMAX Cinema

This 500 seat cinema is a comparatively simple and clean statement. It takes the form of a glass drum sat within the centre of a large traffic roundabout (but accessed at a lower level, from the Southbank) and has thus become an instant, self-advertising land-mark of the kind that is still quite rare in London. It is also an important part of proposals to renew and revitalise the whole of the South Bank cultural area. The photo shows the building in context (Farrell's Embankment Place can be seen across the river, at the top left). Unfortunately, they clothe the outer face of the drum in art, as if this were somehow better than plain architecture, a celebration of cinema, or even advertising.

15.

OXO Development, South Bank, SE1
Lifschutz Davidson, 1997
Tube: Waterloo

OXO Development

Another Coin Street development by the same architects as for Broadwall, this time as a redevelopment of the old OXO building (whose idiosyncratic tower remains). The cherry of this 15,000 sq.m. mixed-use development is the riverside restaurant, bar and brasserie on the top floor of this reinvented 1928 building. It's rather late 1990s yuppie (managed by Harvey Nichols), but the views from the terrace are superb, even if its north-facing aspect makes it less than the warmest place in town. The ambience of the restaurant is affected by overhead motorised fins which change the ceiling colour and alter both lighting and acoustics. Other floors include 78 apartments designed for the Coin Street Housing Association.

16.

Bernie Spain Gardens, Belvedere Road, SE1
Lifschutz Davidson, 1994
Tube: Waterloo

Broadwall

Coin Street Community Builders are the non-profit making developer behind this scheme of 27 units, now in the hands of a housing cooperative. Eleven of the homes are for families, in 3 storey units; walk-up flats are at the southern end of the row in a 4 storey block (no lift); other small flats are concentrated in the 9 storey northern tower. The street side has well-handled access and nominal buffering from passers-by. The garden side is stridently articulated with flues (additional winter heating) and the whole thing has an evident Danish inspiration that is refreshing on the British scene. The scheme is worth comparing with the more Barcelona-cum-Georgian enthusiasms of the more recent Haward Thompkins scheme (see below).

Iroko housing

This Coin Street community scheme sits above an underground car park and bounds the block with tight terracing that forms (or will do when the fourth side is complete) and private inner sanctum for tenants. The model is vaguely Holland Park from the early C19, as reinvented at Milton Keynes, now translated and tightened up for this urban setting, and given a rather Spanish-inspired aesthetic - a well designed simplicity that is quite rare in London. The project provides a total of 59 dwellings and includes 32 family houses which can each accommodate up to 8 persons, the balance of accommodation is made up of a mix of flats and maisonettes. All dwellings are for rent and are managed by a housing co-op formed by the residents. Access is via a common balcony. A simple series of principles have been established in planning the dwellings. All the houses have street level entrances and private gardens opening on to the communal courtyard. All the flats and maisonettes have large balconies and each of the bedrooms overlooking the courtyard has a balcony. Bricks are used externally and timber within the courtyard. The buildings have been designed on low energy and sustainable design principles with the overriding objective of producing elegant buildings that are simple for the occupants to use. Passive solar panels have been included in the scheme to provide domestic hot water for each dwelling. A lightweight, low embodied energy solar panel on each roof preheats the water to the hot water tank in the house, providing free hot water for most of the summer months and contributing greatly to reducing the demand on the heating system for the rest of the year.

17.

Belvedere Road, SE1
Haworth Tompkins, 2001
Tube: Waterloo

The internal court contrasts with the exterior, setting up a multi-level duality of uses, finishes, etc.

18.

Bankside, SE1

Herzog & de Meuron, 2000

Tube: Blackfriars, Southwark, St Paul's

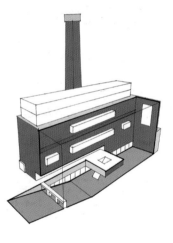

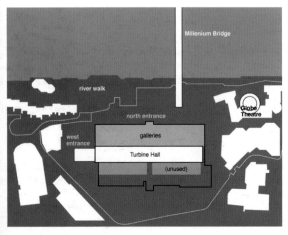

Tate Modern

The English appear to suffer from the need to house their new institutions in buildings formerly intended for something else (perhaps as reassuring remembrance of the past). Banking halls become wine bars, pumping stations become restaurants and, in this instance, a not very old power station made from 4.2m bricks has been transformed from utilitarian purpose into an edifice devoted to the consumption of art. As such, the Tate Modern - perhaps more than any other London building - embodies the transformation of our economy from manufacturing goods to manufacturing sources of entertainment (as well as a recent and novel propensity among the English to patronise foreign architects - a fact the Swiss architects were aware of and, apparently, not an experience they are keen to repeat).

Bankside was designed in 1947 by Sir Giles Gilbert Scott (1880-1960) and completed in 1963. Being oil powered it was closed in the late 1970's after the 1974 oil crisis and the economic crisis that followed. It was then quickly forgotten and ignored, despite its scale and location. In part, this was because the Thames itself had been forgotten and partly because the local area was on the wrong side of the river - self-evidently a poor cousin to the City on the opposite, northern bank.

In its present guise the building has been hollowed out internally whilst retaining the massive brick walls and chimney (some parts still await future funding and conversion). The massive turbine hall has been reinvented as a monumental, top-lit lobby space accessed by an equally generous ramp sliding down into the sunken ticket, information and educational areas, adjacent to which is one of London's largest bookshops. Access escalators, lifts, new gallery floors and other accommodation - including cafes, restaurant, an auditorium, a members room, etc. - are stacked along the adjacent, northern side of the building, overlooking the Hall.

All of this is terminated by the two floors of a 'light beam' that sits upon the brick stack and serves as the principal external device signalling the changes; within it is air conditioning plant, restaurants, etc. New entrances on the north and west sides lead visitors into the vastness of the Turbine Hall, itself dominated by projecting 'light-boxes'. Escalators then lead to a sequence of upper level gallery spaces of varied dimensions and characterized by a daring (but subdued) palette of architectural materials and finishes (including raw oak flooring). The success of the whole experience is mixed but always unique, making this an exhilarating scheme equal of the Parisian *grand projets* that are its precedents, but something less than the architectural wonder the media would have us believe. Having said that, it has been hugely successful.

Externally, public areas are concentrated around the northern (shaded) side and the Millennium bridge termination on the riverside walkway that now runs along the Thames.

18.

The heart of the Tate Modern is the former Turbine Hall, reinvented as London's most monumental space, with retained hints of its past role as part of an industrial building (notably the rivets of the columns and the overhead gantries). The back-lit projecting boxes are wonderful ornaments to the space, but the Tate often switches them off! The north wall fronts the galleries, etc.; the south wall is blank.

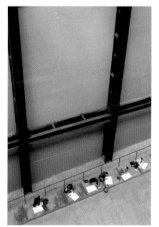

19.

River Thames
Foster and Partners; Arups; Anthony Caro, 2002
Tube: Blackfriars, St. Paul's

Millennium Bridge

A major design criterion for the bridge was that users would have unobstructed views - hence the notion of 'a blade of light'.

The bridge is terminated by two major attractions: St Paul's and the Tate Modern = lots of traffic, especially on a weekend.

The southern end of the bridge is structurally elegant but rather user-awkward. Crowds have to turn back on themselves and are deposited very near the river edge, causing difficult interactions between those entering and leaving the bridge, and people moving along the river walkway.

This design for a 4m wide suspended footbridge between St Paul's and the new Tate Gallery and Globe Theatre on the other side of the river – the first new bridge across the Thames in one hundred years – has undoubtedly been a popular route across the river, enlivening two river banks that have been rather blighted by poor access.

Construction started in May 1999 and was completed in 2001. Well, almost . . . the bridge wobbled so alarmingly under its loading from hugely enthusiastic crowds (up to 250mm) that it was closed within two days and twelve months were spent identifying the exact nature of the problem and then installing dampeners. Problem solved. From beginning to end - including the difficulties - it had been a case of brilliant engineering.

Arups explain the bridge as follows: "In 1996 the Financial Times held an international competition . . . to design a footbridge crossing the Thames between Southwark and Blackfriars bridges. A long span bridge, as needed to cross the Thames at this point, is a pure expression of engineering structure. A city centre footbridge, however, is equally about people and the environment - a piece of public architecture. When considering a link between Tate Modern and St. Paul's Cathedral another element is vital: the pure sense of physical form that drives a sculptor" They continue: "A unique collaboration was formed . . . [The competition had asked for a collaborative exercise between an engineer, an architect, and a sculptor] creating a minimal design that gives pedestrians unrivalled views of London . . . The 4m wide aluminium deck is flanked by stainless steel balustrades and is supported by cables to each side. These cables dip below the deck at midspan enabling unimpeded views of London. The bridge is a very shallow suspension bridge where the highly tensioned cables sag 2.3m over the 144m of the central span, a span to dip ratio of 63:1. This is around 6 times shallower than a conventional suspension bridge."

Was it also a case of very intelligent answers to less than clever questions? Clearly, the competition-winning architect (Foster) and collaborating artist (Anthony Caro) - intent upon the concept of a low-profile 'blade of light' - had landed the engineer with quite an engineering problem which they handled brilliantly and elegantly. But one can't help but feel that a certain cultural dimension has been overlooked - considerations that Lifschutz Davidson's almost contemporaneous bridge upstream at Hungerford offers in bundles (perhaps by default). Whereas the latter welcomes a stroll across the bridge as an urban boulevard, the Millennium Bridge has been argued to have the refined instrumentality of a Gucci trouser belt.

The northern end flows easily into the street pattern at that end and peters out near St Paul's (although interrupted by a road) whilst the southern end has severe difficulty in terminating itself within the space allowed. The engineering solution that literally grounds the cables is impressive and elegant, but height problems force a return that plonks bridge users right on top of people flows along the river's edge (a feature of the bridge that was a point of serious broadcast controversy between Foster and Herzog & de Meuron, designers of the Tate).

Bankside Lofts

CZWG long ago established reputation for combining a throwaway, irreverent wit (of the 'gonna die before I get old' variety) and (a developer driven) commercial opportunism. Their buildings usually have character and maintain an upbeat note. These 130 apartments, offices and a cafe adjacent to the new Tate Gallery combine old and new buildings and are a more complex and Modernist design than the practice usually offers and it is possibly one of their more successful designs, especially in the way variations in construction and materials are mixed and employed to culminate in a yellow, spiralling tower overlooking this part of London.

(There is another CZWG building nearby on Southwark Street / Summer Street corner - not nearly as successful.)

20.

Hopton Street/Castle Yard, SE1
CZWG, 1998
Tube: Blackfriars, Southwark

21. *The Globe Theatre (Pentagram Design, 1995), just east of the Tate Modern, is a London peculiarity not without attractions: a re-creation of the 1599 theatre near to where Shakespeare's plays were performed, complete with oak timbers, an open air pit, and a thatched roof (with water sprinklers in case of fire, of course). But, make no mistake, this is serious theatre, not Disney. It's also not a performative experience to be undertaken lightly: whilst some of the audience sit in the surrounding balconies on hard benches, others stand in the circular* 'pit' for the entire performance.

22. *The Jerwood Gallery (Paxton Locher, 1998, 171 Union Street, SE1) and studios is a scheme refurbishing existing school buildings, providing rehearsal spaces for theatre and dance, offices, apartments, and a strip of gallery space (converted from the old bicycle sheds) together with an adjacent outdoor sculpture court and an adjacent cafe. It is the kind of scheme they are good at: a development equation that balances the client's core 'wants' with the necessary developmental* 'needs' which make such projects viable. The spaces to visit are the gallery and cafe since the rest of it is effectively private. The Tate Modern is minutes away.

23. *Hays Galleria, Battlebridge Lane, SE1, is a 'U' shaped arrangement of refurbished Victorian warehouses that once grandly formed the surrounds to an inlet into which river barges could come in for loading and unloading. Much of this has been retained in the design of Michael Twigg-Brown & Partners (1986), except the water has infilled to form a mall and the buildings are now offices for a bank. The scheme has a naturally-ventilated, open-ended, roof structure enclosing the central area. The ground floor periphery is shops and cafes and has become quite popular. Views to the City, across the river, are very good. From here, you can easily walk west to the South Bank, or east to Butler's Wharf.*

24.

The Queen's Walk SE1
Foster and Partners, 2002
Tube: London Bridge, Tower Hill

City Hall

Dubbed by one newspaper as 'Foster's testicle', the City Hall that serves the Greater London Authority and the Greater London Assembly (yes, confusing . . .) stands in apparent, grand isolation until one realises that the sunken facilities adjacent to the 'blob' tap into an underground service road that caters to the surrounding set of office buildings also designed by Foster for a commercial client who provided the Hall and clearly saw it as the 'strawberry' (as the Japanese would call it) in the development equation. It adds to values but, cannily, only on the basis of a 25 year lease. (One wonders what will happen then; such is PFI.)

The building was commissioned on a design and build basis from the Civil Service some two years before the electoral elections brought the left-wing Mayor Ken Livingstone into power. And then - half-way through completion - the client (the GLA) arrived, with its own interpretation of need. That Fosters were able to adapt such an extremely difficult design on the run, and in such circumstances, is a serious compliment to the practice and the partner in charge, Ken Shuttleworth. (Without computers it would have been impossible to imagine, represent or construct, but employs the kind of difficult circular geometry that First Year architecture students are told to avoid like the plague.)

The Hall is rooted in what the practice did earlier at the Reichstag in Berlin: a glazed assembly chamber acts as an ostensible symbol of transparent democracy; above it soars a spiralling stepped ramp that leads to what is called 'London's Living Room'. Visitors can get to the second floor and see in; they can enter and listen to debate. But they can't use the ramp or access the Living Room for security and noise reasons. In any case, the Living Room is rather disappointing (especially the most peculiar ceiling Foster's office ever put its name to). One expects this Room to face toward the river but it doesn't (although views from the surrounding terrace are otherwise excellent).

The experience of the ramp is (obviously) better coming down, when the visitor (who was able to access the Room and can exit without disrupting the Assembly below) can see into the surround of office spaces. In fact, this is the ramp's most useful function: to enable staff to focus upon it and see everyone who comes and goes between floors. Having said that, its varied, stepped spiralling induces the most peculiar gait!

The entry low lobby area (with another idiosyncratic suspended ceiling) engenders an equally circuitious circulation in order to access the lifts or get to the lower floor (where there is usually a splendid model of central London).

On the exterior the spherical form (in pursuit of the Buckminster Fuller equation of minimum surface area: maximum internal volume) leans to the south in order to avoid solar gain and the hi-tech cladding of unique parts elicits admiration. But one has to ask: is it all the rather clever resolution of a not very clever question? On the other hand, is this is true post-modern architecture: a compound of glamour and symbol in the public sphere (no pun intended)?

24.

The entrance lobby of the GLA is not its most successful space (which can also be said of the upper 'living Room'); circulation is literally circuitous and offers security problems. However, the ramp up to the chamber and the views from it are much better, although the detailing suffers from the design & build procurement route.

The (ostensibly public) internal ramp (together with the Chamber) is the highlight of the building; however, it's not actually accessible for obvious reasons such as security and disruptive clatter, chat, etc. However, it does serve a useful internal purpose in making movements between office spaces visible to everyone (people can take a lift or use the central core stair as well). The roof terrace (right) offers good views, but not to the north.

More London

25.

Tooley Street, SE1
Foster and Partners, 2001-2003
Tube: London Bridge

This speculative business park (195,000sq.m.) utilises the Canary concept of a diagonal underground service spine (with pedestrian route above) that terminates at City Hall (a direct London Bridge Station to Tower Bridge route). The six office buildings (plus a hotel, shops, etc.) to either side are typical of office factories, mostly large footplate structures, sometimes with a central atrium. The architectural equation is competent, simple and reliant upon fit-outs by other designers to lift the interiors into habitability (no doubt talking excitedly of 'new ways of working'). Apart from the site planning, most of 'the architecture' is the novelty of sliced off ends to the glass facades of buildings oriented and engineered to persuade planners that they follow historical precedent and the riverside walkway is not excessively over-shadowed (described as 'fingers'); compare it with Chiswick Business Park. The site has been empty for too long, and its regeneration and integration into the larger fabric of London all around - helped by extensive 'public' areas and an urban design scheme that makes great claims for itself - has to be welcomed.

The More London site plan employs a diagonal that clearly seeks to pull movements away from Hays Galleria (to the west). The GLA building is just as clearly important in lifting the status of the office park, ameliorating its capitalist instrumentalism within an injection of civic significance (note the sunken area on its west side). The hotel, retailing and a modicum of residential content are along the road to the south.

26.

Shad Thames

Not so many years ago, Shad Thames was grotty and crowded, bearing marks of the questionable romance of East End working class history. Now it is pristine and literally sweet smelling – pleasant and gentrified, especially in the form of the renovated and refurbished Butlers Wharf warehouse, now a large apartment block facing the river. The street has been expertly reinvented, complete with some of the many bridges that once linked the outboard to the inboard warehouses and this small stretch of narrow space between former warehouses from the late C19 has been restored to include a ghetto of Conran restaurants (he lives around the corner, at the top of the former David Mellor building designed by Hopkins).

27.

Design Museum

It used to be among the dreariest of river warehouses and then Conran Roche transformed it into a piece of pseudo-Gropius, circa 1930, complete with white render, horizontal windows, etc. One doubts if historic theming was anywhere near the minds of these forthright Modernist architects designing a museum dedicated to mythologising that C20 invention called the design professions, but it might have been. Perhaps the museum takes itself too seriously? Perhaps it should have gone all the way and invented some ostensibly forgotten Modernist author from that era, faking the whole thing: background, associations, ouevre . . . Why not? The ground floor has a shop and cafe; the permanent museum and the gallery are (somewhat concealed) upstairs and the Blueprint restaurant fronts the first floor.

28.

The Circle

The Circle is typical CZWG's inventiveness: a concoction of throwaway pieces rooted in a single idea and put together with panache: in this instance a blue forecourt feature of glazed bricks at the heart of this 302 unit apartment complex, created out of the notion of a huge glazed jar, broken into pieces (in reality, more reminiscent of towering and threatening owls!) The other key feature is a series of balconies ostensibly propped by large timbers. It's all very serious in attempting not to be conventionally serious, but even if the informing meanings are inconsequential and loaded with contradictions, they are at least entertaining. However, inside, the apartment plans are ordinary and the corridor-access unpleasant, betraying the facade as quick-fix, one-liner architecture. And for that there is no excuse but to blame the developer.

Horselydown

Julyan Wickham's late father-in-law was Aldo van Eyck and one detects vaguely Dutch motifs in this fine development of apartments with shops and offices on the ground floor. The forms and their detailing are inventive, and unconventional, offering us an unusual English building with some superb compositional plays. Having said that, the piazza at the development's heart is less than successful, being devoid of the vegetation that would have made such a huge difference in this part of London (there is a car park underneath).

29.

Horselydown Square, Butlers Wharf, SE1
Wickham & Associates, 1989
Tube: Tower Hill, London Bridge

Mellor Building

This building started as a Hopkins design for the kitchen utensil man, David Mellor, and ended up as Terence Conran House, with his set-back shop at the bottom (so that a short colonnade is formed) and penthouse at the top. It is well-proportioned, powerful and understated – perhaps one of the best small buildings in London, making excellent use of its site and materials (principally an exposed concrete frame, large areas of glass and side panels of lead). Try and see it from the water side, if possible. In contrast to the road side, it opens up and reveals its inner life, especially at night. The very similar white block next door is a contemporaneous building by Conran Roche; in contrast, it was never occupied and bastardised into apartments in 1998 – after which it immediately sold. What small things make such a massive difference?

30.

Shad Thames, SE1
Michael Hopkins & Partners, 1990
Tube: London Bridge, Tower Hill

China Wharf

This small apartment and office building has a strong river facade whose red, cut-out and profiled frontality wilfully adds to the scenic qualities of the river edge. Its vaguely Chinese (?) quality is striking, but the most bizarre touch is the rear end of a boat, set cantilevering from the building and acting as a balcony at about the right height for it to float on a (very) high spring tide – probably among the more genuinely witty touches CZWG has offered because it is rooted in context rather than being a throwaway feature. The land-side, responding to different conditions, is simpler but equally characterful: white concrete and deeply fluted (apparently a reference to long-gone silos), with inset windows angled to catch views and any available

sunlight. Its less noticeable eastern facade steps an array of windows and plays perspective games with an inset that joins the building to its neighbour, Reed Wharf. It is a successful design. *Immediately to the east is another Gough design on the river's edge: a riverside house complete with cantilevering stairs and well worth a look (2000).*

31.

Mill Street, SE1
CZWG, 1988
Tube: Tower Hill, Bermondsey

32.

Fashion and Textile Museum, Bermondsey
Street SE1
Ricardo Legoretta, 2002
Tube: London Bridge

Fashion Museum

This will put you on the spot: a hot Mexican number plonked down in a street of small warehouses in Bermondsey, designed by an AIA Gold Medal winner, and a museum that 'will be the first of its kind to showcase the talent of local and international fashion and textile', and to be a venue for exhibitions, shows, etc. The upper floors are apartments, helping to fund the project at the two lower levels.

In reality, this colourful number (as eccentric as its sponsor, Zandra Rhodes) is a proverbial 'black box' that gives little away about its programme and, in this sense, is similar to the Laban. It's another shed and looks as if it could actually be fighting the heat of a Mexican summer. Or is that its defensiveness? So, on the one hand it's wonderful and colourful andhas done wonders for south London. On the other hand, it's possibly as bizarre as a Rhodes outfit. One suspects that the test (as with Stratford Circus, Peckham Library, the Wapping Project, etc.) is in the relationship that evolves between the building and its inhabitation.

33.

Shad Thames / Mill Street SE1
Nicholas Lacey, 1997
Tube: London Bridge, Tower Hill

St Saviour Dock Bridge

Apparently people steal the parts off this intricate, swivelling, pedestrian bridge and even cut the wires. Perhaps it's a way of saying it is rather overdone and needs pruning back. Nevertheless, it is a virtuouso example of stainless steel design, especially pleasant when the tide is low, mud is revealed, and boats in the inlet (once berthing a dense pack of barges nestling up to the warehouses) sit at odd angles whilst they await the return of the tide and the heavy timbers which stop boats crashing into the bridge are fully exposed. (It is easy not to see these as a part of the design). **New Concordia Wharf**, on the east side, was one of the first warehouse conversions in the area (Pollard Thomas Edwards, 1981–83).

Docklands Notes

The area downstream of London Bridge, around the Tower of London, used to be known as The Pool: a densely packed scene of ships, boats, warehouses, every imaginable kind of associated trade and not a little criminal activity. In a boom-time London of the late C18 congestion became so bad that the idea formed of developing the flat, marshy areas to the east and in a period between 1790 and 1830 a remarkable series of engineering undertakings gave London an array of tidal docks and new, secure warehouses, many protected by high walls and defensive moats. Beyond these arose the East End – an area of housing for the workers who toiled in the docks and the sometimes foul industries which made the place into a backyard for London, its pollution removed from the rich merchants in the City and the politicians of Westminster by the prevailing south-westerly winds.

Managerially, the docks were never a success. Even at the height of the British Empire, when the Port of London Authority was formed to administer the wealth imported from the world's first global empire, the docks remained problematic. And so matters remained until well after WWII, even after awesome wartime damage. However, change was coming. Whilst traffic was at its historical peak, in the 1960s, the revolution of mechanisation and containerisation was about to change everything. By 1970 most of the docks had closed, traffic was going through new container docks at Tilbury, at the mouth of the Thames and London was confronted by a vast area of derelict land.

What to do? The first ideas were mixed. Mysterious fires burned down some fine warehouses. Well meaning managers and politicians infilled many of the docks, hoping to create large, flat areas of land suited to industrial sheds. An autonomous 'development area' was formed, free from what was seen as the reactionary, left-wing instincts of local boroughs and their concerns with traditional forms of employment. Backed by tax breaks, newspapers were attracted from their historic location in Fleet Street to decant into new facilities, taking the opportunity to reform outmoded labour practices (in the process engendering serious riots).

Slowly but surely a vision of what was possible became more optimistic and more ambitious. In the 'bubble economy' of the mid-1980s Docklands became a minor boom town in itself, making and breaking developers' fortunes. Industrial workshop schemes turned into proposals for offices and studios. Housing opportunities were eagerly grasped, particularly by the newly enriched 'yuppies' desirous to live adjacent to the City, by the river, and in warehouses now lent romantic overtones (the loft phenomenon had arrived from New York, even as graffitti went up in Wapping encouraging the locals to 'mug a yuppie'). At the heart of it all was the Canary Wharf scheme that had lifted the stakes as high as they could go – presuming that is, that the infrastructure could get commuters in and out. However, by 2002 the capacity of the DLR had been extended, the Jubilee Line Extension had been constructed, the London Docklands Development Corporation had handed everything back to the local boroughs, and housing developments were everywhere. There was much to criticise, but a huge part of London's urban fabric has been renewed, leaving the East End as the local memories of a disappearing population and a stronger virtual reality in the form of a popular TV soap opera.

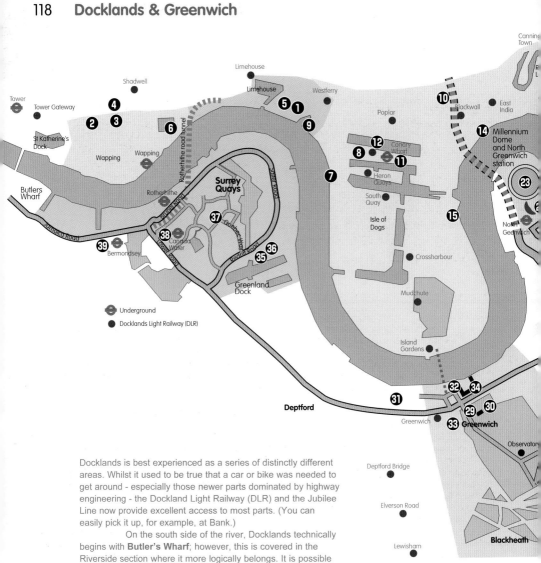

Docklands is best experienced as a series of distinctly different areas. Whilst it used to be true that a car or bike was needed to get around - especially those newer parts dominated by highway engineering - the Dockland Light Railway (DLR) and the Jubilee Line now provide excellent access to most parts. (You can easily pick it up, for example, at Bank.)

On the south side of the river, Docklands technically begins with **Butler's Wharf**; however, this is covered in the Riverside section where it more logically belongs. It is possible to walk beyond that point through Rotherhithe to **Surrey Quays**, but most people will find it easier to take public transport.

It is possible to get to **Greenwich** village across the river at Island Gardens, at the bottom tip of the Isle of Dogs, through an old Victorian pedestrian tunnel. To get to the **Greenwich Penninsula** (effectively the eastern boundary of central London) you will have to take the new Jubilee Line extension (which is very convenient and quick) or one of the river buses being made available. You can also get river boats from the West End and City to Greenwich and the Dome.

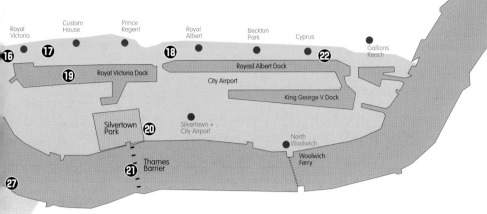

North Areas

Wapping
An historic area from St. Katherine's Dock (see City section), stretching east to Shadwell Basin. There is a pleasant walk along Wapping High Street, past Wapping Pierhead and Oliver's Wharf, past other warehouses, old and new, Metropolitan Wharf to the riverside Prospect of Whitby pub and the adjacent Wapping Hydraulic Pumping Station (now an excellent cafe, restaurant and one of the best galleries in London), both adjacent to Shadwell Basin. Many of the warehouses on the river side will be original ones, since the planners have long since enforced riverside access and prevent new development on the river itself.

Limehouse
Now a small, land-locked community on the west edge of the Isle of Dogs. Use Westferry DLR station. There are a couple of old riverside pubs here that might interest the traveller.

The Isle of Dogs
The 'flagship' of Docklands redevelopment: a satellite of the City, centred upon the private realm of Canary Wharf (now a significant shopping venue). The new Jubilee Line Extension to Foster's Canary Wharf station has made the area much more accessible and, together with extensions to the DLR, Canary is becoming integrated into the rest of London. The DLR also takes you down to the southern tip of the Island and over the river into south London, but you might want to get off at Island Gardens and take the old, pedestrian Victorian tunnel under the Thames to Greenwich (or vice versa).

The Royals and Beyond
The Royal Docks (Albert and Victoria) are the last area to be redeveloped and therefore the least complete. They are also the most inhospitable and many of you might want to avoid them in wet, windy and cold weather (we're serious - it's exposed out there, but let your enthusiasm temper our warnings). This is also where the City Airport is located. Beyond the Royals lies Beckton, a suburbanised part of the former docks. We suggest the DLR to Royal Victoria and taking the Lifschutz Davidson Bridge across the huge dock to the southern side, then continue through the housing to the Thames Barrier Park and the Thames Barrier itself.

South Areas

London Bridge to Tower Bridge (see Riverside section)
The Dockland redevelopment area technically came all the way through here, including Hays Galleria and London Bridge City, but the area has changed so much that this is effectively disguised.

Butlers Wharf (see Riverside section)
Butlers Wharf area now effectively concludes the riverside promenade that begins at Vauxhall Bridge and is dealt with in that section, but it was also a part of the Docklands redevelopment area.

Rotherhithe and Surrey Quays
A large area on the south side of the river, opposite the Isle of Dogs. Early schemes were distinctly a part of the more suburban ideas fashionable among planners during the 1970s and 1980s, lending the area a 'new town' feel in its central parts (quite peculiar for a place so near central London). However, one can walk through to here from Butlers Wharf, into Rotherhithe, on the western side of the Surrey Dock area. Current building work reflects a more appropriate, urbane and physically dense concept of how the area can be redeveloped – something the new Jubilee Line Extension has encouraged.

Greenwich, Greenwich Penninsula and the Millennium Dome
Greenwich and its park are an oasis in this part of London. The Millennium Dome site is again a distinctly separate area, best accessed by the Jubilee Line.

1.

Ropemaker Field, E14
Proctor Matthews Architects, 1996
DLR: Westferry

Limehouse Houses

This terrace of 11 town-houses, with their 'layered' facades, stands out by being simple and self-evidently well-designed. Elements such as the entry gate, concealment of utility meters and bins, balconies to a first floor *piano nobile*, the grouping of windows and the cornice-like attic storey, indicate careful composition and detailing. The pergolas to balconies are typical of attempts to provide a sense of comfort and security, their wood detailing corresponding to that of the windows so that the various elements are unified. The contrast is with an ostensibly more novel and upbeat CZWG scheme around the corner. The problem is that both schemes have suffered from developers who insist they know what customers want for the interior fit-out – from which the architect is banned. Also see their housing on the Greenwich Penninsula.

2. *Lumiere (Pennington Street, E1; Rick Mather, 1992; tube: Tower Hill)* is spec office building striving to be different, but not really making it despite a cornice punctured by over-scaled occuli and a rear facade that plays with projecting, triangular windows slim 'Roman' bricks from Denmark and the like. It suffered in the recession but is now occupied by News International

(Murdoch), who have built a bridge from their building, crossed the road and punctured their way into Mather's design!

3. *Tobacco Dock (Pennington Street, E1. Terry Farrell Partnership, 1987; tube: Tower Hill. DLR: Shadwell)* was a commercial failure but remains interesting: the original Georgian, high-tech sheds, with wonderfully thin and elegant roof members, together with impressive brick vaulting at the lower level (all 1806); and also for Farrell's restoration work and the creation of steel and cast-iron facades for the shops. The massive surrounding brick wall is original, indicative of how defensive the docks once were (pilfering was big business).

4. Nicholas Hawksmoor's baroque church, **St George-in-the-East** *(1714–29)*, is a haunting burned-out shell, within which there nestles a much smaller, 1960s church. It sits opposite Tobacco Dock, on The Highway, E1 with a dark, brooding quality that belongs to a church programme intended to bring moral order to the irreligious masses of early eighteenth century London. This is Hawksmoor expressing that notion of the Divine as something wonderful and sublime, but somewhat 'terrible'. Details have a chunky, robust and brooding quality. **St Anne's**, Limehouse, is another Hawksmoor church dating from the same period. Also compare with St Luke's *(p161)*.

5. **Roy Square,** in Narrow Street, E14 (Limehouse), is an Ian Ritchie design from 1987. The scheme is an exception to the neo-Victorian blocks that were also being constructed at the time. Ritchie has created an urbane 'hollow block' of 77 units formed into four pavilions accessed from a shared, central garden court that is also a podium above car parking. The formalism owes much to Georgian precedent and aims for a similar, calm regularity. It is worth looking at, but there is a security gate and visitors are not usually welcomed into this self-contained development.

Wapping Project

6.

Shadwell Basin, E1
Architects Shed 54, 2000
Tube: Wapping

The Wapping Project at Shadwell Basin is the reinvention of an old hydraulic pumping station (1890), one of five that used to serve the West End, now converted into a restaurant and art gallery by Jules Wright and her architect husband, Joshua (Shed 54). It's a superb conversion - a balance of old and new, where knowing 'intervention' (why do architects use that aggressive term? policemen intervene, not designers) or its avoidance manages to produce an authenticity that is all too rare, especially where food and art are concerned. The entry space and the adjacent hall (bottom right) were given a new timber roof and diners sit on Charles Eames chairs midst the machinery. Beyond that is a large space for exhibitions and installations. These parts are linked to upper parts by an external galvanised stair and upper deck that links to large old water tanks awaiting future conversion.

Wright's imbues her gallery with a 'no bullshit' undertone affecting everything about the place and it is surely one of the most worthwhile projects in London. And, since the restaurant is actually good and its profits enable the art programme to function, you should have something to eat when you go there!

Also take a stroll around the area, around Shadwell basin, its housing (old and new), maybe pop into the Prospect of Whitby pub opposite.

Cascades

7.

West Ferry Road, E14
CZWG Architects, 1986-88
DLR: Westferry, Canary Wharf

Cascades (compare it with Rogers' Montevetro) is one of the most successful CZWG designs, towering high even before Canary Wharf arrived and a breakthrough against high-rise living prejudices well before towers once more became appealing to popular tastes. In the late-1980s it was a yuppie symbol but during the recession prices had plunged low enough so that the local authority was purchasing them as housing the homeless. Now we're back where we were. The long, spinal diagonal – important to the difference with conventional towers – can be explained as a fire escape but its form derives from the way apartments have been arranged and oriented to obtain good views. Much effort has gone into breaking any monolithic qualities the tower might have had.

Just north, at Westferry DLR station, on Milligan Street E14, is another CZWG job: a neo-Venturi building of live-work units, complete with proclamatory signage.

8.

Canary Wharf, E14
Masterplan by Skidmore Owings & Merrill
Tube/DLR: Canary Wharf

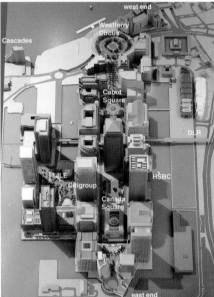

Canary Wharf

This instant Gotham City (master-planned by SOM in Chicago) started off almost accidentally during the early 1980's and grew into a speculative North American vision profoundly challenging to British architects as well as to the City of London. The first phase (around Cabot Square) up to the 1990 recession - was almost entirely North American: the initiatives, the money, the designs, the construction management. When this ended the banks took over a bankrupt development, only to have the original speculators buy it back and bounce into a booming second phase initiated in the mid '90's. What has been crucial to this success has been the Jubilee and DLR extensions. Significantly, the maturing development now incorporates some apartments, a hotel and extensive retailing (the mall is now a major East End venue) as well as additional offices. About 25,000 people worked here in 1999 and 55,000 by 2002 (set to rise to about 90,000 at full potential).

The gloriously dominant building of the first phase was the stainless steel clad Canary Wharf Tower (One Canada Square), 50 stories and 114,751 sq.m. (net), floating on a raft 4m thick, in turn supported on 22 piles going another 30m into the ground, designed by Cesar Pelli, who also designed the first stages of the central shopping building and the DLR station. It was an instant London landmark, now unfortunately absorbed by surrounding towers. The squat, first stage lower buildings surrounding the Pelli tower were by a variety of architects: Pei, Cobb, Freed & Partners; Kohn Pedersen Fox; SOM; and Troughton McAslan (the lone British firm). All are undistinguished, although interesting for their Po-Mo values and mish-mash of Chicago-Paris values that pretend to be English: real power-dressing of the kind that frightened and offended the native architects.

During late '90's Canary's second phase Foster built a tower for Citibank (the triple-glazed, 52,284sq.m. net, 33 Canada Square) and put One Canada Square under competition with a 41 storey building of 102,191sq.m., designed for HSBC on the north side of Canada. Immediately to its west is an SOM building for Credit Suisse (46,450 sq.m. net); to the east is another SOM building (55,740 sq.m. net). To the east of that is an HOK building of 99,902 sq.m. The Citigroup tower on the south side of Canada Square is by Cesar Pelli (111,852 sq.m.), who also have another three buildings along the southern edge of Jubilee Gardens. To the immediate east of the Citigroup building is another SOM design (50,632 sq.m.). Most tenants are in financial services. Terry Farrell has a building on the south side of Westferry circus (at the west end of the development).

This instrumental, global capitalist equation - an office park pretending to be a vibrant part of the city - might scare you. The hotel and few apartments don't really change anything and the shopping mall could be anywhere in the universe. Which brings us to that contemporary palliative of instrumental capitalism: art. To be fair, it's a lively programme aimed by its curator at 'a bit of intimacy within these enormous spaces'.

8.

The first phase was dominated by the Cesar Pelli tower, but was already served by a central DLR station (photo right) linking the development back into the City. The buildings were all Po-Mo American redolent with symbols of power and wealth that scandalise English architects to this day (although they are used to it by now).

The realities of strategic infrastructure were at the heart of early, high-level machinations aimed at ensuring Docklands was a success. The arrival of the Jubilee Line (with support from the Canary bankers) helped enormously.

Below left: Foster's Citibank. Below centre; Pei Cobb Freed, first phase; SOM / Koetter Kim Associates / Perkins & Will, at Westferry Circus; general view, first phase.

9. *Dundee Wharf (Dundee Wharf, Limehouse, E14; CZWG, 1998 (DLR: Westferry) is a large, quirky block of 160 flats is argued to be contextual, polite to neighbours and properly responsive to its position on a river bend. The apartments form a 'U' shape on plan, enclosing a private access and parking space conceived of as a 'new urban square'. The design is actually its*

'kerb appeal', principally achieved by the likes of idiosyncratic brick coping details at roof level and a daringly disconnected 11–storey tower of balconies (said to refer to travelling dockside cranes). Other balconies, being 'V' shaped, are ostensibly a reference to ships' loading booms. It's fun. Isn't it?

10 *Robin Hood Gardens in Cotton Street and Robin Hood Lane, E14 (DLR to Blackwall) by Peter and Alison Smithson is one of the few projects that London has seen from this team (see the Economist, in St James's). No student of the 1950s–70s would offer them less than hero worship and this polemical scheme is all about streets in the sky and attempts to make medium to high-rise housing work. Strangely, even when built it was an oddity, surrounded by a moat concept - now a secure defensive barrier. It's a sad, bleak place and no amount of lyricism about its authors can ameliorate its failures, so typical of many '60's housing schemes.*

11.   Canary Wharf JLE station

Canary Wharf JLE Station, E14
Foster and Partners, 1999
Tube/DLR: Canary Wharf.

The Jubilee Line Extension project gave London eleven excellent, architect designed stations (heavily assisted by a JLE team that receives less credit than it deserves). Foster's grassed-over **Canary Wharf** station design owes something to its precedent at Bilbao and a bit to Stansted as well, but this one is much larger in scale and capacity (it is intended to serve up to 40,000 people per hour, served by twenty escaltors - more traffic than Oxford Circus). Underground, it is a huge hall (280m long by 32 m wide and 24 m deep; about as long as the Canary tower is tall), typologically similar to that designed by Will Alsop adjacent to the Millennium Dome, but bigger. Much bigger. Above ground, it manifests as a double-curved glass canopy that belongs to a family of such forms the Foster team adapts to a variety of projects at a variety of scales (e.g. the air museum at Duxford) - like a swollen airplane cockpit bubble. Below ground is veritably Piranesian: gigantic forms, given flow, elegance and the scale of a Italian fascist train station! It's superb. The aim (characteristically) has been simplicity and clarity, avoiding a clutter of signage and producing a calm ambience enhanced by the sweeping curves of the concrete structure. Lighting has been an important feature of the design and the entry bubbles scoops enable daylight to penetrate the interiors and draw travellers out into Canary. Station servicing is via concealed gangways, entirely behind the scenes. Lighting is by Claude and Danielle Engle. The total area is about 31,500sq.m.

12.   Pontoon bridge

North Quay/West India Quay, E14
Future Systems, Engs: Anthony Hunt, 1995
DLR: Canary Wharf

This is an especially elegant footbridge, particularly by night when its integral lighting is displayed. The floating concept lends the design a metaphorical 'liveliness' to set against the ponderous formalism of Canary Wharf's first stages. However, although it looks as if it could float away (or be taken away overnight), it is necessarily anchored on sliding connections to concealed concrete piles under the water. The central portion is hydraulically operated (assisted by counter-weights) and opens to allow boats through. And there is a curiously neo-militaristic undertone - as if some romantic, war-weary 'band of brothers' was about to march over. The engineers were Anthony Hunt Associates.

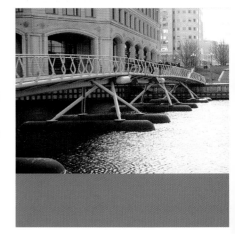

Container City

The LDDC designated this part of the Docklands - Trinity Wharf, once owned by the people who trained lighthouse keepers on site - as a place for artists to let cheap space. Its developer (shame it's not a cooperative . . .) uses redundant containers as a relatively cheap and quick way of doing this. It's all based on the UK economy's import-export inbalance that leaves quiet parts of the country stacked with empty, old containers. Windows are cut, doors fixed open to support balconies, external staircases added, insulation sprayed on the inside, plasterboard linings put in place ... It's all fairly straight-forward. Interestingly, the first phase has been 'architected' by Nicholas Lacey. This makes sense, but somewhat knocks the edge off a naive romance about shanty towns in London. Local planners have been supportive (but probably traumatised).

Container City could be seen as part of an English seaside tradition of cheap 'n' cheerful shanties - not entirely plausible, but some PhD student is probably writing it up as we speak.

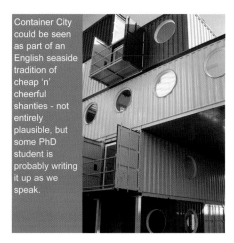

13.

Trinity Pier, Orchard Place, E14
Nicholas Lacey and Partners, 2002
DLR: East India

Reuters

There is something defensive and castle-like to many of Rogers' designs and this is no exception. It sits against the river, has multiple power connections and back-up systems, and is characterised by an air of paranoia which surrounds the place with guards, fencing and cameras. The building houses telecommunications equipment for an agency whose services are crucial to many finance houses – information worth millions. And they don't want anyone thinking it might be easy to knock the building out. It's really a big machine, with a few inhabitants, a relatively low-cost shell but expensive internals. These qualities are emphasised by the massive air-conditioning plant taking up the two upper levels. The architect's ability to be more playful is restricted to perimeter escape stairs and a separate cafeteria pavilion with riverside views.

14.

St Lawrence Street, E14
Richard Rogers Partnership, 1990
DLR: Blackwall

15.

Stewart Street, E14
John Outram, 1988
Tube/DLR: Canary Wharf

Pumping station

This has to be one of the challenging and daring of London buildings: one that some people find offensive to their sensibilities and ideas of architectural propriety, but it is a building full of ideas, challenges and enjoyment - a most peculiar mix of fun, seriousness, erudition and skill.

What you see on the exterior is the wrapping to a massive engineering pump installation that discharges surface water into the Thames. But what fun Outram has had. He explains the design almost mythologically: the pediment is like a mountain; the columns are trees on the mountain; water runs from a cave (the fan) and down to the plain where the water runs over the area around the buildings as different coloured blocks; and the sides of the building are layered as if ground strata. The front gate includes a middle-eastern 'evil eye' (we are not sure what it is warding off) and the decorative scheme is pure *beaux arts* (in the manner of recreated painted, classical temples) with a slight Chinese influence. There are even references to the work of Alvar Aalto in the way the side pilasters have been clad in half-tiles.

Nevertheless, whatever Outram's rationale, the fan and pediment have the formal playfulness of a 1950s child's drawing of a propeller-driven aeroplane and the colouring is like a cross between Classicism and a Chinese pagoda.

On top of all that, Outram is sincerely concerned with honest, explicit construction of an entirely Modernist manner. He desires everything to be functional and he wants you to know how it's all put together. For example, he uses the columns with pre-cast capitals ('blitzreig' concrete made from redundant broken bricks) as duct risers, the fan is entirely functional, exhausting any build-up of methane gas, and the outer walls are bomb-blast proof.

All in all, it's a rich architecture, not only erudite in its search for meaning, but significant at the more immediate level of an experience of the thing itself, in all its directness. Few architects - anywhere in Europe - have dared to employ such an agenda and play such a game. To call the work Post-Modernist does Outram a disservice.

16. *This **pumping station** at the Royal Docks (west end, Tidal Basin Road E16; Richard Rogers Partnership 1987) looks utterly different to Outram's, but they are both equally expressive besides sharing the common denominator of brightly coloured paint. Outside, it is all pipework, industrial railings and ducts like ship's ventilators. Inside, it is basically the same, although the engineer's plans do look more elegant. The aesthetic is reminiscent of an architect's idea of either ship or an oil rig (take your pick) and, in that sense, is profoundly romantic as well as functional and instrumental. From that perspective, the design is not so far away from that of Outram as at first seems (see above).*

17. *Excel is a worthy enough building (a huge exhibition hall sitting on the north side of the Albert Dock) but the small area of landscape on its west end (designed by Patel & Taylor) is the real reason why you might head down to this windy part of London. There's a real continental sensibility informing their designs and their 'waving' lights are a delight.*

From here you can go across the Lifshutz Davidson bridge to their work at the Thames Barrier Park.

Regatta Centre

This club and adjacent boat house - described by its architects as a 'robust intervention' - could have been one of the finest buildings in London (sited at the end of an Olympic standard 2000m rowing course within the old dock), but site, an adjacent DLR line, the windy bleakness of the Royal Docks and a poor fit-out all fight that notion. But the architecture has some very fine qualities and is worth visiting (especially on a sunny day).

       The centre comprises two buildings: a Boathouse and ancillary workshop of approximately 1150 sq.m., and a Clubhouse which includes changing rooms, gym, restaurant and bar facilities, and short term residential accommodation for athletes. The Clubhouse has a unique, powered rowing tank which utilises flowing water to simulate open water rowing. The architects structured the design to flank parallel lines of gabion walls which define spaces within which the buildings nest. With the boathouse, the building is defined by the free standing gabion walls and a lightweight stiffened catenary stainless steel roof. The clubhouse building sits back from the north-side gabion wall to create an access buffer zone spine running the length of the building. Terraces on the second level project over the gabion providing interesting viewing from the bar and restaurant.

18.

Royal Albert Dockside Road, E16
Ian Ritchie Architects, 1999
DLR: Royal Albert Docks

Royal Docks Bridge

This competition-winning Royal Docks bridge has been offered in two stages. The first provides a purely pedestrian link across the dock and the second will add an enclosed, travelling car slung beneath the bridge. At the moment, it's a gesture awaiting potential users among those who will live along the Royal Victoria Dock. The southern termination is at a small, semi-circular apartment block leading through to the first of the housing developments. It is quite a structure and comparatively large, but shrinks against the massive scale of the dock.

19.

Pedestrian Bridge, Royal Victoria Dock, E16
Lifschutz Davidson, 1999
DLR: Custom House

20.

North Woolwich Road, E16
Groupes Signes, Patel & Taylor, and Arup Engineers 2000
DLR: Prince Regent, Custom House

Thames Barrier Park

We are familiar with the park in its manifestations as Renaissance garden, the apparent informalities of the English landscape tradition, and the dense, formal cuteness of the Victorian municipal garden. Within the Renaissance tradition, mannered artifice was everywhere self-evident, mostly as geometry coloured by symbolism and myth. In the English tradition, artifice is at once concealed as an 'improved' nature and made explicit as contrivances such as the resident hermit, grotto, folly, and ornamental cottage - aesthetics devices less concerned with ratiocination and its manifestation as something eruditte and clever.

The Thames Barrier Park is the post-modern municipal park returning to the explicit formalities of the Renaissance, now in the guise of public art, Anglo-French style. After a long absence, geometry has returned as the tool of artifice and contrivance. The folly is there as public loo and café (an elegant neo-Miesian exercise in timber from Patel & Taylor), with the equivalent of the band-stand, now as floating canopy propped with irregular columns vaguely evocative of a farmed pine forest. The tradition of the walled villa garden is now a huge slot (appropriately reminiscent of a dock) that wilfully slices through the landscape and manifests a taming and repression of the underlying industrial pollution, dominated by playful geometric delights and fragrances that thrive in its microclimate, and oriented toward the Piranesian engineering act that keeps modern central London from drowning: the Thames Barrier. Even the edge of terraced housing (by Goddard Manton) is reminiscent of the grand terraces of Regents Park (now with nautical overtones).

This is the culture of the West End coloured by Francophile influences and introduced into the formerly industrial docklands of the East End as a civilising act of vision and reform serving a programme of urban reinvention within the new Town tradition. However, the place is simultaneously a local park - somewhere to walk the dog and play with the kids - and deeply embedded within a London tradition of open spaces that have always served the needs of a growing, changing city: a successful ornament to London.

The Design

The designer's task was to create a park from a heavily polluted wasteland adjacent to the City Airport, linking it into a larger urban design framework of urban renewal and regeneration that includes an extension of the Docklands Light Raiilway (DLR) along the park's northern boundary. The key elements of the park include the green dock, a permeable eastern edge of housing (originally intended to be a series of pavilions rather than the solid terrace implemented and fenced off by Barratt), a water feature, the street entrance, a plateau of greenery and trees with subtle changes of level, a network of paths that cross the park and leap the dock as steel bridges, and a riverside walk and performance area. Other axes link to surrounding developments prompted by the 24 acre park, potentially giving a local population of about 30,000 people who could use the park. The 'dock' is a topographical slice between the direction of the bridge over the Royal Dock and the Thames Barrier, emphasising a potential linear movement from barrier to the

20.

DLR and Excel centre on the northern side of the Royal Victoria Dock. The formally planted dock is 6m deep at one end and 4m at the river end, creating a microclimate a few degrees warmer than the surroundings. A 100m rebuilding of the river wall and adjacent walk area (separated from the plateau by a ha-ha), where a dock was once located, includes a tall canopy (The Pavilion of Remembrance) propped by a random set of steel columns simulating a grove of trees. Another pavilion serves as toilets and a cafe, and has a concrete service part married to a green oak frame with glazing inbetween.

21. *The Thames Barrier is London's flood defence: the end of central London and its true river gateway with a very serious defensive role to play. If necessary, water flow can be stopped by six huge steel gates (1500 and 750 tonnes) which rotate up from the river bed. The gear for all this is within the zinc-clad sculptured housings that straddle the river. It's an impressive sight, underscored by the massive dangers to life and property if the system doesn't work when the occasional mix of conditions arises that places central London at risk of flooding. The engineers were Rendel, Palmer & Tritton (1984). A visitor's centre is on the south side (Unity Way, off the Woolwich Road), but you'd be better off just seeing the engineering itself, probably from the Thames Barrier Park side.*

University campus

22.

Cullinan's University of East London Docklands campus design for 3,000 students is strung out along the northern edge of the Royal Albert Dock. At its core is a building described as a 'pedestrian hub '- meaning a stubby east-west 'street' that feeds into the various facilities on either side. Along the (windy) dock edge itself, a series of brightly coloured, isolated residential towers lend an identifying theme to the campus. One suspects that a design strategy predicated on the idea of pavilions keenly rationalised in terms of net:gross and available funds - rather than a network of outdoor spaces and people places - is at odds with the exposed conditions. Bring back the cloister!

Cyprus Roundabout, Royal Albert Way, E16
Edward Cullinan Architects, 1999
DLR: Cyprus

23.

Gate 1, Drawdock Road, SE10
Richard Rogers Partnership, 1999
Tube: North Greenwich

Millennium Dome

The Dome - an attempt to receate the success of the Great Exhibition of 1851 in 2000 - was a brilliant way of doing something inherently meaningless. The Dome's fundamental problem was that it became a symbolic act founded upon an abstraction (the number 2000), and a set of arbitrary forms madly searching for an appropriate, celebratory content (required to be at once meaningful, significant and entertaining). In reality, the project became its own content (the only authenticity about the whole thing). The Rogers part (the driving partner was Mike Davies) included the tent, the peripheral plant housings, the interior comfort pavilions, and the central arena, together with overhead gantries, lighting rigs, etc. It was gutsy stuff. The basic figures include coverage of more than 8 ha, over 12,000 piles, 12 bright yellow masts, each 90 m long and stacked on 10 m high steel 'quadrapods', holding the 400m diameter cable-net structure which is about 50m high at its apex. Because the site was formerly a gas works, the engineering included the careful isolation and capping of more chemical nasties than one likes to think about – resulting in a profoundly symbolic equation combining a balance of dream and nightmare. So, the real heroes of the phenomenon were surely Buro Happold, the engineers on the project. At the time of writing, the Dome appears to have no plausible future.

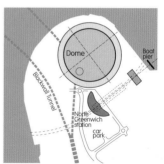

River art

Take a walk around the edge of the Greenwich penninsula and you'll see sculpture of a scale to suit the river. 'Quantum Cloud' (left) is by Antony Gormley; the 8m ship part is called 'A Slice of Reality' by Richard Wilson.

Millennium Housing

Greenwich Millennium Village, John Harrison Way, SE10
Ralph Erskine (with Proctor Matthews), 2000
Tube: North Greenwich

24.

Ambitious plans for inhabiting the Greenwich Penninsula have been master-planned by Rogers and taken to a detailed level by Erskine Tovatt Architects, with EPR and Proctor Matthews (who designed the second phase of housing with the Erskine framework) as executive architects. Like BedZed, it's a very green scheme with 'low energy impact' ambitions and much talk about 'self-sustainability' [sic].

Essentially, the scheme is a series of taller apartment blocks surrounding low-rise terraces with mixed accommodation types. The former are in concrete and the latter are timber and steel framed. Efforts have been made to keep the car at bay whenever possible, but this surely runs against the grain in such an environment. Even though the Jubilee Line is ten minutes walk away across the peninsula's pleasant but wind-swept park designed by Robert Rummey, this remains as implicitly car-based as any suburbia. The designs are certainly upbeat and well considered, but (as with BedZed) one has the feeling that the fiercesome, extrovert cheerfulness of it all and the symbolic proclamation of values might overwhelm the less extrovert personality.

School / Health Centre

25.

50 John Harrison Way, SE10
Edward Cullinan Architects, 2001
Tube: North Greenwich

Cullinan's school and community building extends this architectural practice's impressive portfolio of social work and has many of the old Cullinan features, updated by a younger generation in the office. Designed to provide education, health centre and act as a community centre (with creche, one-stop advice centre, sports facilities, etc), the more private sides of this the low-energy building face south to landscaped garden areas; the more public faces are faced in 'rippling' vertical larch boarding and introduce a timber fortress keynote that is at once playful, endearing and bizarre.

26.

Horn Lane, SE 10
Chetwood Associates, 1999
Tube: North Greenwich.

Sainsbury

This is not a bad supermarket building, but its claims for being super-green are an affront to one's common sense. The overall design, the berm walls and the rooflights surely help the energy equation and it's a very pleasant supermarket (if you like that kind of thing), but the cars in the car park outside and the two playful windmills with additional solar panels make this palliative to the suburban shopper's guilt complex less than what it pretends. And the design also didn't anticipate the locals climbing up onto the roof, so security fencing has been added. But we carp: if one has to have a large suburban shed, then this is probably as good as it gets.

27.

Old Greenwich Yacht Club, 1 Peartree Wharf, SE 10
Frankl & Luty, 2000
Tube: North Greenwich

Yacht Club

Designed to exploit panoramic views, this yacht club building (unusual in London, but the club was founded in 1908) is possibly an example of sububia creeping in and linking up with the docklands redevelopment (and welcoming visiting sailors): the river here is wide and useable in a manner hardly feasible further upstream. Whilst the building itself - the social focus of the Club - sits 45m offshore on an existing jetty, the boatyard and parking area is on the land side (on the other side of the riversdie walkway recently constructed). And Clare Frankl, one of the designers, is even a member of the club!

28. *North Greenwich Jubilee station has two parts: a massive underground concrete box, 400 m long, 30 m wide and 25 m deep, by Alsop Lyall & Stormer and, above ground, a bus station beneath a curved, flowing, metal roof designed by Foster & Partners. Alsop's gutsy, Piranesian design employs huge diagonal struts covered in blue mosaic. These carry the roof structure and the suspended concourses, whilst blue glass panels screen ducts help and lend the interiors an especially lively spirit. The Foster station is designed as a large, bird-like, curved roof that draws vehicles beneath sheltering arms, low on one side and opening up on the other, the curved, 'shell' roof appearing to be 'draped over' (not propped by) a forest of structural 'trees' is not entirely convincing and it is not until one is in an aeroplane taking off from the City Airport, when the 'big roof' idea become readable and convincing, taking on the form of some beautiful giant moth hugging the ground.*

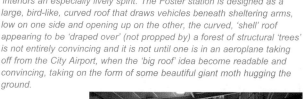

Maritime Museum

Romney Road, Greenwich, SE10

Rick Mather / BDP, 1999

DLR: Cutty Sark

29.

The National Maritime Museum is a part of the Greenwich Palace and Naval Hospital complex designed by Sir Christopher Wren and adjacent to the Queen's House designed by Inigo Jones, with access from both the north front of the building and the west colonnade of the Queen's House. In addition, it sits on the edge of one of London's finest parks and an old village area now accommodating the Cutty Sark and offering a very busy weekend market. Access can be via the DLR at Greenwich or via the old Victorian pedestrian tunnel under the Thames between Greenwich and Island Gardens (another DLR station).

    The key to the design is Mather's enclosure of the central courtyard and the insertion of a single storey building with an upper podium (where a cafe is located). Together, these elements hold the complex together and, from all points, give a central reference. The design is simple and robust and Mather even provides an uncharacteristic, seamless extension of the existing classical detailing.

    Visitors enter through the triumphal arch of the existing building, into a lobby area and then out into the lofty enclosed courtyard where there is a central block and cafe mezzanine (the roof – at 2,500 sq.m. – is claimed to be the largest free-span glass roof in Europe; see his similar but smaller exercise at the Wallace Collection). From here, there is direct access into two floors of galleries, where Mather's hand is always evident, sometimes in spite of the tacky entertainment quality that typifies some of the gallery exhibits. Other accommodation includes a restaurant, library, shop, etc.

30. *Immediately adjacent to the Maritime Museum is Inigo Jones's **Queen's House** (1616–35; enlarged by John Webb, 1662), England's first Palladian villa, described by Pevsner as being shockingly chaste and bare when constructed. For some peculiar reason concerning convenience, Jones's design straddles the former road to Dover, making it novel as well as architecturally pretentious (the road was diverted north in 1693). The colonnades linking the building to the NMM are by Daniel Alexander, 1807-16. Inside, there are some impressive (if sparse) spaces (esp. the central cubic hall). The entry (and misc. disabled access issues) were dealt with by Allies and Morrison.*

31.

Laban Centre, Creekside, SE8
Herzog & de Meuron, 2003
DLR: Greenwich

Laban Centre

The Laban is the kind of brief and project content most architects would die for: some 8,000 sq.m. of facilities for the country's premier dance school. Tight budget, yes, but Herzog and de Meuron have injected the project with the kinds of decision-making that carefully allocate available funds. It's cheap 'n' cheerful, but with elegance and wit - a refreshing place to visit. It is, as the architects claim, respectful, sensitive, and engaged. Having said that, it's also a dual personality building, with one architectural narrative on the outside and another on the inside.

These narratives are inter-linked in a manner that is quite rare in architecture, but one has nagging doubts about claims for the fundamental site strategy. One can see the logic of a compact, low-energy, low maintenance shed. But how to make it sing? What the architects have attempted is to create a dialogue with the environment - principally in the form of a curve to the frontage that also orients the entrance toward Thomas Archer's St Paul's Church, Deptford (1713-30; a superb work) - and to develop the concept of interior arrangements as an urbane village, with streets, courts, views (for example, to the church again) and the presence of nature.

The curved front facade of the Laban, with the cafe on the corner, behind the black glass. Right: the cafe interior. Bottom right: upper level plant. Below: view from the Creek.

Intended as the catalyst of regeneration, the new building sits astride Deptford Creek and reinvents a former refuse depot, populating it with a 'pavilion in a landscape'.

Jacques Herzog describes this as a 'figurative' building rather than a 'systems' one - a building that is 'a vibrant, inspiring focal point for the community, accessible and welcoming all'. In fact, it comes close to communicating itself as a proverbial black-box fortress with constant CCTV surveillance, set well behind a tight perimeter security fence and defensive landscaping - all this disguised and glamourised by softly tinted polycarbonate and the long curve to the principal facade. For example, on opening, there was still a large squatter encampment is next door, complete with caravans, old vans and buses and aggressive dogs. To them, as well as most other people, the Laban signals a welcome by invitation only, underscoring the area's social issues (the borough is one of the most deprived in the country). This even affects internal arrangements. Take the publically accessible corner cafe: it's on a south-west corner off the (security) lobby and is glazed in black-tinted glass that doesn't open up. The external landscaping may be discussed in terms of its potential as an external amphitheatre, but the reality is a camera-scanned no-go zone. All this is hardly unreasonable, but it's a sad reality at odds with the PR-speak.

It is not until the light fades that the vibrant richness of the interior is revealed: a place of colourful streets and courts and internal transparency, with 13 dance studios, offices, a 300 seat auditorium (with public programmes), a dance health suite, long ramps and all kinds of internal delights tempered by the consultancy of artist Michael Craig-Martin. It is here that the architects have been able (despite the budget restrictions) to exercise ambition and real skill.

The roof of the two-storey concrete structure is pitched (and also the place of deliberately cultivated inhabitation by rare Redstart birds!), so that the upper interior studios all have different configurations and personalities. These (as well as offices and other rooms that subtly background themselves) are accessed from wedge-shaped 'streets: carefully considered corridors dealt with as sensuous, lively spaces that feed one's ears as well as one's eyes, their geometries informed by alignment with the Creek and the main street, thus generating the wedge geometry.

It's all a rare kind of architectural gamesmanship that offers genuine satisfaction and commands admiration: an inner, as well as an outer, landscape rooted in the idea that the interior is as much an urbane village as the outside community is - the former described by Harry Gugger, a partner of Herzog & de Meuron, as "an urban life within the envelope".

Despite all this there remains an even larger strategic issue. The Goldsmith's campus, where the Laban was located (and retains a building), would have been hugely and more plausibly improved by a new building like this in its midst. Instead, we're going to have to await Will Alsop's new arts building there for that kind of injection.

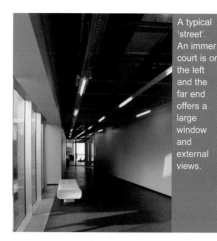

A typical 'street'. An immer court is on the left and the far end offers a large window and external views.

31.

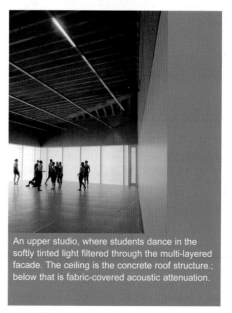

An upper studio, where students dance in the softly tinted light filtered through the multi-layered facade. The ceiling is the concrete roof structure.; below that is fabric-covered acoustic attenuation.

31.

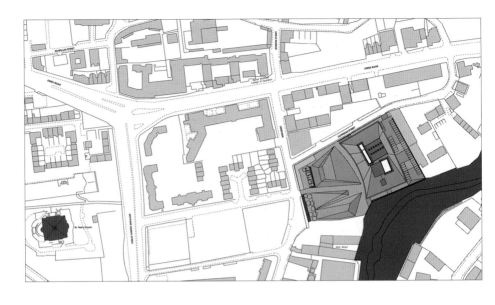

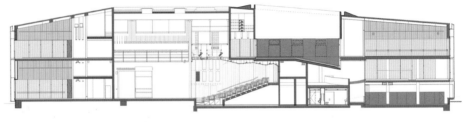

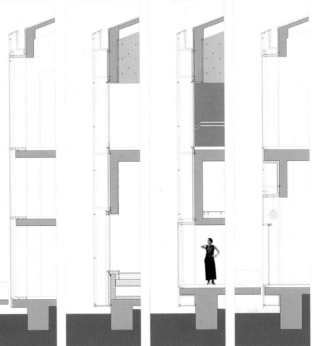

Sections through the whole building and the cladding of the Laban begin to suggest how complicated this ostensibly simple shed actually is. The site plan (Top) also indicates the 'reach' of the site concept.

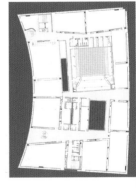

Trinity College of Music

32.

Uni. of Greenwich, King William Walk, SE10
John McAslan + Partners, 2001
DLR: Cutty Sark Gardens

TCM (a distinquished music school) occupies the east wing of King Charles Court (in what became the Greenwich Naval Hospital), designed by John Webb, 1662-69. The interiors were always utilitarian and McAslan continues in this mode with a low-budget conversion. There are plans to roof over the central courtyard.

33 / 34. *Across the road to the Maritime Museum (on the east side of Greenwich village) is the former* **Greenwich Naval College and Hospital,** *a palatial, axial scheme now partly taken over by the University of Greenwich. Much of it was planned by Sir Christopher Wren (1696–1702); other parts are by Nicholas Hawksmoor, James Stuart, Yenn, and John Webb (son-in-law of Inigo Jones). As well as being listed Grade 1, the building is a World Heritage Site (see the Painted Hall and the Chapel).*

The Greenwich Observatory (Wren & Hooke, 1675-6) is just up the hill, in Blackheath Park (from which you'll get splendid views).

Another significant building here is Nicholas Hawksmoor's church of **St Alfrege** *(bottom left), built 1712–18 (Greenwich High Road, SE10). It was bombed during WWII and the interior is a reconstruction, but the exterior still bears Hawksmoor's trademark. The pedimented portico onto the street is especially impressive.*

35 / 36 / 37 *Richard Reid (responsible for some notable housing designs and **Epping Town Hall**, 1990) designed **Finland Quay** (at Onega Quay, off Redriff Road, SE16, Surrey Docks) as a 'necklace' of 7 pavilions designed at a time when Po-Mo architects felt they were rediscovering a warm and comfortable vernacular tradition. (The housing market didn't discover Modernism until the mid '90's.)*
The Lakes *housing scheme, designed by Shepheard Epstein and Hunter, 1990, Norway Dock, Redriff Road, SE16. An unusual scheme: many of its detached, suburban villas are romantically surrounded by an area of shallow water which lends the development a special character.*
Wolfe Crescent *(CZWG, 1989) includes some pleasant 4-storey apartment brick towers that sit adjacent to a canal. Their nearby terraces are also interesting.*

38. *Like North Greenwich, this station in Surrey Quays designed by Eva Jiricna is in two parts: the **Canada Water** JLE (1999) underground platforms and a bus interchange above ground. The main part of the scheme is a large, cantilevering bus shelter and ancillary accommodation. Below ground works, are by the Jubilee Line Extension Architects, who engineered and detailed a concept design by the late Ron Herron (a typical procurement route for most of the Jubilee Line stations).*

39 *Ian Ritchie has designed **Bermondsey JLE Station** and three nearby vents: one in Ben Smith Way, of wavy concrete forms; one in Durands Wharf, looking like an up-market pill-box (both these designs close the vent with cable-net) and one in Culling Road, adjacent to Southwark Park. The latter is perhaps the most interesting, being an exercise in playfully cladding the large vent with bands of pre-patinated copper cladding – apparently, to keep the nearby funeral director happy. The station itself is most interesting inside.*

Outer Ring:
North &
East

Outer Ring:
South &
West

Outer Ring:
North &
East

M25 Motorway

North & East

M40

Heathrow
section

Outer Ring:
Heathrow

South & West section

Outer Ring:
South &
West

Finchley

Kenton

Hendon

Hampstead Garden
Suburb

38 20

Highgate

33 Hampstead
Heath

29

Neasdon

28

35

30

Wembley

Hampstead

31

18

Swiss
Cottage 17 7

32

35 23
21 22
26   27

St John's Wood

Willesden

5

9

15

Camden

Kilburn

2

12 Regent's
Park

10

North
Kensington

6

3   4

13

14 16

8

11

1

Hyde
Park

See South & West
section for this area.

Edmonton

Tottenham

60

19

Stoke
Newington

49 58 Clapton

39

50 Bethnal
46 Green
52
34 53 41
43 51
37 42

54 56

57

See City
section 55

Stepney

Stratford
New
Town
62
61
59
63 West
Ham 64

Stratford
Marsh

Bow

65
Millmeads

Plaistow

s between
d Tower bridges
e section.

Paddington Basin, W2
various architects, 2002-2005
Tube: Paddington, Edgware Road

1. Paddington Basin

Paddington basin is a kind of mini-Canary Wharf, in West London, set upon former railway land and around a barge basin of the Grand Union Canal, just to the north-east of Paddington The development is four distinct parts: the station; the Paddington Healthcare Campus, around St Mary's Hospital; Paddington Central, to the north of the station and alongside Westway; and an area between the Westway and the canal, called Waterside.

The site's problem has been its isolation, inaccessibility and consequent blight. As master-planned by Terry Farrell, the site (with the exception of Paddington central, master-planned by Sidell Gibson) has been linked back into surrounding areas and the station has been re-oriented from the south to the north-east, where the Heathrow link will terminate (this part to be designed by his ex-partner and architect responsible for the Eurostar building at Waterloo, Nicholas Grimshaw).

Paddington Central has two parts: one by Sidell Gibson and the other (on the west) by Sheppard Robson and Kohn Pedersen Fox.

Waterside is to have buildings from: Terry Farrell (offices), Munkenbeck + Marshall (flats), Richard Rogers (flats and offices), Jestico & Whiles, HOK (a Hilton hotel) and Broadway Malyan (flats).

SOM are involved on the Healthcare Campus. Alsop Architects are lined up for a new CrossRail station to the west of Paddington Station.

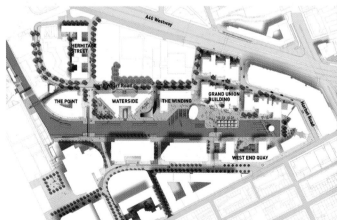

Above left:
The Point (Terry Farrell; 20,657 sq.m. of offices)
Grand Union (Richard Rogers Partnership; residential)
Waterside (Richard Rogers Partnership; 20,526 sq.m. of offices)

Urban School

English education has become a strange scene, prompting developments such as this, in which the school sells off some prime playground for private housing in order to raise the capital for a new school that includes a marvellously successful set of stacked playgrounds that form the buildings key architectural feature of this 3,400 sq.m. building. The triangular plan for the Hampden Gurney School is simple, symmetrical, and splits entrances between a nursery and the school for older children. Four play decks are provided, together with another play area to the rear at ground level. The realised housing is, as they say, undistinguished.

2.

Hampden Gurney School, Nutford Place, W1
BDP, 2002
Tube: Edgware Road, Marble Arch

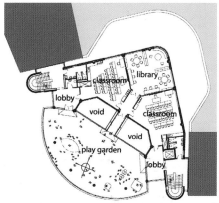

Lisson Gallery

Lisson appears to be one of the few galleries that has not moved to Hoxton and parts east, and is another example of Modernist contexturalism, managing to skilfully blend old and new. In this case, it's a two-stage minimalist conversion and extension to an art gallery which is L-shaped in plan, wrapping another, existing corner building. The first stage came through from Lisson Street; the second met it from Bell Street. The Bell Street facade attempts to reconcile disparate neighbours and, perhaps, does it so well that the game appears incidental to more interesting features. Huge sliding glass doors allow access for large art pieces and an upper loading door loans the facade an industrial overtone. The upper level is a studio.

3.

Bell Street, NW8
Tony Fretton Architects, 1991
Tube: Marylebone, Edgware

4.

27 Broadley Terrace, NWI
Michael Hopkins & Partners, 1986
Tube: Marylebone, Edgware

Hopkins Studio

The thinness and transparency of these simple, hi-tech, prefabricated 'Patera' sheds sits incongruously, but not unpleasantly, within the brick fabric of Marylebone. A key aspect of the shed design is the exposed roof truss and the employment of similar, gasketed, metal-faced sandwich panels for walls and roof. However, dwelling on the technical aspects of the Hopkins' offices runs the danger of missing its key architectural quality: an informal grouping whose inbetween spaces are almost as important as the buildings themselves.

Two sheds, an entry pavilion and an existing building to the rear of the site (used for workshops, stores, printing etc) are linked by a fabric covered awning that runs down the length of one boundary. The spaces around and inbetween are dealt with as garden relaxation areas that have an almost Continental air about them, suggesting lazy summer meetings and vino stained table cloths. In other words: this is a very pleasant urban grouping concealed behind the gates and in spite of conversations about Hi-tech, prefabricated architecture.

Hopkins' fans might like to know that there is a small office building by the practice, originally designed for IBM in the mid '80's, in Lodge Road, just to the north.

5. *Rebuilt after a fire, the **Tricycle Theatre** (Buckley Road, NW6;Tim Foster Architects, 1999; Kilburn Tube) has Hollywood stars as founding members (Costner, Travolta, Spacey, etc.) lending the place glamorous undertones. What it's really about is the cinema as a social place – somewhere to eat, drink and meet friends before and after performances. The accommodation includes the cinema (which also serves as a theatre) a rehearsal studio, art studio, offices, and a cafe/bar. Architecturally, it's bold and interesting. It won't knock you out, but every local community should have a place like this.*

6. *This housing in **St Mark's Road**, W10, is by Jeremy Dixon and was completed in 1980. It comprises 44 family units and attempts to be contemporary whilst contexturally offering a traditional London arrangement, e.g. half-basements, walk-up steps to a piano nobile, etc., in a terraced format with a stepped gable overhead.*

*Another scheme by Jeremy and Fenella Dixon is at 171–201 **Lanark Road**, W9 (1979–82) – a scheme that is also in radical contrast to those being designed only ten years earlier.*

Sarum Hall School

7.

15 Eton Ave, NW3
Allies and Morrison, 1995
Tube: Swiss Cottage, Belsize Park

This is typical Allies and Morrison: considered, well mannered; fussed over but not fussy; unrhetorical, carefully composed and detailed. It's a contextural design, conscious of its Arts & Crafts, leafy, domestic surrounds near Primrose Hill, one that bring together a variety of features in one building. For example, the entry porch, canopy and gateposts take ideas from neighbours (but keep the language contemporary) and the architects have arranged the accommodation so that repetitive elements are on the rear and varied ones are on the street. It is an attractive and satisfying school building that has one celebrating this kind of design skill in an era where it is all too rare (Allies and Morrison have somewhat inherited the mantlee of YRM and are among London's foremost, late 40's, respected architects). Interestingly, however, their work makes some people hanker after the counterpoint of a certain rudeness and irreverence. This is not to criticise A&M's work – quite the contrary. But after soaking up a few works like Sarum Hall School, the architectural tourist might enjoy an architectural poke in the eye from the likes of Will Alsop.

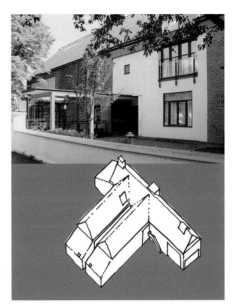

8. *Trellick Tower, by Erno Goldfinger (1973) sits in Golbourne Road, W10, overseeing west London in the form of what was once the tallest block of flats in England. It was an experiment in access (one external corridor serving three maisonettes) and 'brutalist' architectural form. Now it is an icon. Architects love it, partly because it has a content of professional expertise, in part because of its peculiar beauty, and partly because it's such a*

radical design statement. Whether that makes it good housing is another issue. However, since it was constructed, people have grown to love the city once again and the Trellick has become an admired model for metropolitan living. Best seen from afar.

9. *The massive social housing development of Alexandra Road, NW8 – the last of a series of 'infrastructural' housing schemes promoted by Camden Council and designed by Neave Brown) had a brief for 1,660 people in 520 units, developed into the form of two curving, raked concrete terraces, facing one another. The resulting canyon is both incredible and frightening – testament to how architecture can go badly wrong. It is worth comparing such developments with Lubetkin's Hallfield Estate in Bishop's Bridge Road, W2 (1951–59).*

10.

St. John's Wood Road, NW8

Mound Stand, Sir Michael Hopkins & Partners, 1987. Grand Stand, Nicholas Grimshaw & Partners, 1998.
Cricket Shop, English Cricket Board offices, and Indoor School, David Morley, all 1996–8. Media Centre, Future
Systems, 1999. Tube: St. John's Wood

Lord's Cricket Ground
summer in the city

It is difficult to reconcile oneself to the idea of the gentlemen of the Marylebone Cricket Club (the MCC, formed in 1787) becoming patrons of contemporary architecture. However, encouraged by an architect-member called Peter Bell, they have given us a number of modern buildings that, in turn, have helped to revitalise the game at Lord's, home of English cricket.

As a spectator sport, cricket is a million miles away from soccer: a summer ball game lasting all day leaving the pitch and stands at Lord's unused for much of the year, only coming alive as a venue on only 10–12 days a year when international matches are played – also when corporations indulgently entertain valued clients and customers from within their own boxes and less favoured enthusiasts bring luncheon boxes from which to picnic. Importantly, cricket at Lord's has - like other sports - become fodder to the international media machine.

When completed in 1987, the **Mound Stand** designed by Michael Hopkins' office was notable because it offered us an architect pigeon-holed as Hi-

The Mound Stand sits above an existing stand of 1899.This has been retained, but its load-bearing brick piers have been extended (using reclaimed bricks from a demolition site). The additional seating at the upper level is held up on six columns at 18m centres, giving minimal disturbance to the existing structure as well as views of the game. Below the open upper deck sits a structural box incorporating some storage and service facilities. below that is a mezzanine housing private boxes. The translucent fabric roof is a PVC coated glass-fibre weave with an additional PVDF flouropolymer topcoat. The Stand is a simple construction and, by 2003, it was looking somewhat tired and in need of renewal, but it's still an excellent building to visit.

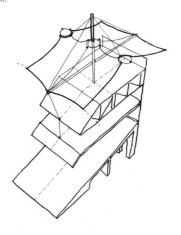

tech betraying both contextural sensitivities and an enthusiasm for dealing with a range of low-tech constructions. Observers were surprised by Hopkins' acceptance of the existing stand, together with his embrace of its brick arches (and their extension from six in number to a row of 21, all properly built as load-bearing), as well as by the acrobatics of the new overhead structure. They were also suspicious that an inspiration for the scheme was not only technical and instrumental, but the notion that an expansive, white, tensed fabric roof had a symbolic appropriateness to the ambience and traditional sartorial garb of summer cricket.

Just after the Mound Stand, Hopkins also completed the **Compton** and **Edrich Stands** that stretch around the east side, beneath the Media Centre. These are simple concrete raked decks that sit upon a more complex arrangement of tubular steel arms.

Cricket has no need of summer at David Morley's **Indoor Cricket School** (1994), an exhilarating interior of green plastic carpet, white finishes, masses of daylight filtered from above, huge powered doors that open in summer, and lots of eager kids properly kitted out for their practice sessions. The entry side incorporates its own viewing terrace and seating, looking over the Nursery Ground.

Morley also designed the 275 sq.m. single-storey Lord's **Cricket Shop** next door (1996), with inflated roofing panels made of continuously pressurised, translucent ETFE foil cushions. Beside this sits a third Morley design: a simple, but elegant, 1,200 sq.m.. two-storey office building for the **Test and County Cricket Board** (1996) with an exterior dominated by large 'light-shelves' which push daylight into the interiors.

Opposite the Mound Stand sits the **Grand Stand** by Nicholas Grimshaw (1998). His team offers the same basic arrangement as Hopkins, but eschews the tensed fabric motif and provides the structural acrobatics we have come to expect from this firm in the form of a two-storey spine truss and two 50m span roof trusses supported on three columns. It has many structural similarities to the Mound Stand and, like it, was

10.

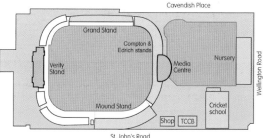

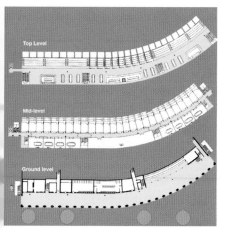

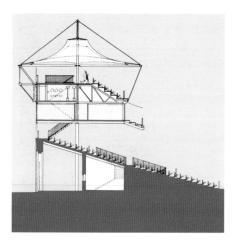

10.

constructed in two winter phases so as not to disrupt the summer games. It is a splendid design, a sophisticated and elegant structure that is well detailed and built (better, in these terms, than the Mound Stand), but misses the emotional connection Hopkins touched upon and Grimshaw would probably dismiss as sentimental design motivation – what John Pringle, the job architect on the Mound Stand, describes as 'a five-day boat cruise', complete with upper promenade and steerage class passengers.

The most interesting building at Lord's is the newest: the **NatWest Media Centre** (1999) designed by Future Systems – architects with a name reeking of 1960's technological optimism who are into designing 'things' (complete with obligatory rounded corners) and who marry retro and progressive postures into a single and skilled post-modern stance. Propped upon two concrete access towers, the structure accommodates special desks plus alcoholic support from a bar at the rear and characteristically an inhabited architectural blob with the exotic, sensuous, other-world quality of Hi-tech engineering (racing cars and yachts, combat aircraft, etc.), from which it borrows its forms and techniques. Taking the form of a 'semi-monocoque' aluminium yacht construction poised high above ground at the east end of the luscious green field, the Centre reads as a UFO dropping in for the splendid sights offered through its massive 40m front window. This is carefully raked so as to avoid reflections back onto the field and so that the media people can easily see out and be fed 'ambient sound'; however, the BBC considered an air-conditioned box as an affront to their commentating history and insisted on a small openable window for themselves so that they could actually hear the crack of leather on willow (a distinctly Heath-Robinson affair; see photo on right).

In fact, most journalists appear to dislike the place. The *Independent's* columnist comments, "You cannot feel the match: the mikes don't work properly and you don't get a proper sense of what's happening. And it's so very bright that you can't see your laptop. We just need windows that open and better tellies (for the replays). And *The Times* man says, "There's a bank of televisons above our heads and for the second half of the day you're looking into the sun and can't see them" Being high up in a glass-faced, westward-oriented pod is clearly not their idea of fun.

Overall, Lord's has become a part of the capitalised, globalised, telecommunicating cultural stream of commercialised contemporary sport. If the Media Centre, for example, were simply an instance of advanced engineering techniques transferred to building it would be less interesting. However, as an unconscious embodiment of so many contemporary cultural streams, this object comes alive and, for a while, will speak to us and echo our dreams.

Above: David Morley's office building and indoor cricket school. below: Grimshaw's stand.
Right: the rear of the media centre; interior of the BBC's window; view out through the rear bar; the raked journalists' seating and the big window, vents on the journalists' desks, a window glazing detail; an end stair up to the mezzanine (there are two of these); and another shot of the journalists' desks.

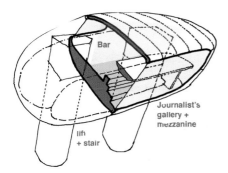

Bar

Journalist's
gallery +
mezzanine

lift
+ stair

10.

The **Media Centre** is constructed from 26, pre-fabricated aluminium sections of 3–4mm thick plate, shipped to site and welded together. CAD and numerically controlled machines were crucial to analysis and the fabrication carried out by yacht builders. The structure – acting as a semi-monocoque of ribs and skin – is supported on two concrete stair/lift towers clad in GRP panels (the architects originally wanted one, but members said this would spoil their view of exisiting trees). The top half rests on these towers, with the bottom half bracketed off concrete ring beams. Internally, the accommodation is principally a raked bank of journalists' benches and an upper, mezzanine level of small rooms (one being for the BBC, with its openable window that is, apparently, rarely used). The rear part accommodates the all too necessary bar. The internal mezzanine floor is hung from the roof and the 9 m high raking glass front (made of 12mm laminated glass plus a layer of 9mm annealed glass and designed so as to be both safe and not dazzle players) rests into the floor but is supported by the mezzanine, requiring carefully designed movement joints.The powder blue interior is argued to result from the need to avoid any distractions to players; to say it is impractical would be an understatement. In a gesture of '60's mannerism, doors are formed as hatches, complete with curved corners. Overall, it's a stunning design, despite its failures. The engineers were Ove Arup.

11.

Marylebone Road, NW1
John McAslan + Partners, 2002
Tube: Regent's Park, Baker Street

Royal Academy of Music

Another piece of architecture that is mostly subterranean, with a large roof with glazed ends popping up above ground on the Marylebone Road frontage. Beneath this is a new concert and recording hall, the focal part of a much larger remodelling and extension programme described as 'a living museum', archive, teaching and practice facility as part of the 1820's John Nash building occupied by the RAM.

12.

Six private villas. Three of them – the Veneto, the Gothik and the Doric – were built in 1992 and have since been added to by three more. Located in the north-east corner of Regent's Park, on the Outer Circle, they are designed by Erith and Terry in a tradition of English eccentricity married to latterday Establishment values, Post-Modernism's reactionary undertones and a good dose of hi-tech carefully hidden away. They supplement the five villas realised by John Nash in the 1820s and straddle the edge of the Regent's Canal adjacent to Hanover Lodge in the north-west corner of the park, providing a conspicuous display of architectural taste that attunes the lifestyles of affluent owners with that of the Ancients who gave us a symbolic classicism. They're an example of an ostensibly light-hearted approach from a serious classicist.

Education Centre

27 Sussex Place, Regent's Park, NW1
Nicholas Hare Architects, 2001
Tube: Baker Street

13.

The Royal College of Obstetricians and Gynaecologists' Education Centre is a fairly large but almost entirely subterranean building - the only parts above ground are a series of large cones illuminating conference and educational spaces below. The project extends facilities in a Louis de Soissons '60's building and required the

excavation of 7,0000 cubic metres of material to accommodate a lecture theatre for 250p and a series of seminar rooms around a central atrium space (lit by the large cone). Above ground, the Centre becomes a garden design with lawn and pergola.

14. *Denys Lasdun's **Royal College of Physicians**, 1960–64, on the Outer Circle and St Andrew's Place, NW1, is a design in the spirit of Le Corbusier married to the English Baroque. One has to imagine an institution with medieval roots, small but hugely influential, dragged into the post-war National Health System and, by the late '50's, ready to attempt a move from a neo-Greek building in Trafalgar Square into a contemporary design. Professional, ceremonial and mundane functions are expertly conjoined into a pavilion terminating terraces along this side of Regent's Park whilst similarly acknowledging context on the eastern side, where administrative offices form part of an existing terrace. Most accommodation is ceremonial and highly symbolic (library as head and cultural memory, initiation room (Census) as heart, central tall hall with its central stair as lungs, dining areas as gut, roof top air intake as mouth and boiler exhaust as . . . (you guess); the auditorium to one side reads as a speech bubble on plan, etc. Bizarre. All of it self-evident in plan and section, but there is hardly a revealing word from Lasdun and an institution who will go no further than admit to the architect's interest in Harvey's concept of blood flows (equals architectural circulation). During the late 1990's, Lasdun was asked to add another 'pod-like' addition opposite the Census room and the College has been linked into nearby buildings to form a latterday educational precinct for the profession. This includes a neo-classical building to the south by Nicholas Hare. Go here and then head north to the Nash terraces of Regent's Park (possibly on to Park Village and Camden Town).*

15. *London Zoo, Outer Circle, Regent's Park, NW1, includes • The **Aviary** in London Zoo is attributed to Cedric Price, Lord Snowdon and the engineer Frank Newby and is a by-product of enthusiasms for Buckminster Fuller's geometries and tense gritty structures designed during that era, and is one of the first pieces of acrobatic modern architecture in London. • Another cool, acrobatic architectural work to see in London Zoo is the **Penguin Pool** (1934–35) by Tecton and Berthold Lubetkin.*

• A third project is more recent: the **Ambika Paul Children's Zoo**, by Wharmby Kozdon Architects (1995), a 'green' children's educational facility.

16. *Office building, Euston Road, NW1 (Warren Street tube; Arup Associates, 1998). Architectural practices typically evolve from 'brightest kids on the block', to 'expert professionals', to 'delivery firms'. Arup Associates have remained experts for a long time, but the role can engender designs that are easy to respect, yet difficult to feel emotional about. This might be such a building, with its references to early Jim Stirling in Stuttgart and the fashionable floating architectural planes. Centre in Paris. It's well done, but go to the rear to see **Broadgate Club West**, by Allford Hall Monaghan Morris (1998), to see something with as much character as style.*

17.

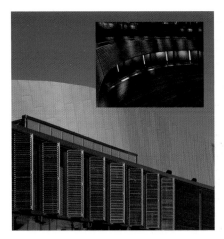

Hampstead Theatre, Eton Avenue, NW3
Bennetts Associates, 2003
Tube: Swiss Cottage

Hampstead Theatre

HT- London's first new theatre since the National opened in 1976 - is an 'egg-in-a-box' (like the Royal Festival Hall) scaled down for more local audiences, the outsides aninated by lots of glass, wood shutters and lighting design by Martin Richman. The auditorium with adaptable seating for up to 325p is slung above the foyer areas and an underground level provides additional facilities. It has been criticised as too 'business park', indicative of how our contemporary tastes and the notion that an architecture has to be expressive of purpose - in this case, as a house of imagination, story-telling, fantasy, illusion and, of course, drama. Put into the context of 1930's Odeon cinemas, latterday multiplexes, a media age and our insatiable appetite for narrative, it's a point to ponder over. At the root of it all are some age-old appetites.

18.

105-119 Brentfield Road, NW10
Sompura, C.D., 1995
Tube: Neasden

Hindu Temple

If Future Systems redream 1960s technological optimism, this Hindu community centre, Shri Swaminarayan Mandir, redreams community and spiritual harmonies, having thoroughly researched their subject in order to recreate this Hindu jewel in Neasden. The focus is upon the incredible craftsmanship of stone-carving that was imported from India, but the heart of this place is a community/prayer centre that includes a column-free space for 2,500 worshippers. What you experience here is not some Disney recreation, but investment in the power of architecture to be a sign and a symbol, to represent a whole gamut of values. To experience this architecture is also to experience a community spirit – which is what most good architectural experiences are about.

19.

Wightman Road, N8
Inskip & Jenkins, 1993
Tube: Manor House

St Paul's Church

The diagrammatic qualities of this church's massing bear comparison with John Nash's All Soul's at Langham Place and, like the Nash church, it works. The key (as always) is context – in this instance, a hilly, Victorian domestic suburb, with pointed gables and dormers. The geometry gives the church a real presence and the simple interior is well handled. It's not only the church's name that draws a comparison with St. Paul's in Covent Garden, but also its 'barn-like' qualities. There aren't many contemporary churches in London, so it is worth a visit if you are in this area.

Lawn House

'The Lawns' is the conversion and extension of a house originally designed by Leonard Manasseh in the '50's. The new work - mostly in glass - entirely engulfs the old house and doubles its size with expansive, double-height spaces, so that the new is played off against the old. And a complete new floor is added, replacing the former pitched roof. For historical and planning reasons the house is set well back from the street - generating a large forecourt and underscoring a space syntax that elevates the house's status as the visitor parades to it or swings into the car area. The house was short-listed for the Stirling prize in 2002.

20.

South Grove, Highgate Village, N6
Eldridge Smerin, 2001
Tube: Highgate

Arad Studio/Shop

Arad has to be one of London's best designers: a man who prefers customers (for his chairs and other products) rather than clients (who end up having to be nursed) and a man whose work is inherently rhetorical yet (ostensibly) devoid of any intent to impress for the sake of it – a rare characteristic that applies to his studio as well as his product designs and craftsmanship. The studio is the conversion of an old warehouse tucked in a mews and has a positively Dickensian approach guaranteed to put off the casual visitor to the Fagan-like character hiding away up there behind the peeling paint. But it is worth the effort of climbing the decrepit access stair to see the way the studio has been formed in a marvellously whimsical yet wilful manner, the wavy wood floor and the superb furniture in the showroom.

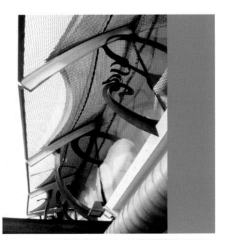

21.

One Off Studio, 62 Chalk Farm Road, NW1
Ron Arad Associates, 1991
Tube: Chalk Farm, Camden

22.

Camden Road, NW1
Nicholas Grimshaw and Partners, 1988 Tube:
Camden

Sainsbury's
battleship supermarket

This is an admirable development with an aggressive note to it, something other than the battleship grey steelwork (latterly softened in some areas to greyish baby blue - a mistake, apparently) and grey aluminium cladding, perhaps betraying the technocratic concerns and military roots of Hi-tech. (Although Sainsbury's low maintenance standards don't help.) The architect's brief was to design an inner-city supermarket that really wanted to be out-of-town. He provided an entirely column-free shopping area, together with loading areas, administration facilities, underground car parking and housing along the canal, on the north side of the development. Two features stand out. First, the main facade makes an attempt to build up the massing of the supermarket shed and to provide a bay rhythm corresponding to the Georgian terrace of late eighteenth century houses opposite – a sound move, realised with the aid of characteristic Grimshaw structural acrobatics. Second, the terrace of maisonettes along the canal have only northern light (their southern side being directly onto the service yard), yet Grimshaw manages to cope well, providing a double height space with garage doors giving onto canal balconies.

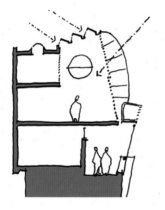

23. *The facade of **MTV** (Formerly **TVAM** – now MTV; Hawley Crescent, NW1; Terry Farrell Partnership; Tube: Camden was once one of the most exhilarating in London – straight into an architectural tradition going back to Googie coffee shops of '50s L.A. and even the spirit of the 1950s British Pop movement reinvented in latterday terms: the converted garage reinvented as a metaphor of the rising sun, complete with a dark horizon (the base) and layers of diminishing textures rising into the sky. At the centre is a rising sun/arched entry, its 'keystone' scrawled in neon. The egg cups on the canal-side are fun but less successful. Inside, the original scheme was well-planned, but eclectic and thematically over-the-top and emphatically global locations from where the news was coming.*

Just like those Googie coffee shops, TVAM was here today and a memory tomorrow. TVAM lost their licence and in came MTV who toned the whole thing down, stuck roundels over the TVAM logo at each end of the sweeping facade, and generally ruined the whole thing in homage to good-designer taste. For a while Camden had the only pure Pop building in the UK. And it is still there, just beneath a surface of denial, out of

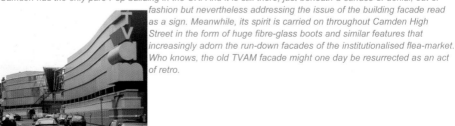

fashion but nevertheless addressing the issue of the building facade read as a sign. Meanwhile, its spirit is carried on throughout Camden High Street in the form of huge fibre-glass boots and similar features that increasingly adorn the run-down facades of the institutionalised flea-market. Who knows, the old TVAM facade might one day be resurrected as an act of retro.

The Place

The Place is a major dance school and performance venue in mixed accommodation that stretches itself between two streets: an old entrance on Duke Street and a new one on Flaxman Street.

The new entrrance is the result of A&M's focus upon the identity of the institution, the performers' and students' facilities, and the dance studios, providing a new and dramatic entrance with a stretching area in front of the glazing to create a shop window-like effect for the School with passers-by viewing the dancers' silhouettes in motion. Other work increased the number of studios and improved the quality of existing ones, and improved the public areas.

24.

16 Flaxman Terrace, WC1
Allies and Morrison, 2001
Tube: Euston

Straw House

Two architects build a very green dream house - literally, using straw bales as a key constructional material for some walls, as well as sand bags and duvet quilting (although the gabion piers are false, concealing a concrete frame) in pursuit of a passive energy equation and sustainable living in an urban environment. There's Modernism in the manner the house is lifted on stilts so that the garden runs under it (and is combined with a grassed roof) and a hint of Rudolf Schindler in the handling of the upper storey. There's even romance in the form of a reading and lookout tower (described as a 'thermal flue' and natural vent, as well as 'a book stack'). But apart from all this (and determination against all odds), the design exhibits some real architectural skill. For 'green' read some true architectural wit and inventiveness - and on a comparatively large scale for a domestic property.

25.

9-10 Stock Orchard Street, N7
Sarah Wigglesworth & Jeremy Till, 2001
Tube: Caledonian Road, Kings Cross

26. *CZWG's Green Building in Camden (2001) comprises apartments above a ground floor of retail units. Unusally for such a location and building type, huge amounts of glass have been used (which certainly helps to lift an area that can sometimes be less than salubrious).*

27. *David Chipperfield's studio (Cobham Mews, NW1) is in a similar location to Arad's – tucked away in a mews – but meaningful correspondence stops there. Chipperfield goes for a more cool, architectonic aesthetic, for a simple play on materials and abstract surfaces also evident in his designs for shops like Equipment (now closed) or the Wagamama restaurant in Soho. The Maison de Verre influence is again evident in the way the facade cladding has been handled.*

28. *These terraced houses built by* **Erno Goldfinger** *at 1–3 Willow Road, NW3, in 1938 are a fascinating and intricate design that marries 1930's Parisian avant garde values with design traditions informing the London terrace house that stretch back to the late 1600's. In Goldfinger's design, Modernism as an ostensibly radical lifestyle found a place to root and nest within cosy Hampstead. Elegant living and salon conversations enthusing about Surrealism and socialist politics found resonance in spaces profoundly indebted to the good manners, tastes and support from the invisible servants of London's 17th.c Georgian terraces. The fundamentals of their architectural form – especially the 'vertical living' between party walls (as opposed to a 'horizontality' between floors characterising Continental apartments) was enthusiastically taken up by this talented architect and his wife who saw no difficulties in attempting a synthesis of tradition with Modernism. No. 2 Willow Road epitomises a distinct period between quite different eras in England's architectural history: between architectural traditionalists sceptical of the new ideas coming from the Continent and architectural*

values that were to be at the heart of a large post-war programme of urban regeneration; and also between pre-war and post-war social values. Here, in this small, pre-war family house in Hampstead, overlooking Hampstead Heath, the Goldfingers literally and demonstrably brought the issues home, set stylistic themes and standards that were to be copied by many post-war architects and lived a life that manifest the kinds of social changes that saw their servant's quarters modified into a family apartment. Goldfinger's own unit is now owned by the National Trust and is open to visitors. Tel 020 7985 6166 for daily opening times and tours.

29. *John Winter's own home at 81 Swains Lane, N6, sits opposite the gates to Highgate Cemetery (where Marx is buried). It's a marvellous three-storey design (completed in 1969), with piano nobile at the top, bedrooms in the middle, and kitchen / family / dining on the garden level. Its rusting Corten steel cladding and large panes of clear glass peek above crusty brick walls, looking at once aged and modern. The influences are North American again, this time the California Case Study houses of the late 1940s and early 1950s, and the work of SOM, for whom Winter worked in the 1950s.*

30. *The two-storey* **Hopkins House**, *at 49a Downshire Hill, NW3, was completed in 1975 and stood as an understated model of Hi-tech and eccentric living for many years (somewhat in the manner of the California houses built after WWII by Entenza, Eames et al, from which it drew inspiration). The former came from its simple, 3.6 m span, steel and glass structure; the latter came from a home / work equation that optimistically placed a lot of reliance on louvres for spatial divisions, foreshadowing the latterday enthusiasm for loft spaces and similar non-prescriptively defined spaces that are easily changed and adapted.*

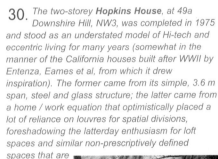

31. *The* **Burton home** *(1989), 1b Lady Margaret Road, NW5, around the corner from Kentish Town tube), is a two-person, timber framed house by and for Richard Burton, of ABK. It is pushed against its northern site boundary, facing south in order to benefit from solar gain. But this is more than another timber-framed / highly insulated eco-exercise. Burton manages to give his*

home extremely livable qualities totally integrated with the technical strategies.

32. *Of these two* **houses**, *44 & 42 Rochester Place, NW1, designed by David Wild from 1984 on – Wild's own (no. 44) was built first and a neighbour loved it, asking him to do one for them. This is architecture on a budget, without grandiose gestures, and indebted to the London Georgian house (piano nobile with bedrooms above), le Corbusier (the city villa type, with ground level undercroft parking and a roof terrace) and Adolf Loos (who advocated non-rhetorical aesthetics). Private London has many small, local works like this (e.g. in nearby Camden Mews). Wild plans another new house at no.40.*

33. Camden's rich legacy of social housing from the 1960s and 1970s is epitomised by this development of a hillside in Hampstead Village, tucked away in **Branch Hill**, NW3. Designed by a local authority whose programme gave young designers marvellous opportunities, this scheme (designed by Gordon Benson and Alan Forsyth, 1970–77) bears reference to Corbusier's beloved Mediterranean hillside villages as reinterpreted in Switzerland by Atelier Five.

35. **Camden Gardens** (Jestico Whiles, 1994), is a difficult site opposite the Grimshaw housing on the Sainsbury site, with five villa-like apartment blocks (18 units) tightly squeezed onto it. Three villas face the street, and further accommodation provided in a terrace that faces onto the canal. Ground floor units in the terrace have gardens, but there is otherwise no private open space, although a central, rolled-gravel garden is provided behind the central villa. Europeans might wonder what the big deal is, but London has all too little of this kind of housing.

37. They don't come much thinner than this insinuation into the urban fabric (**125 Golden Lane**; Joe Hagen, 2000). The house is about 3.5m wide and 5 stories plus a roof terrace, with no rear views or access. Compact, as you might guess, and it's all served by a lift as well as stairs. The house has a steel frame sitting on 15m deep concrete piles and the gable wall hanging over the corner pub is clad in timber.

34. This is one of the better warehouse conversions in London, although the most interesting parts – zinc-clad roof pavilions and the central court – are not readily accessible. The building, located in 10-22 **Shepardess Walk**, N1, fills a whole block and is centred around an open court fitted with new access balconies, a glazed lift, and minimal landscaping with Scottish beach stones and three silver birch trees (parking is underneath). The ground floor is commercial space and the upper levels are 50 apartments. It is all very direct, no gimmicks, with robust, consistent detailing and very satisfying. The designers are Buschow Henley (1999; see their TalkBack building in an earlier section).

36. The **studio** of Jo van Heyningen and Birkin Haward (1998) at Burghley Yard, Burghley Road, Tufnell Park, NW5, is the conversion of a former warehouse into one of those equations that pays the studio bills. The front half has been converted into apartments and studios are provided at the rear. Intermediate structural bays have been removed to provide a courtyard inbetween and the rear wall has been demolished and rebuilt one bay in, in order to provide the studio with a patio. It's necessarily an economic design, but sensitive and carefully considered. The pruning manages, for example, to retain the roof trusses and boarding, complete with the patina of age and wear, thus lending instant warmth to the simply arranged, main studio space at the upper level.

38. The **Highpoint** flats in North Road, N6 have an almost suburban location, high above London, with terrific views. Berthold Lubetkin and the Tecton group designed them in 1936–38 as exemplars of modern rational thinking. Highpoint 1 offers us all of le Corbusier's 5 Points (car port, piano nobile on piloti, roof garden, free plan with minimum columns, and horizontal windows). Highpoint 2 further echoes the example of le Corbusier, with double-height studio spaces. The entry porte coche is daringly held up by neo-classical caryatids copied from the Erectheum in Athens – a gesture that some people have considered to be facetious and incomprehensible, but that lifts the spirit.

39.

40 Douglas Road, N1
Future Systems, 1994
Tube: Highbury & Islington

Glass House

This house sits at the end of a Georgian terrace, its four storeys straddling the two flank walls and wrapped in a 'skin' that rises as a front wall of glass block on one side, over the roof, and down the southern garden side as a splendid, falling wall of glass. The front, with its glass blocks (vaguely Maison de Verre), stepped stainless steel approach to the threshold across a 'void of stones' (vague undertones of aeroplane access stairs providing access to a parked industrial object) and groovy 1960s, round-corner entry door (hatch) is probably the most interesting because it gives much away about the values and enthusiasms of these designers.

40.

Rosebery Avenue, EC1
RHWL and Nicholas Hare Architects, 1998
Tube: Angel

Sadler's Wells

This reinvention of a 1931 theatre is aimed at providing an intimate performance space with links to the local community. Its accommodation includes a new, large auditorium designed for watching dance performances and the refurbishment of the small, Lilian Baylis Theatre, together with an education centre, rehearsal rooms, etc. – a veritable community of facilities packed into the site. Internally, the designs are direct and functional, with an emphasis on simple finishes, glass and steel. Nicholas Hare Architects were involved as advisors on the exteriors.

41.

Blue House, Garner Street, E2
FAT (Seran Griffiths), 2002
Train: Cambridge Heath

Wood House

FAT have a neo-Venturi programme that comes across in a contemporary manner and the '**Blue House**' (actually pale turquoise; and it's not wood either, but fake wood boarding) betrays its author's PoMo enthusiasms (plus a touch of Arts & Crafts). "We are more interested in the effect the thing has, than how you might produce it", says the architect.

Contexturalism here is a purely cerebral, trans-Atlantic game that refuses parochialism: the house is two small apartments pretending to be a villa in Maine, deriving every possible benefit from its tight site and given odd features such as an end elevation capped by what is supposed to be an Amsterdam skyline. Like Venturi's work, the house deliberately obfuscates the boundary between fun and high architecture: 'the windowseat [on the stair rising to the first floor] may be Loos on the inside, but on the outside it refers to the Amsterdam red light window, with its game of seeing and being seen'. (And if architecture is not to be a game, then what is it?) One would like to see this thinking extrapolated to a whole group of houses.

Tin House

This house off Brick Lane is an indicator of how the area has recently changed: cheek by jowl with Pakistani restaurants sits this galvanised steel and glass beast that manages to blend in surprisingly well. The lower floors are bedrooms and the top, double-height space is the living area. It's very elegant and comes across like a polite English version of the houses Frank Gehry used to put up in Venice (LA).

42.

Bacon Street, E1
William Russell, 2002
Tube: Liverpool Street

St Luke's / LSO

St Luke's Church was a derelict shell without a soul: broody, romantic (John James; wonderful obelisk spire by Hawksmoor; 1728). But now it has been revitalised as a music education centre (serving a programme called LSO Discovery) and at the heart of the new body is the Jerwood Hall: a large, galleried rehearsal and recording facility for the London Symphony Orchestra, able to accommodate an audience of 350p.

    A new steel structure of internal 'trees' props and frames the new roof and underground excavations to either side of the church (in the crypt and former graveyards) provide ancillary accommodation.

    Acoustics, of course, were a prime concern and a silent (as the grave) heating and ventilating system utilises 100m deep undergound bore pipes and the stable conditions at that depth. It's impressively done, but also a polite English interplay with an important old building that avoids real dialogue across time. The interior is impressive, but externally, the new work is almost entirely suffocated by the coffin of the old shell.

43.

Old Street, EC1
Levitt Bernstein Architects, 2003
Tube: Old Street

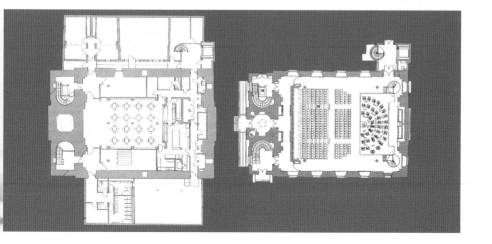

44.

60 Farringdon Road, EC!
Allies and Morrison, 2002
Tube: Farringdon

Visitor Centre

The idea of a Visitors Centre and Archive Centre for both Guardian and Observer newspapers is without precedent in the UK. The concept, instigated by the need to house all original documentation from the papers' histories, dating back to 1821 and 1791 respectively, developed to become an expression of the ethos of the papers, embodying specific social and political values through its core activities of exhibition, education and archive. A colonnade has been formed behind the existing brick façade by removing and rationalising the jumbled assortment of openings. A new glazed screen is set back behind the colonnade to give a continuous, light façade to the entrances to the Newsroom and independent offices on the upper floors. Two strips of rooflight over the central exhibition space (originally a courtyard) admit natural daylight, and a new concrete structure at the rear is pulled back from the rear boundary wall to create a lightwell, providing light and ventilation. These elements occur in the three successive zones of the building, which become progressively more private on the main route through the building. The first zone is the entrance area and a public café, which can be opened independently of the Newsroom. The second zone forms the heart of the building, where the exhibition space is bordered by a temporary exhibition space (which can be converted into a lecture theatre via a series of moveable partitions and a retractable seating unit), and the highly environmentally controlled archive vaults which hold all the original photos and paper documents. The third band of accommodation houses the more private education rooms, a study relating to the archive and ancillary areas. It's worth a visit.

45. *It's difficult to give social housing the attractiveness of other architectural projects. This urban block of housing (**Killick Road**, N1, Avanti Architects, 1998) fights on two fronts: decent housing design; and the media promotion that feeds on sexy images. It is relatively high density (170 beds per acre) and helps to rejuvenate an area that has been sorely blighted for too long. The 16 family units, 48 apartments, and 9 apartments for 'rough sleepers' are compactly planned and mixed together. It adds up to being an expertly designed scheme that still manages to incorporate architectural features into an area that sorely needs them.*

46. *The **Rushton Street Surgery**, on the south side of Shoreditch Park, N1 (Penoyre & Prasad, 1999) divides doctors over two floors around a central, top-lit mall running through the centre of the plan and the street facade offers itself as the presentable face of the building, embracing on-site parking, whilst the rear (south) side is quite plain – architecturally, a layering of accommodation along the central axis. It is the kind of design that is deeply considerate of users' needs, operating costs, etc., although some details have suffered from a procurement process that, at the final stages of the job, distanced the architects.*

47. *This folly in Farringdon (44 Britton Street, EC1 **Janet Street-Porter** / CZWG, 1988) sits on a corner site in an area better known for offices and studios. The design emphasises the corner, plays vaguely contextural games with window arrangements, inscribes huge squares, offers an un-London blue glazed roof, and adds 'log' lintels that some critics have likened to a 'knowing' comment on the Abbe Laugier's notes about architectural origins(!). The brickwork was Porter's idea of cast shadows and descriptions of the interiors by the owner are daffy, joyful and dominated by a jokey desire for the place to look 'wrecked'. It was an existential statement. But, for some reason architecture and frivolity invariably make poor bed-fellows. But it is clever and it is fun. Then the owner moved on.*

48. *Finsbury Health Centre, designed by Tecton, 1935–38, Pine Street, EC1, belongs to a beginnings of a former age of Modernism when architects and their patrons were overtly socialist and humanist and there was a belief in the power of architecture to contribute to the well-being of others, especially the deprived and disadvantaged. They believed in a different future, mediated by a design that would throw away the past and embrace a new, egalitarian future of well-being. The key designer among the architects was Berthold Lubetkin (his partners were well connected ex-Architectural Association students he had teamed up with in 1932,*

after coming from Russia via Warsaw and Paris). As a young practice, they had managed to design and exhibit a clinic design seen by people from Finsbury - then one of London's poorest boroughs, with appalling health problems. English social connections, left-wing politics and European inspiration with a mix of impeccable sources (Russian Constructivists to Perrault and Le Corbusier) had made an unlikely meeting.

The outcome was a remarkable Modernist exercise in the tradition of 'art leading the facts of science'. Two wings (exhibiting with self-evident beaux arts symmetries) house administration and consultation rooms, and a central mass houses reception, waiting areas and an upper lecture hall - all designed so that services, accessible from outside, could rise at the blank ends and run along the facades, into the accommodation. The framed construction and the way it is serviced and organised is a model of rational design, an example to the profession of how architecture could be at once modern, instrumental, at the service of the people, and beautiful. And yet there is an odd note indicative of the period: the basement was designed as a processing and delousing unit into which coach-loads of children would be driven, mattresses brought and burned - a concept with undertones reminiscent of the functionalist, ethnic cleansing machines of National Socialism!

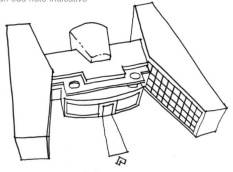

*Sadly, FHC is a rather neglected building but, together with Tecton's Highpoint buildings and the **Penguin Pool** at London Zoo, it is a rare example of a European-inspired modernism intruding into a London scene otherwise preoccupied. It was a design that married instrumentalism and aesthetics into a model architectural configuration that remains as a bench-mark for contemporary architects.*

Clissold Leisure Centre

49.

63 Clissold Road, N16
Hodder Associates, 2002
Tube: Arsenal

Steve Hodder's leisure centre for Hackney was the project from hell: 3 years late and £20m over budget (it started at £7m; some say the outcome is actually £34m) and symbol of Council incompetence. Was it worth it? said the headlines. Well, it's actually an interesting piece of design based on a rather confused brief that sought to please everyone. Which, of course, it doesn't. The lofty spaces, the two 25m pools and the problematic glazed screen between them, issues of ambience (concrete, glass and stainless steel; complaints that the building is unsure whether it's an art gallery or a leisure centre), issues of management . . . and the rest make this a fascinating case study in what can happen to a good architect in the wrong place at the wrong time. The community even has a battling web site about the place. 'Beautiful but badly designed' said the Audit Commission. Eh? You figure that one out.

50.

Kingsland Road, E2
Branson Coates Architecture, 1998
Tube: Liverpool Street, then 149/242 bus

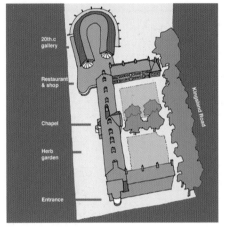

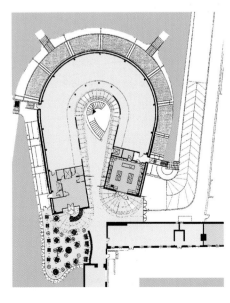

Geffrye Museum

The Geffrye Museum is a pleasant London oddity. Formed from what were once almshouses and devoted to the history of our domestic interiors, the Museum sits on the edge of the East End, on a busy arterial road. But leave that urban grittiness behind and we are at once in a village-like setting. Tall trees define the boundary; beyond them is a green forecourt, and arrayed around three of its sides are the cottage-like former almshouses, calmly dominated by what was once a chapel at the architectural focal point of the grouping. It feels as if the old folk should still be living there. They're not. But the keynote of the Museum and the recent Branson Coates extension to it - a two-storey 1,900 sq.m. extension that almost doubles the Museum's size - continue in this vein and provides displays on C20 interiors, a restaurant, a temporary gallery, a design centre for locally made furniture, educational rooms, and a book shop.

    The visitor approaches the Museum off the busy Kingsland Road and enters the tree-lined and grassed forecourt of the almshouses built in 1715. The entrance is in one corner. From here, visitors progress along the frontage of the almshouses, following an architectural promenade on a temporal theme, through what was once a individual series of homes, now transformed into room sets displaying domestic interiors from different historical periods, beginning in the C17 and ending at the C20. This promenade terminates at the opposite end of the array, in the corner where a new focal space has been created between three brick gables. This space – formed beneath a roof that spans between the gables and conceived as if it were an exterior space - houses the restaurant (now revealing a view back down the rear herb garden of the Museum) and a shop, and it is also a foyer space that leads on to the C20th. new gallery itself. One of the three gables is a termination of the almshouses, where they turn the corner. Two of the gables are actually the ends of the same, horse-shoe planned building. One leads into the shop the other forms an entrance to the restaurant kitchen. Entering into the new gallery, the visitor has the C20 sets arranged in an arc, all around. The backwall is solid masonry and the roof structure is a heavy, open timber truss, At the centre of this top-lit space is a grand, curving concrete and glass staircase that leads down to a lower set of rooms mostly used for educational purposes. From the outside, the new addition is a blank, two-storey, brick-clad building, with a sheltered ramp wrapping around the outside.

• The Flemish bond external brickwork of the extension building is made of spiraling brickwork that follows the line of the 1 in 12 ramp which goes around the exterior and is 80m long, without a break.

• This external wall is very thick - 680mm in total! It comprises a 215mm inner brick leaf; a 250mm cavity with 180mm of insulation; and a 215mm outer leaf. The reasons are entirely to do with energy conservation and control, providing the building with insulation and thermal mass.

• The brick arches in openings (such as the gable end in the restaurant) are phoney: brick slips stuck onto concrete arches. It would have cost considerably more to do it in the real, traditional manner.

Lux Building

This was designed as a small cinema and art gallery for the Film Makers Co-operative and London Electronic Arts in a trendy location within 'up and coming' Hoxton, just north of Broadgate. Contrived to look as if the accommodation is in two separate buildings, the blue, composite brick/concrete structure (which is a composite of both precast and *in situ* concrete) has an intentional heavy, industrial quality whilst the large windows promote a continuous 'dialogue' between interior and exterior. It is worth a visit if, as a contrast to the manifestations of global capitalism at the heart of the City, you are prowling peripheral areas in search of authenticity. The cinema went bust in 2002.

51.

2–4 Hoxton Square, N1
Maccreanor Lavington Architects, 1998
Tube: Old Street

Hackney College

This large 'community college' in Hoxton, just beyond the northern edge of the City and adjacent to Hoxton Market, serves about 14,000 students. It mixes brick, timber, metal louvres and stretched fabric sails as key features of buildings that race around the perimeter of a large, 2.8 ha site, defining a landscaped and colonnaded inner courtyard at the heart of the complex whilst ensuring the outer edges maintain a definition of surrounding streets. The aesthetic is crisp and fresh, although the understandably heavy security presence contradicts the open arms, community message. Hampshire County Architects, experts in this field, are responsible for the scheme; Hawkins Brown refurbished two included Edwardian schools on the site. Artists were brought in to design gates and screens, courtyard benches, water features, etc.

52.

Falkirk Street, N1
Hampshire County Architects/Perkins Ogden
Hawkins Brown, 1997
Tube: Old Street

53. *2002 saw an two-storey addition to the top of* **White Cube***'s building in Hoxton Square, N1, designed by Mike Rundell and providing additional office, conference and related spaces for this trendy gallery. It's an incongruous addition, but quite elegant and appears quite appropriate both to the gallery and in this area.*

54. *The obvious comparison to make with the library at* **Queen Mary & Westfield College** *in the East End (Mile End Road, E1, designed by Colin St John Wilson, 1989), is the same architect's design for the British Library at St. Pancras. The 'bagged' brickwork on the exterior is more timid than Lewerentz's precedent of St. Mark's in Stockholm, but it is the only example you will find in London and always takes courage. The interior is comparatively cheap-and-cheerful, as one might expect for a contemporary university library.*

The Student Union building on the campus (1999) is by Hawkins Brown.

55.

Old Castle Street, E1

Wright & Wright Architects, 2001

Tube: Aldgate, Aldgate East

The Library sits behind the facade of what was a derelict Victorian wash-house: a loaded symbol of women's roles in the C19.

Women's Library

Housing a significant international collection, the WL uses a layout that responds to the client's requirements for highly accessible and secure private space coupled with the need for stringent environmental control in some areas. The building consists of an exhibition hall, seminar room, educational facilities, reading room, archives, cafe, offices, friends' room and garden. The most public spaces are on lower floors, with increasing security as one moves up through the building. Servicing requirements, coupled with the need for primary spaces such as the exhibition hall, led to the plan form. This consists of a series of large rooms, one on each floor, framed by two structural cores, which contain the circulation and services. This is set back from the washhouse wall, with ancillary accommodation between old and new. The combined resolution of the structure, environmental control and functions of the building led to a complex section of heavyweight construction. The spaces intertwine in section so the uniqueness of each of the building's main functions is reflected architecturally. The spatial manoeuvres within the building are highly complex to reflect this uniqueness. For example the exhibition hall consists of overlapping spatial relationships and axis, while the reading room, a calm, white room is the only symmetrical space in the building. Design ideas are carried through from the strategic design to the smallest details, such as ironmongery and window details.

Nine artists worked with the architects, eight of them making staircase panels representing a well-known woman.

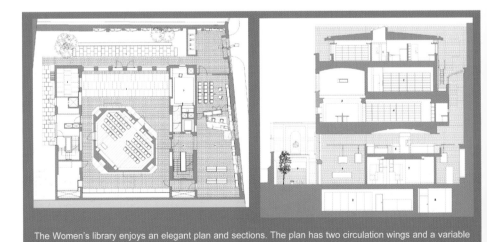

The Women's library enjoys an elegant plan and sections. The plan has two circulation wings and a variable central space inbetween; the section plays with single and double height spaces. At the heart of the ground floor is a seminar room surrounded by an exhibition area. Above the seminar room is a 'multifunctional' deck linked to the kitchen on the same level. Above this is the library. Offices are at the top.

Mile End Park

This East End park is a fascinating example of regreening: an area bombed in WWII, grassed over, left to dereliction, and reinvented with the assistance of lottery money and the energies of a local charity (Environment Trust) together with the local authority, etc.

The park sits alongside the grand Union Canal its linear development is zoned for play, ecology, art, sport, etc. Since a main road crosses the park, it was decided to build a 'green bridge' (CZWG) so as to lend the park continuity (an appropriate and well executed idea that isn't half as novel as it's authors pretend) and which includes retail accommodation in glazed green bricks.

The Ecology Park includes two half-buried buildings whose open side fronts the canal by Jonathan Freegard Architects. One is an education centre and the other is an arts gallery, both trumpeted as having 'been designed to be as energy efficient as possible using a 'Passive annual heat storage sysstem' (PAHS)'. Another two are planned.

56.

Mile End Park, E3
CZWG/Jonathan Freegard, 2000-02
Tube: Mile End

57. *Percy Thomas Edwards' **Swanlea School** (Brady & Durwood Streets, E1; 1993) is for 1050 pupils, built within a visually nondescript area, designed as a series of rooms off a long, large mall that acts as a 'spine' to the design. It is self-consciously 'new', a regenerative statement in that optimistic, Modernist sense, albeit on a low budget. The intention is that the local community can also use the school facilities. The architectural forms are indebted to the kind of steel bending technologies that would have been expensive not so many years ago and passive solar gain has been utilised in order to contribute to an economic thermal strategy.*

58. *The **Raines Dairy** project is another Peabody trust modular, prefab housing project (61 flats, including 8 live-work units), by Allford Hall Monoghan Morris (2003; Northwold Road, Stoke Newington, N16). The 127 steel-framed modules were 3.8m wide and 9.6-11.6m long, mostly forming 2-ved units (with some 3-bed units to the rear). Access is by rear access 'deck'. Time on site was a 40% reduction on normal construction.*

59.

Stratford Station, E15
Chris Wilkinson Architects (concourse)
Troughton McAslan, 1999

Stratford Station

This is quite a statement and just what Stratford needs (the place is virtually a large, inhabited and isolated roundabout designed by highway engineers). The main building – serving as an interchange and terminus for the underground and DLR – is a soaring, curved roof structure and a simple solution to a complex design problem with design criteria for crashing trains and collapsing roof beams, and the accommodation of underground trains and a river. In addition, the big volume acts as a simple solar ventilator, drawing air from the shed and the lower passages. But it's the way Wilkinson plays off the big statement against considered detail and a thoughtful use of materials that makes this building sing. The ceiling, for example, is almost invisibly lit and appears as a gigantic ribbed and shimmering surface. The JLE platforms are by Troughton McAslan.

60. *Stuck out in the middle of nowhere on the edge of the Lea Valley area (Ferry Lane, N17), **Tottenham Hale Station**'s cheap and cheerful design by Will Alsop is typical of his striving to make a statement from difficult material. 80% of the 'architecture', in the sense of what you go to enjoy, is in the curved aluminium tube down one side of the station, punctuated by large portholes.*

Stratford Circus

A successful project conjoins many things together. To isolate any one would be unjust. And yet the design of this building is clearly a major part of what makes the Circus such a lively and valuable community resource (much like Peckham Library). The Circus' programme is focused upon the performing arts, on schools and out-reach projects. At the heart of the building is a central hall with a cafe and a suspended gallery level, off which there are studios, dance and theatre spaces (Circus 1, 2 and 3). It's tight (clearly too small) and buzzing. Every community should have one of these.

When there, also look at the adjacent Picture House by Burrell Foley Fisher, 1998, a place with a restaurant and bar as well as cinemas. Like the station, it's a welcome, fresh design for the area.

61.

Theatre Square, Salway Road, E15
Levitt Bernstein, 2002
Tube: Stratford

62, *The huge **Stratford Market Jubilee Line Depot**, serving the underground trains, was designed by Chris Wilkinson Architects and engineers, Richard Fenton Associates (formerly Acer Consultants). It was completed in 1997. It's a bit remote, but is impressive and sometimes open for **London Open House**.*

63. *Opposite the station is the **Stratford Bus Station** designed by London Transport (below).*

64.

Plashet School, Plashet Grove, E6
Birds Portchmouth Russum, 2000
Tube: East Ham

Bridge
Plashet gem

Technically, there's not a lot to say about this pedestrian bridge for Plashet School in Newnham: an artfully propped, prefabricated, 67m, blue painted steel construction, covered with tensed fabric, linking two halves of a girls' school across a busy road, (one from the 1930's, the other an eight storey 1960's building).

But it's where utilitarianism ends and the enjoyment of designing a contrived artifice begins that this simple link bridge elevates itself into the alchemy that transforms the mundane into the valuable. It's a joy to see, to pass under, to walk through, giving the anonymous school buildings a new identity. The sinuous curve (argued as necessaary to preserve an existing tree, but they would say that wouldn't they?) is interupted by an intermediate hang-out with steel benches.

It's cheerful, inventive and - in the details that incorporate lighting and get rid of rainwater - distinctly quirky. You'll either rank this, together with Alsop's Peckham Library, as two of the best pieces of London's contemporary architecture - or dismiss it as over-wrought mannerism posing as instrumentalism. We hope you'll join with us in seeing this as the celebratory *act* that is good design: entirely rooted in its substance, in contingent factors and it is and does. This is architecture at its simplest and most sophisticated: on target; both appropriate and authentic (two words that are difficult to employ these days).

Doesn't it have any problems? Well, of course: in particular, the magazines never show you the most difficult and unresolvable part of the equation: the ends where the new bridge hits the two schools. And its smaller than you think. And the fabric gets dirty. However, few designs can induce the feeling that such criticism is carping.

Pumping Station 'F'

65.

Abbey Lane, E15
Allies and Morrison, 1997
Tube: West Ham

The Lee Valley is not the most attractive part of London, but it does possess a curious, post-industrial authenticity that latterday ecologists wax lyrically over and protect as nature reserves. And there, midst a landscape that could be anywhere in industrial England sits a gleaming aluminium beast of exquisite design: the enclosure to hi-tech pumping machinery that deals with some of London's prodigious waste. Pumping Station F is a large industrial barn, some 57m long, 29m wide and 23m high. What you see is a gleaming enclosure to sophisticated pumping machinery, the fifth of a series of sewage pumping stations built here since 1869, in this instance using state-of-the-art submersible pumps that halved the normal costs associated with such installations.

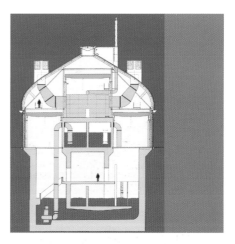

The enclosing superstructure comprises lightweight steel 'A' frames at 6m centres, bearing internally upon a square frame that carries the travelling cranes necessary for maintaining the interior machinery. It is this square structure that is at the heart of the design and becomes the key to the expression of the gable ends. Four sewers are brought together into one large concrete culvert that forms the base of the entire building. Using 16 submersible pumps with a 2 cubic metres per second capacity, the sewage is then pumped up 13m and discharged into the upper level culvert, and from there into the 1869 main outfall sewer and the treatment plant at Barking (in the same manner it has been done since that time). Four diesel generators - sitting in the middle of the building - power the whole affair whilst a central gantry and two side-aisle travelling cranes are for lifting the submersible pumps and other machinery for maintenance.

Externally, the roof is penetrated by four vent cowls for the machinery. Louvres all along the roof ridge provide ventilation to the barn itself. The sides are also louvred.

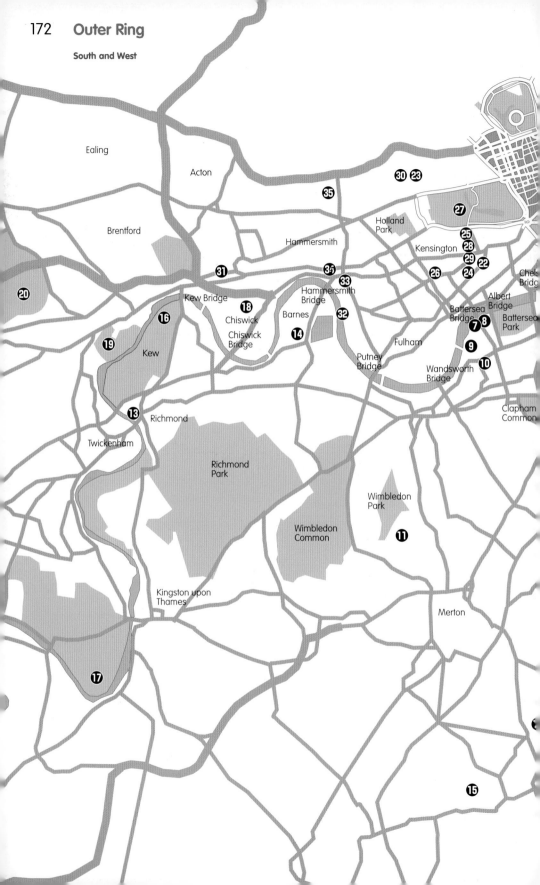

Ealing

Acton

Brentford

Hammersmith

Holland
Park

Kensington

Chels
Bridg

Kew Bridge

Chiswick

Chiswick
Bridge

Barnes

Hammersmith
Bridge

Battersea
Bridge

Albert
Bridge

Battersea
Park

Kew

Fulham

Putney
Bridge

Wandsworth
Bridge

Clapham
Common

Richmond

Twickenham

Richmond
Park

Wimbledon
Park

Wimbledon
Common

Kingston upon
Thames

Merton

1.

Horniman Museum

The Horniman was originally designed by Charles Harrison Townsend in 1901 (he also did the Whitechapel Gallery and the Bishopsgate Institute) and the A&M work was part of a long overdue dilapidations and extensions programme that called for an exhibition space, education facilities, a shop and cafe. It also called for clearing away unsatisfactory extensions and attempting to make a connection between the interiors and the surrounding parkland. The result is a delight, both in terms of what A&M have done and what the Horniman now is.

Townsend's building is now a small complex of inter-linked pavilions in a park. From the street it reads as four: (two belonging to the Townsend design, the gable end of the A&M extension, and a 1994 Centre for Understanding the Environment, from Architype (actually quite a nice 'green' pavilion in itself, complete with the obligatory grass on roof); on the rear is another (a glass-house). Inside, the Museum is a mix of old and new and the collection is, on the whole, a superb and idiosyncratic mix of ethnographic pieces. The parts handled by A&M are excellent (especially the new music room) and one only wishes the funding could have extended to a revamp of all spaces. (Perhaps that it didn't remains a part of the pleasure of the place).

This is A&M at their best: picking up contextural themes from the existing parts of the Horniman - particularly the barrel vaulting - and reinventing them. The detailing and proportioning is, as always, superb (vaguely Scarpa inspired) and the scale is (again as always) well handled. It's a lively mix, often thronged with children and the place offers the especial pleasures of expert but non-monumental architecture somewhere out there in suburban London. if there is a sour note it's that frequent English disparity between cultural and design intent, and management actions - manifest here, for example, in the stink of frying chips that fills the otherwise fine cafe.

(Go to the Dulwich Picture Gallery on the same visit.)

The parade of paviliions front the road. The Architype pavilion is nearest; the 1901 clock tower is in the background. Below: the frontage of Townsend's building - all vaguely H.H. Richardson in flavour. The front iincludes a large mosaic by Anning Bell on the topic of 'Humanity in the House of Circumstance'. The two--storey lectuure hall was an annexe of 1911.

The Horniman from the rear (park) side. The 1901 building is on the left. The end of the Architype building can just be seen on the right.

1.

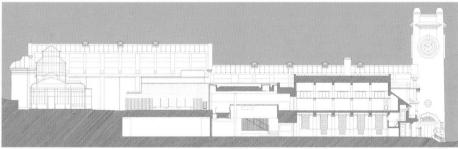

Below left: the street gable. Right: the rear, park, gable.

Below: the new hall

2.

Gallery Road, Dulwich Village, SE21
Rick Mather Architects, 2000
Rail: West Dulwich, North Dulwich

Dulwich Picture Gallery

A public picture gallery that is simultaneously a mausoleum for a painting collection's founding ménage a trois is surely a circumstance to which architectural talent must adapt itself. Dulwich Picture Gallery is a celebrated London landmark and was England's first public art gallery, designed and completed by one of its most famous and respected architects, Sir John Soane, between 1811-14. Given Soane's status, it is understandable that Rick Mather's recent extensions and alterations are sensitive, contextual, and respectful of what exists, complementing both Soane's work and the old Dulwich College buildings that form a back-drop to the Gallery.

Mather's design strategy at once leaves Soane's pavilion alone and stands back from it, whilst simultaneously entangling it in a new architectural composition that reaches out to the boundaries, engages the old Dulwich College buildings (especially the Christ's Chapel), the existing gateway and boundary brick walling, whilst introducing a new site concept focused upon the empty space between the buildings (in fact, a lawn) rather than the buildings themselves.

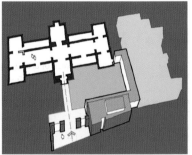

The built device that is employed is an old fashioned one: the idea of a cloister that wraps around the perimeter of the site, runs along the older College buildings and connects to the gallery pavilion (see plan below right). In fact, it is more of a 'half-cloister' because one half is implied rather than constructed. Nevertheless, it acts as a kind of tactful armature off which the other buildings hang, whilst the cloister itself provides an alternative means of access or egress to the gallery. A new café, new exhibition space and education rooms are neatly insinuated into and around this perimeter device. And as visitors perambulate this corridor they are given superbly framed views of the gallery building before they reach the side entry door to the gallery. This simple cloister / corridor becomes the key architectural piece binding the assembly of parts. But it is the green lawn – the void at the heart of this equation – that becomes the new spatial heart of the architectural parts. In this sense the idea of a cloister has been used cleverly and given its traditional role.

The older gallery spaces themselves have been entirely refurbished, the roof lights renewed etc.

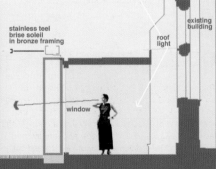

stainless teel brise soleil in bronze framing

existing building

roof light

window

The nucleus of the collection in the Dulwich Picture Gallery began when paintings were bequeathed to the College in 1626. These were added to in 1811, when more paintings were bequeathed by Sir Francis Bourgeois. He had been associated with a Mr & Mrs Desenfans, and the latter collaborated with the College in commissioning John Soane to design a picture gallery for the collection, together with an intended mausoleum for Bourgeois and both Desenfans. In addition, Soane was to design almshouses for six elderly women displaced by the new works. Soane's design - evidently constrained by economics – provides a sequence of five, top-lit gallery rooms arranged on a long axis (three square in plan and two oblong).

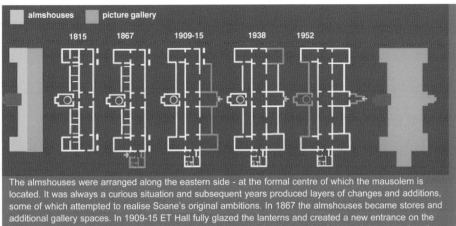

almshouses **picture gallery**

1815   1867   1909-15   1938   1952

The almshouses were arranged along the eastern side - at the formal centre of which the mausolem is located. It was always a curious situation and subsequent years produced layers of changes and additions, some of which attempted to realise Soane's original ambitions. In 1867 the almshouses became stores and additional gallery spaces. In 1909-15 ET Hall fully glazed the lanterns and created a new entrance on the south side. In 1937-8, H S Goodhart-Rendel provided an additional room that balanced the west elevation and later became lavatories (recently altered again). In 1944, severe bomb damage to the east and the mausoleum was repaired and a new porch - designed by Austin Vernon & Partners - was added to the west side.

Band stand

3.

This is one of the better examples of architectural design in London – a witty, considered exercise in using Corten steel to blend the accommodation and protective/sound reflecting structure of this moated, summer band 'platform' into the landscaping of the park. It is redolent with C18 landscaping values and also references to Richard Serra's work, but it has an almost abstract, quality, as if Ritchie had produced the simplest diagram possible and built it (a diagram for a presentational platform, protected against vandals, with massive, built-in electronic acoustic support, principally from two speaker towers at either side of the platform). It is at once sculptural and practical, heroic and intimate. But try and see it on a summer's day, when a band is playing.

Band Stand, Crystal Palace Park, SE26
Ian Ritchie Architects, 1997
Train: Crystal Palace.

Goldsmith's Library

4.

This is a simple, direct building of 1,500 sq.m. of accommodation. Internally, it is designed with economy and offers exposed concrete surfaces and natural ventilation to the users. Externally, it has a long, robust facade coping with the orientation and a busy road outside. The large fins are solar protection and stiffening for the glazing, but also lend image-quality to the building. As always, the design is elegant and well composed – the work of a firm who will probably be around long after more strident and fashionable firms have come and gone.

Goldsmith's College, Lewisham Way, SE14
Allies and Morrison, 1997
Train: New Cross

5.

Peckham Hill Street, SE15
Alsop & Störmer, 2000
Train: Peckham Rye.

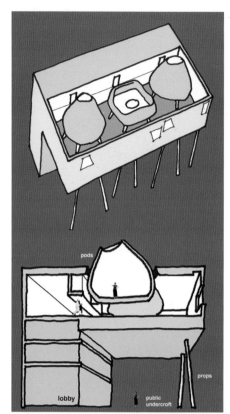

Peckham Library

Peckham Library has been a major success, but the building itself is simply one part of a larger story that embraces the initiatives of local planners (under Fred Manson, former Director of Regeneration) and the local Head of Library Services, Adrian Olsen, as well as the architects. The library building is the third part of a plaza that terminates a new urban park (Burgess Park) as it meets the local Peckham High Street, aiming to give civic dignity to the locale as well as useful places and spaces. Apart from the park itself, the first part of the equation was the arching shelter designed by Troughton McAslan - a gateway to the park, a place to linger, to protect market stalls, and an art-work in coloured lighting. The second built part was the Peckham Pulse, the local fitness centre. The third part is the Library. Together, they help to form component parts of a larger architecture aiming at urban renewal in what is has been (and mostly still is) a deprived and run-down part of London, currently experiencing 'gentrification' and the rising property prices that accompany major infrastuctural change (e.g. new rail links). The Library itself has been a significant success in social terms - a dimension of the project architectural magazines frequently neglect, but one that a visit will make self-evident. It is in this larger sense that the architectural design is all the more remarkable and unique, especially since it comes from the office of an architect's architect hardly known for community credentials. And, make no doubt, it is a terrific piece of architectural realisation: at once dramatic, economic and sensually rewarding. The Library stands together with a handful of other London building projects of the last ten to twenty years whose authenticity sets them apart.

The Library makes a number of simple and bold architectural moves from which subsidiary features are generated. Rather than nestling down snuggly into the ground, it rises up to stand tall above its surroundings. It then dares to locate its raison d'etre - the lending library - on an upper floor, requiring lift access. By doing this, the design realises a large open space at ground level that integrates itself to the adjacent plaza and also offers a massively protected area akin to standing within the giant orders of some neo-classical, pedimented portico (where people can meet, gather, trade, etc.). Alsop attempts to underscore this experience by wrapping a woven stainless steel mesh up the inner facade and across the underbelly of the library above. The job architect explained that, "We elevated the library above the ground so that it would be a little bit apart from the normal humdrum life of Peckham". (He might have added: a pretty lively and sometimes threatening 'humdrum'.) "People would come out of the lift and into another world. We wanted to reveal views of the city that people wouldn't have seen before. And we wanted the library to be like an attic, where people can concentrate without distractions". The exterior sports a large white 'Library' sign and the dark red prow of the roof-light roof (described by one critic as 'like a beret') - adding sculptural effect to the copper-clad L-shape of the main block. The rear of the block - facing north, over a large builder's yard and toward the not-so-distant towers of the

City - is glazed, using a pattern of differently coloured glass sheets that arguably enliven the interiors rather more than the urban context.

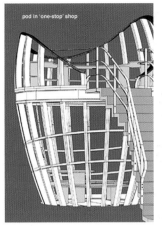

pod in 'one-stop' shop

5.

The Pods

Autonomously located within the overall Library building, the pods of Peckham Library are seriously fun elements that have attracted much attention: sexy as well as impossible to imagine, draw, detail or construct without the aid of computers, as well as occupying a place within fashions for 'blobby' architectural shapes. In reality, the pods are quite simple. They are constructed from pre-shaped timber ribs, assembled on site, clad in OSB (oriented strand board) and then clad in stained, thin, 1.5mm plywood sheets cleverly sized and arranged so as to overlap in a simple geometry that also accommodates the curves and takes up construction tolerances. Inside, the construction is lined with white painted board. They were apparently inspired by the work of the sculptor Richard Deacon, and the original intention was to use leather, but this proved too expensive. There is an office / interview room pod on the ground floor, study pods on one of the intermediate floors and three large 'pod rooms' within the main library hall, propped on concrete legs, each of them accessible from the upper gallery. Two of the library pods are fully enclosed and top-lit by roof-lights with internal 'butterfly' hinged louvres: shaped plywood panels that are operated by pulleys and small electric motors, so that a degree of black-out can be achieved - crude but effective. Fun has been had with some of the 'sculptural' light fittings that look as if they are giant 'Brillo' pads.

The central pod is open, like an egg with the top lopped off and it can be accessed directly from the library hall. Above it is a circular set of clearstorey lights raised above the ceiling level. (Whose roof features as a prow poking beyond the front facade.)

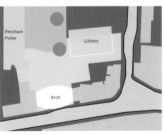

6. *Quay House by Ken Taylor (Kings Grove, SE15; 2002) is a builder's shed and yard converted into the architect's home, a studio for him and another for his partner, Julia Mannheim, together with street-frontage flats that are a fine example of how inventive architects can be in imaginatively transforming derelict sites. It's all very upbeat and cheerful, complete with bedrooms designed as first floor 'beach huts' and two mini-galleries on the street (M2 and 2M2, reflecting their sizes at one and two metre cubes). A good example of putting such things together.*

7.

Hester Road, SW11

Foster and Partners, 2003

Tube: Sloane Square

Albion Riverside

This shiny metal beast adjacent to the Foster studios is the same developer as Rogers' Montevetro scheme, on a possibly even better site. But this is more compact and sensuous, more formal and traditional in its relationship to the river, where a concave facade promotes more people in about 190 apartments having balconies and good views. The residential accommodation is raised up, with shops, restraurants and a gym at ground level (where arrangements even follow space syntax consultancy guidelines!). Every apartment was designed as a shell for adaptation to specific customer requirements.

8.

22 Hester Road, SW11

Foster and Partners, 1990

Tube: Sloane Square

Foster Studios

This has to be one of the most pleasant architectural studios in town: designed for London's most successful architect as a double-height space, 60m long and 24m wide, overlooking the river through a tall wall of glass and accessed by a long, slow stair that Alvar Aalto might have been proud of. The rest of the building is comparatively ordinary, built as speculative offices below and apartments above, in order to finance the development. Compare with the Rogers' riverside studio further west, at Hammersmith. The studio is often open during **London Open House**.

9.

Church Road, Battersea, SW11

Richard Rogers Partnership, 1999

Train: Clapham Junction

Montevetro

This rather controversial block (the name means 'glass mountain' and the neighbours were certainly intimidated by the very idea of it) is similar in concept to Cascades (CZWG): stepped apartment block with roof terraces and river views for all apartments. Sitting alongside St Mary Battersea (1777), the 103 units (including penthouse owned by Marco Goldschmied, a RRP partner) are organised as a slim block divided into five parts, with access towers on the land side and full views on the river side. A key aesthetic device is the use of terra-cotta cladding, first used by Renzo Piano on apartments in Paris, and now a proprietory system. The great irony of this private, gated community is that it should come from Lord Rogers of Riverside, left-wing promoter of popular causes. You can't get in, but don't worry: you can intrude from the river side.

Gwynne Road

10.

2–4 Gwynne Road, SW11
Walter Menteth Architects, 1999
Train: Clapham Junction

Around the corner from the luxury of Montevetro is this housing association design that sparkles like a Mediterranean jewel transported to south London. Eight units are gathered together into a garden pavilion beside the railway line, surrounded by 500 mm 'gabion' walls (dry-stone encased in mesh). White walls are played off against bright colours and slim aluminium window details. It is simple, cheap and cheerful, formal whilst still domestic, considerate and sensitive to both client and users. If only London had more like it . . .

Menteth has designed another housing scheme in **Holcroft Road**, *Hackney (1994). It features a superb entrance stair that had a large hanging fabric screen – cut down by a tenant who complained it was stopping the sun getting to the potted plants placed outside his front door!*

Pawson House

11.

82 Arthur Road, SW19
Terry Pawson Architects, 2002
Tube: Wimbledon Park

Pawson's house is a delightful, robust addtition to just another inter-war London surburbia of semi-d's - truly an 'ornament' to Wimbledon. He makes the most of the narrow, sloping site and provides a fitting end to the street and a most elegant plan (which he describes, enigmatically, as 'a modern reworking of Sir John Soane's terrace in Lincoln's Inn Fields' (meaning a series of inter-locked volumes that play with perceptions of space, compressing and then opening out in unexpected directions to create a sequence of changing and ambiguous volumes). At 5m (one room) wide and 80m long, the house has a concrete substructure, with timber framed and clad tower, and steel framed rear section clad in engineering brick. The rear is has a vaulted and grassed roof, with a fully glazed end, opening out into the garden.

12.

Beddington, Sutton (A237, Hackbridge)
Bill Dunster Architects, 2002
Train: Hackbridge; Mitcham Junction tramlink

BedZed

They're not much greener than this: an impressive 'zero-energy' development on a 'brownfield' site (a former sewage works), providing 82 dwellings in a mix of flats, maisonettes and 'town houses', plus 2,500 sq.m. of workspace and community accommodation, including a health centre, cafe, nursery, etc. (Density is 187 people per hectare.) All this is set out in five long, south-facing rows of 3-storey buildings with narrow spaces between the rows (the 'gardens' have become 'sky gardens' on the south face; town houses have a small bridge to a roof-top garden on adjacent units, similar to the Branch Hill project). Walls are 300mm wide, stuffed with insulation; other construction is in concrete, bricks and blocks. Rainwater is used, baths are low-volume, toilets are double flush . . . and the entire scheme is served by a central heat and power plant. Nothing, it seems, has been overlooked in promoting a sustainable way of living (including schemes for community electric vehicles).

Wherever possible, natural, reused and local materials and contractors were employed - argued to increase local employment, cut down on transport costs, reduce pollution and reinforce local identity. (Grand claims crying out for justification, but BedZed takes itself very seriously e.g. everything is carefully researched and materials are sourced within a 35m radius.)

The roofs provide photovoltaic panels and are topped by cowls that scoop in fresh air and discharge used air (employing a heat-exchanger in the process - a functional but rather Mickey Mouse feature that proclaims the development's green credentials). This is, by the way, a Peabody Trust development and many of the houses are part-owned or rented.

Riverside offices

This large, speculative complex of offices (10,000 sq.m.), apartments and shops is a skilfully designed exercise in the picturesque wrapping of the ostensibly unacceptable commercial realities that lie within. Terry attempts to disguise a larger truth as an organic aggregation off small, Georgian buildings (parts of which are actually genuine). Criticism of this masterful deceit has been strong, but Terry has at least (unknowingly and against his inclination, one suspects) bridged the gap between popular enthusiasms and office practises. Such architectural packaging raises questions concerning our appetites for both theming and truthfulness, and the boundaries at which a lack of authenticity becomes architecturally unacceptable. Still, it's good theatre and Ron Herron of Archigram would have appreciated it.

13.

Hill Street/Bridge Street, Richmond
Erith and Terry, 1986-88
Tube: Richmond

14. *The original church of **St Mary's**, Barnes, in Church Road, SW3, suffered arson damage in 1978 and Edward Cullinan gave it a new architecture as well as a new, complex roof and extensions in a vaguely ad hoc, Arts & Crafts manner so typical of his work. Although the church's original architecture was reformed, the best of the historic fabric was retained in a design process closely involving the local community. The aim was to produce a space for congregation and worship that could continue the tradition established on the site in the eleventh century, but without pastiche.*

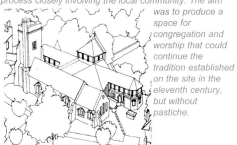

15. ***The Charles Cryer Studio Theatre*** *by Edward Cullinan (1991), in the High Street, Carshalton, should have been a celebrated building, but it had an unfortunate project history that dragged it out and got bogged down in changes. But you just have to look at the engaging way Cullinan has handled the problem of adapting an old theatre and transforming it into a new work of architecture to get a feel for just how well things might have worked out. It is a 'might have been', but well worth a look if you're this far south.*

Some others places to go out west:

16. *The **Palm House** at Kew was designed by Decimus Burton (1844-48) and is a marvellous iron and glass structure in the Royal Botanic Gardens.*

17. ***Hampton Court Palace**, East Moseley, 1514–1882. Work by Wren and William Kent. Train to Hampton Court.*

18. ***Chiswick House**, Hogarth Lane and Burlington Lane, W4, designed by Lord Burlington (1725–29), who did Burlington House and inspired by Palladio's Villa Rotonda.*

19. ***Syon House**, London Road, Brentford. Internal remodelling by Robert Adam (1761–68).*

20. ***Osterley Park**, Isleworth. Another remodelling by Robert Adam (1763–67), this time of the entire house.*

21.

Tite Street, SW3
Tony Fretton Architects, 2002
Tube: Sloane Square

Red House

Not your average house, but a design for an art collector within the more than average affluence of Chelsea. The design is mindful of the street history and plays contextural games that politely front an interior arrangement that is distinctly pre-WWII: an entrance to the left for staff, a car bay in the centre and the owner's entrance on the right (compare with Goldfinger's house). The double height *piano nobile* ('salon') echoes the traditions of the Georgian London terrace house, but is clearly for entertainment, with a 'small living room' to one side and a concealed mezzanine library above. An attic storey is set behind a parapet - a retreat for hedonistic pleasures, with guest bedrooms and an outdoor 'tropical hot-tub' with planted courtyard. All this is faced in a sensuous red limestone. The interior rooms were worked on with Mark Pimlott.

22.

60 Sloane Avenue, SW3
YRM Stanton Williams, 1994
Tube: South Kensington.

60 Sloane Street

This was Stanton Williams's first major job (assisted by YRM). The challenge was to convert and extend an existing 1911 building of some character. The outcome is an elegant marriage of old and new, the latter betraying distinctly Catalonian architectural traits as it marries itself to the older 5 storey block and integrates itself behind and above the two-storey wing, as if the old facade had been 'peeled back'. Retail content on the ground floor is about 3,350 sq.m. and the offices above comprise about 7,150 sq.m.

23. *Wild at Heart (49 Ledbury Road, W11; Future Systems) is a 1997 Future Systems design that makes the most out of a small commission in a Notting Hill street serving a local community. The facade treatment is one, large sheet of glass, partly screen-printed to offer a beautiful, curved 1960s shape, penetrated by a central door accessed from the obligatory FS aluminium stepped ramp. It's a cool design, carried through into the interior as smooth curves and a sexy, red, built-in seat. But it is also a peculiar, guillotined separation of inside and out that denies context (one wonders what Terence Conran would*

*have done – you might groan, but that's a serious question). A more recent shop by FS is **Marni** in Sloane Street.*

24. *The mosaic wrapped **Ismaili Centre** near South Kensington station (Cromwell Gardens, SW7; Casson Condor, 1983) is an unusual piece of Modernism in the Islamic tradition - sounds awful, but it's actually very good and in no way a pastiche of anything. It sits as an island, scaled to nearby houses, chamfered to give them daylight, with a top floor garden, with escape stairs at each corner (see Foster's 10 Gresham Street for a larger, office version of the same format) and the content of the design strives for an Islamic spirit without obvious quotation.*

Imperial College

There are two buildings to see on this densely packed, urban campus: Sir Norman Foster's **Alexander Fleming Building** (1999; for medical and biological work), and John McAslan's extension to **Imperial College Library** (1998). The former is an independent, new atrium building, whilst the latter is an extension to a 1960's building by Norman & Dawborn. Both face onto the central quadrangle of the College overlooked by Thomas Edward Collcut's 85m tall Queen's Tower (1887–93). Both buildings are straight-forward, but McAslan's two-storey roof extension (totalling about 4,500 sq.m.) works superbly well with the entirely different base it sits upon. Externally, Foster's team employs brickwork and Portland stone as well as the usual glass and metal; internally, their design makes great use of daylight to the atrium, and even throws in strong colour to complement the more common Hi-tech palette of grey and blue.

25.

Exhibition Road, SW7
Foster and Partners / John McAslan, 2000/1998
Tube: South Kensington

26. *If you are interested in hospital design you'll find food for thought at the **Chelsea & Westminster Hospital**, designed by Sheppard Robson in 1993, in Fulham Road, SW6. Other people might find the art and emphasis upon designer features too much to take, but there are some impressive and expansive features to this National Health System facility. It is getting rather tatty at the edges and its exterior is a strong effort to put you off, but the internal public atria spaces (with their inflated plastic cushion roofing panels) work hard to dispel the tradition of Victorian hospitals.*

27. *John Miller's work at the **Serpentine Gallery**, a 1934 building in Kensington Gardens, Hyde Park, leaves the building looking outwardly the same, but inwardly totally changed (1997). Ad hoc arrangements have been replaced and reorganised, together with air conditioning, louvres to roof-lights, etc., including a shop and education room as well as the galleries themselves. It is an artful piece of work that stays in the background – both its strength and weakness. You can compare it with Miller's work at the Whitechapel Gallery, at Aldgate. Recent summers have seen a series of excellent 'garden pavilions' designed to front the gallery (by Hadid, Libeskind, and Ito)*

28.

Science Museum, Exhibition Road, SW7
MacCormac Jamieson Prichard, 2000
Tube: South Kensington

Wellcome Wing

Deep within the Science Museum, strapped onto its rear end, sits a huge, galleried hall loaded with technology and bathed in blue light. The lighting serves to add drama to the content whilst simultaneously disguising a monumental architectural equation that harks back to 1960's notions of infrastructure and changeable parts floating within it. The former comprises a massive, acrobatic structure and a differentiation of parts, together with exposed services; the latter is a dazzling whizz-bang-press-button set of displays designed to entertain and inform. In principle, the design is quite simple. One has to imagine a gigantic, inverted 'U' shape - this is the side-wall structure and roof. Hung within the inner space is a set of galleries ('trays') that carry the displays and the underbelly of an Imax Theatre with escalators that ride people up into it like something out of a 1930's futuristic movie.

The far end is fully glazed, but obscured to give a hint of the outside but deny daylight any entry. Visitors enter at the opposite open end from the older Science Museum gallery spaces. The wrapping structure is clearly derived from Foster's Sainsbury building in East Anglia: a form of infrastructure that keeps out the weather and whose side wings bear within them toilets, ducts, escape stairs and the like. The infrastructure concept also facilitates the series of galleries (or 'trays') that are slung across the inner space on 'gerberette' column and beams conceptually derived from Rogers' Lloyd's building; these carry the ducted service and cable trays, and have a grille ceiling exposing everything to view (a celebration of the architectural technology). The tall, fully glazed end-wall is a virtuoso exercise of layering that gives a dim view out and awareness of external life whilst admitting a mere 4% daylight.

The exhibits include a series of aluminium pods and all kinds of sophisticated 'interactive' displays that, unlike those at many venues, actually work. A cafe designed by Wilkinson Eyre is on the ground level.

It's rather impressive, the detailing is well considered and the lighting is amazing, although all that artificial blue makes one desperate for normal daylight after a while!

Museum Land

29.

Cromwell Road, Exhibition Road, SW7
Various, 1991–2002
Tube: South Kensington

Alfred Waterhouse's **Natural History Museum** (1873–81) includes two contemporary designs worth searching out: Ian Ritchie's **Ecology Gallery** (1991) and the late Ron Herron's dramatic, stainless steel, structural insertions into the **Dinosaur Gallery** (1992). Ritchie offers an intriguing mall lined in glowing glass and crossed by zoomorphic bridges. Herron's work is especially clever, installing a spinal armature that weaves between the existing columns and is immediately in tune with the subject. 2002 saw the opening of the **Darwin Centre** - a zoology research and storage centre with a collection of some 14m soft-bodied sea creatures housed in ethanol, designed by HOK. The **Science Museum** has two pieces of contemporary design to see: Ben Kelly's basement **Children's Gallery** (brash, cheerful, direct – a successful design); and an 'interactive' **bridge** designed by Chris Wilkinson with Whitby & Bird, meant to demonstrate stresses with sounds and lights (it is a nice bridge design but less successful as something meaningfully interactive).

Lavatory & shop

30.

Colville Road/ Westbourne Grove, W11
CZWG, 1993
Tube: Westbourne Grove/Notting Hill

Perhaps this triangular building, built on the foundations of a Victorian lavatory, is one of the best things CZWG have designed – at once utilitarian, cheerful and frivolous. It is a poised, single-storey design that is simple and makes you glad it is there – not the easiest thing to achieve and something that encouraged a lot of community support against a local authority alternative (including a large donation from a local resident). As with most CZWG buildings, don't expect any internal surprises but (after relief in the lavatory) enjoy the flowers, the polycarbonate projecting canopy, the turquoise glazed bricks and the big clock.

31.

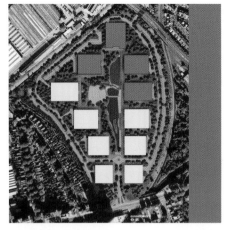

566 Chiswick High Rd, W4
Richard Rogers Partnership, 2000
Tube: Gunnersbury

Chiswick Business Park

CBP is a new generation Stockley Park: more dense and urban (4 stories instead of 2 or 3), characterised by a lean budget that makes the achievements of the Rogers' team all the more remarkable. To get there (keenly encouraged by the demands of Stanhope's, the client), they honed the design equation to a simple set of architectural parts that, nevertheless, look expensive. The 1.5m gridded geomerty is as compact as it comes, the frame is concrete, with post-tensioned floors and plenum access floors; the cladding is mostly glass, screened by high level louvres, access walkways and fire escapes. Net to gross is 87%. Parking is below. Go there and keep telling yourself this was low cost, shed construction. You won't believe it.

The eleven buildings (first phase in yellow) are set around an artificial lake, on what used to be a large bus garage site. cars under the buildings on a site easily accessible by public transport adds to the more urbane character of the place.

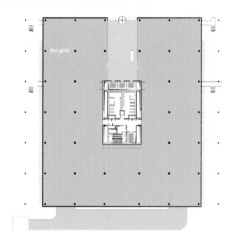

32.

Rainville Road, W6
Lifschutz Davidson & RRP, 1984
Tube: Hammersmith

Rogers' studio

The Rogers' studio is a part of a small complex of buildings. There are three things to see (and do) here:
• See the barrel-vaulted **Rogers' studio**, converted from an existing 1950's brick and concrete warehouse. Other accommodation nearby is rented out to creative trades.
• See the adjacent brick buildings of **apartments** with huge, slung balconies facing onto the river. They include the 'Deckhouse' designed by John Young, Rogers' partner as the ultimate in bachelor pads; look for a glass block bathroom tower on the roof. The riverside is the most dramatic facade.
• Enjoy the (expensive) **River Cafe** (run by Rogers' wife Ruth, together with Rose Gray), located in an adjacent building facing toward the river.

The latter you can do any time; the former two events are usually open during **London Open House**.

The Ark

33.

Talgarth Road, W6
Ralph Erskine, 1992
Tube: Hammersmith

This idiosyncratic, dark, brooding lump serves as a gateway to London as visitors arrive from Heathrow. The exterior might have been even more interesting if the colouring had been different (brown glass of a complex geometry and copper spandrel panels that resist going green), so one has to wait for the breath-taking effects inside: white, airy, light, soaring and exhilarating spaces topped by a huge Douglas Fir ceiling. The heart is an atrium filled with meeting structures inspired by Italian hill villages (corny, but very effective). Around this are stepped, open office galleries. Scenic lifts glide up and down and disappear into the roof, where they pop out to an upper level viewing gallery which offers amazing views over London.

In terms of the stock of office buildings in London, the Ark is hugely significant, breaking conventions and demonstrating alternative possibilities. That was the theory and is the reality, but its curved floor plates were not the rectangles your average agent or facility manager is used to and the building took a long time to find its tenant.

Doctors' Surgery

34.

Hammersmith Bridge Road / Worlidge Street., W6
Guy Greenfield Architects, 2001
Tube: Hammersmith

The planners wanted this doctors' surgery in Hammersmith, tucked under the principal road out to Heathrow, be be a 'landmark' building and were delivered this frontage of tall white, insulating screens to internal corridors serving the accomodation in a two-storey building. The result is a unexpectedly calm interior with top-lighting and slotted views out to the mundane drama of traffic jams. The corridors give accesss to the

medical and other rooms overlooking a courtyard well screened froom the noise and business outside.

35.

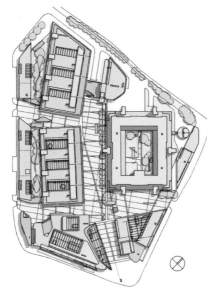

Wood Lane, W12

Allies and Morrison, 2003

Tube: White City

BBC White City

The White City project has the BBC remoulding the city as well as programming much of the media we consume. The first stage of this large complex (mid-2003) will provide some 50,000 sq.m. of offices and production space set out as 18m deep floor plates divided by lively atria and set above a ground level of shops, cafes and restaurants (arrangements in the atria described by the architects as 'provocative, encouraging informal communication between departments'). To mediate the scale of it all with the surrounding urban fabric, perimeter blocks of a different scale have been introduced. Considerately, these also present their fronts to the street, enlivening the streets whilst lending them continuity and a positive relationship to existing residential buildings.

Within the site, the instrumental regularity of the blocks engenders a network of pedestrian, landscaped routes and gardens between the individual buildings (designed by Christopher Bradley-Hole). The facades facing onto these places are enlivened by a colour programme for shutters designed by Yuko Shiraishi; in addition, Tim Head has created a light projection 'piece' visible from the adjacent major highwway (the A40).

36. *The **Putney Bridge Restaurant** building (Embankment, Lower Richmond Road, SW15) is by Paskin Kyriakides (1997) and is a welcome addition to the riverside scenary around here (a good place to go at Boat Race time).*

Heathrow

A number of buildings and developments cluster around Heathrow Airport. Stockley Park is the largest and most successful of the business parks. The World Business Centre is smaller, but the logic is the same. Bedfont Lakes is a mix, part of it being custom-designed for IBM. By the time we get to the British Airways complex, we are at a fully custom-designed office building that is an autonomous world in itself. In between these are buildings like the Compass Centre designed for BA flight crews, the Hilton Hotel, designed for weary travellers who can't be bothered to get into town, and a Visitors Centre intended to keep the tourists outside of the airport perimeter. It is all a part of the vast complex that, together with the M25 and the motorway links, helps to make Heathrow into London's current port. Ironically, midst all the intentional and carefully marketed design, the airport itself is a wonderful conglomeration of unsanitised, historical ad hocism – which is what many people love about the place. Note that all these buildings are best accessed by road transport and that office interiors are almost invariably the private realms of tenants worried about security – access beyond the lobby will be difficult unless it is a public building (as the BA Visitors Centre) or you have made arrangements to visit.

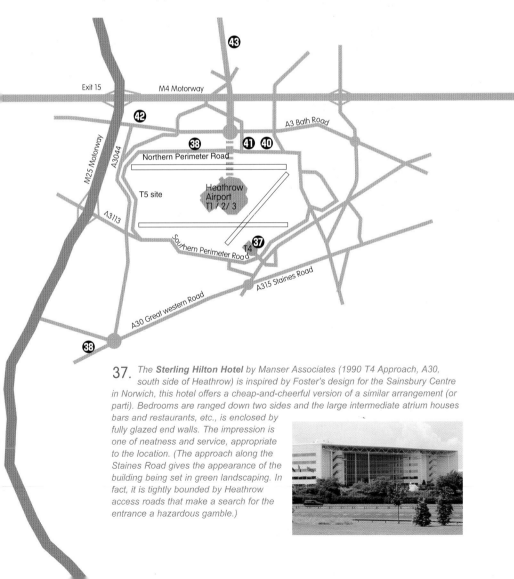

37. *The **Sterling Hilton Hotel** by Manser Associates (1990 T4 Approach, A30, south side of Heathrow) is inspired by Foster's design for the Sainsbury Centre in Norwich, this hotel offers a cheap-and-cheerful version of a similar arrangement (or parti). Bedrooms are ranged down two sides and the large intermediate atrium houses bars and restaurants, etc., is enclosed by fully glazed end walls. The impression is one of neatness and service, appropriate to the location. (The approach along the Staines Road gives the appearance of the building being set in green landscaping. In fact, it is tightly bounded by Heathrow access roads that make a search for the entrance a hazardous gamble.)*

38.

New Square, Bedfont Lakes, Staines Road (A30), south west corner of Heathrow Airport. Michael Hopkins & Partners, 1992

Bedfont Lakes

There are two buildings to see at this office park designed as a set of blocks around a square that might be in Holborn: Ted Cullinan's somewhat less attractive venture into speculative offices; and Sir Michael Hopkins' more than successful exercises for IBM (with, one suspects, a nod toward the 1960's YRM black, steel-framed Cargo Agent's building on the Southern Perimeter Road).

39.

BA Compass Centre, North Perimeter Road, Heathrow Airport
Nicholas Grimshaw and Partners, 1994.

Compass Centre

The interior of the Compass Centre serves air crews 24 hours a day, seven days a week; a facility where operators track planes around the world whilst disoriented crews refresh themselves and get their briefings. The deep interiors (45m face to face, including small atria) feel tight and effective – one of the few buildings where the life of the inhabitants is truly demanding and dynamic, well served by the two accommodation wings either side of a central atrium space. The peculiar facade is meant to diminish the building's radar 'shadow', but the form is similar to another building by Grimshaw and one is suspicious of such a rationale. The interior fit-out, serving 850 employees and about 200 flight crews passing through each day, was by Auckett.

40. *The **World Business Centre** (Bennetts Associates, 1997) is a pair of office buildings facing the runways of Heathrow: architecture as generic building type, costs cut to the bone, generic tenant types offered generic fit-out packages. However, many conventional wisdoms are thrown away in favour of one, major selling point: the impressive view of aircraft landing and taking off. The emphasis is entirely frontal; the south-facing glass facade is kinked inward, dressed in large anti-sun louvres and generally given a confident air. That the landlords can throw aside the facility manager's instrumental mind-set in favour of 'kerb appeal' says volumes about what really matters.*

41. *The **BA Visitors' Centre** (Bath Road, next to the Ramada Hotel; Bennetts Associates, 1995) is a 1650 sq.m. building serving as a public relations facility for Heathrow Airport's management. It enables them to allow tourists to see planes coming and going, to display and lobby for schemes such as the Richard Rogers' design for a new Terminal 5, and to provide some facilities for the local community. Bennetts have provided a strong and simple architectural diagram for the clients to fit out – a central hall between parallel zones on the Bath Road and the Heathrow side respectively. But where the architect leaves off, comparative banality sets in at the level of exhibition design – a recurring problem with latterday procurement policies that split form and content.*

Waterside

This is the office as house of a large corporate family wearing security badges – an independent, autonomous and self-sufficient place referring to a global community. The design is the sibling of a similar building in Stockholm, both of them being a village of office pavilions strung along a shared mall. They are both impressive, but the BA building takes the conversation further, integrating the spatial concepts into contemporary strategies of space-time management, non-territorial working patterns, cultivated cafe-work, and similar themes that make up a latterday theory of office practices. The central street is a huge success and a place whose ambience only the Ark, in Hammersmith, can compete with. However, the interiors of the office pavilions leave something to be desired and are not so radical. On the outside, design excellence continues in the form of extensive landscaping whose idyllic qualities are only disturbed (not inappropriately) by the roar of aeroplanes taking off.

42.

Harmondsworth (off the A4/Bath Road)
Take exit 14 on the M25
Niels Torp Architects, 1998

Stockley Park
sanitised arcadia

Stockley is a successful '80s business park on the northern edge of Heathrow. DEGW did the research and briefing; Arup Associates were the master planners and the architects for many of the early buildings in a place where issues of typology loom large within an equation of two-storey development and 25% ground coverage. SOM have buildings on the west side of the scheme; Foster, Troughton McAslan, Ian Ritchie, Geoffrey Darke, and Eric Parry have buildings on the east side. Everyone struggled with the same developer constraints that offered tenants a carefully structured, shell-and-core option. This strategy culminates in recent Arup buildings at the western edge, where ingenious geometrical variations strive to creatively cope with the realities of architecture as a building type set within a landscape that is the undoubted feature lending the place its character of acceptability. And this is the real, hidden achievement: the reclamation of a heavily polluted area of land and its transformation into the business park and a local authority golf course to the north. Ducks and flowers flourish above the barriers that keep a frightening toxicity at bay. It's a beautiful place where people bring the kids on Sunday to feed ducks and carp. But it is also a place where buildings hide behind bushes, globalised tenants identified only by discrete signs labelled with acronyms and offering instructions with regard to acceptable behaviour. Luxuriant nature hides security cameras and the stealth of guards who slowly cruise in neo-military vehicles looking for those 'who don't belong'. The entertainment of sanitised landscape beauty lulls the mind into contentment and the illusion that all is well in the world. Somehow, even the dull, constant background sound of aeroplanes is comforting. It is very clever, very modern, very strange ...

43.

Furzeground Way, Hillingdon (North side of Heathrow Airport)
Various architects, 1990–2000

Population

In 1100, at the time of the Norman conquest, the population of London was only about 15,000, but growing to about 80,000 two hundred years later. By 1600 it had grown to 200,000 and by the time of the Great Fire in 1666 had expanded to 375,000 - by then a European curiousity divided into three areas: the historic City; a suburban development that stretched along the Fleet Street / Strand axis to Westminster; and outlying areas of market gardens and the like to the north, east and south of the Thames in Southwark (an area that the Commonwealth defenses had enclosed between 1643-47). Foreign visitors would remark upon a curious 'vertical living', like so many birds in a cage and it was at this time that speculative developments established the novel idea of architectural 'regularity' and the brick terrace house in a typological form that even influenced the 1920's semi-detached suburban house. London was already a smokey, insanitary, industrial place.

The late John Summerson described an air-view from 1615 as follows: *Below us is the constant ribbon of the Thames. . . London is one of its shallower curves, a tesselation of red roofs pricked with plots of green and the merlon-shadowed patches which are the lead roofs of churches. Within the blurred margin, the line of the ancient wall takes the eye . . . Away to the west, clearly separate, is Westminster. The abbey church and the cloister are distinct . . Round them is a red-roofed colony, less compact, less imposing, and much smaller than London. . . . Between London and Westminster a line of buildings fringes the river - the palaces along the Strand . . . like Oxford colleges . . . whose great highway and approach is the river itself. . . Within a few years two great rectangles crystallise north of the Strand, in Covent Garden and the fields of Lincoln's Inn; and the houses around them are conspicuous by trim discipline - uniform, ungabled fronts.*

And of the post-1666 developments he says: *Long before the charred patch* [of the Great Fire] *glows again with fresh brickwork there is commotion in the west. The streets around Lincoln's Inn, Covent Garden, and St James' fill up with houses. Squares spring into being in Gray's Inn Fields and Soho, and packed streets close in upon them; new streets shoot northwards, eastwards and westwards.*

After 1720 Summerson comments: *We notice the shabby gabled streets in the inner west end slowly yielding to neatly parapeted rows . . . now the brickwork tends to be grey and brown rather than red. Whitehall becomes truer to the colour of its name, the slow operations for a new bridge are seen at Westminster.* But someone at the top of St Paul's Cathedral would still (on a clear day) have been able to see the entire city.

Between 1700 and 1750 the population rose from 674,500 to 676,750. But by 1801 the population was around 0.9-1.1m, most of them living in terraced housing, many in the fashionable 'Georgian' squares and terraces of west London. The city was rich, powerful and sprawling. By 1831 the population was 1.66m and in 1861 it was 3.323m and the railways were extending the urban area ever outward.

About this period Summerson comments: *1801-3 coincides with the making of the first docks . . . to the dock area come line upon line of brown cottage streets, each carrying the east-end invasion further towards the Essex fields. . . . [T]he perimeter of London has been moving at a ramping, devouring pace. Every outward road, now, is lined with terraces and villas. In the wedges of country between, streets and squares are filling in. London's satellite villages are villages no longer: Hackney, Islington, Paddington, Fulham, and Chelsea are suburbs. . . . [C]an London still grow- and yet be a humane city? . . . The Victorian age provides an answer. Iron fingers point to the stucco terraces in Euston Square, to the fields of Paddington, to Bishopsgate and Southwark.*

By 1921 the population was 7.5m, split between central terraces and apartments, and the new suburbs of detached and semi-detached villas served by rail and road networks. By 1951, it was 8.2m, but by this time the definition of London was increasingly blurred and confused by extensive suburbanisation served by rail and road networks (the peak population was reached in 1939, at 8.6m). London was now an extensive south-east region in which outer residential areas were separated from the heartland ('Greater London') by a 'green belt' where development was not permitted. In 1965 administration of this area was taken over by the Greater London Authority (GLC), later removed by Thatcher's government in 1986. It was not until 2001 that London had its own Mayor and Greater London Authority.

Building Materials

Before the Great Fire of 1666 and subsequent building regulations that sought to reduce fire risk, most buildings were of timber. After that time, new building regulations ensured that the common materials were brick, stone, clay and slate roof tiles. Yellow 'stock' bricks, white Portland stone, and grey slate roof tiles dominate much of the city, particularly for older buildings. The most characteristic building material in London is the London 'stock' brick, which is typically yellow. Originally, these were hand-made and came from the London area itself, with some supplies coming up the river from Kent. By the early C19 most sources had been expended but the new canal system (late C18) enabled the metropolis to be supplied from outlying areas - producing a proliferation of brickfields along the banks of the Grand Union Canal that led one commentator of 1811 to describe London as surrounded by a 'ring of fire'. By the 1840s and '50's machine-made bricks were being brought by rail from sources in the near Midlands (e.g. Bedfordshire). Portland stone comes from the Portland island off the south coast of Dorset and arrived in London up the Thames. In latter years, economic drives and new building regulations and their energy-saving aspirations have effectively superceded this older building tradition, reintroducing London to 'layered' constructions that use render and metal claddings, often offset against large areas of hi-tech glazing.

Architectural Periods and Styles
It may be imprudent, even potentially misleading, but it is also useful and convenient to divide London's architecture into a series of distinct periods:

Early
• **Roman -1615.** *Not much remains of this period, either before the Norman Conquest (symbolised by the Tower of London) apart from a few Roman remains and memories, for example near the Barbican and the Tower (and within quite a few City buildings, including the new ones for Merrill Lynch).*
Taste, Regularity and Romance
• **1615 - 1820:** from Inigo Jones' introduction of Palladianism as Surveyor to the King, to the Baroque of Wren, Hawksmoor, Gibbs et al, through another Palladian revival and a transformative period of 'Georgian' development characterised by the squares and terrace types developed in the late C17. The period - racked by religious dissent, revolution and rebellion - manifest the Industrial revolution and articulated notions of Beauty, the Sublime and the Picturesque, ending with the building of docks and warehouses, John Nash's work on Regent Street and Regent's Park, and Sir John Soane's house - perhaps a fitting private memorial to this remarkable period.
Tumult and Improvement
• **1820 - 1920:** a radical period characterised by stylistic battles that polarised the Greek with Gothic, the utilitarian with romantic, and populating inner London with endless rows of terrace housing and the first social housing developments, now served by new transport systems such as the train, the underground and the omnibus. The period saw the introduction of new building types and a fusion of architecture and engineering. (Although the highlight of the period was the great 1851 exhibition - much celebrated as one of the sources of modernism - some historians see it as the sunset of British engineering expertise.) Good neo-Gothic architecture is epitomised by William Butterfield's All Saints, Margaret Street and George Street's Law Courts in the Strand. The period ended with Empire bombast and the Germanic royal family adopting the English name of the House of Windsor, new sensibilities toward dying crafts and old buildings, and nostalgia for what became known as (an implicitly anti-Palladian and baroque) 'Wrenaissance', with many 'grand manner' buildings in the City.
Inbetweens
• **1920 - 1945**: an intermediate period between the wars when the instrumental values of the C19 were being translated into a new Modernism on the Continent, but with very little evidence in London (except for excellent fore-runners of what to was to come, such as Tecton's Finsbury Health Centre and Highpoint flats, and Erno Goldfinger's home in Hampstead). The alternative was perhaps epitomised by the work of Edwin Lutyens, now undertaking 'grand manner' commercial work rather than the country houses he became famous for in the period before WWI (e.g. Brittannic House in Moorgate and the Midland Bank HQ in Poultry).
Art Leading the Facts of Science
• **1945 - 70:** a time when art (as architecture) was attempting to lead the facts of science in the service of a progressive and optimistic Modernism that had caught up with influences from Scandinavia (Alvar Aalto), France (le Corbusier), and the USA (the Chicago of Mies, the New York of SOM, and the California of Charles and Ray Eames et al), much of it informing large urban redevelopment programmes (exemplified by the work of Camden's architects). Brutalism was discovered and Pop Art invented. The LCC's Royal Festival Hall is an outstanding building from the beginning of the period and Denys Lasdun's National Theatre of the end. Inbetween are iconic housing schemes such as the Brunswick Centre and Alexander Road.
Post-Modernism, Hi-tech and the Invisible hand
• **1970 - 90:** when socially oriented architectural programmes were withdrawn and commerical ones took over, culminating in the boom years of the '80's and the redevelopment of the former Docklands. Architectural 'post-modernism' arrived as a US import in the early 1970's to supplant an earlier socially-oriented modernism that had begun to adapt into Hi-tech (these two forming the major polarisation of the period, both fueled by City deregulation). Buildings by Terry Farrell (Embankment Place), Robert Venturi (Sainsbury Wing), Jim Stirling (Clore), and Richard Rogers (Lloyd's). Broadgate and Canary Wharf embody urban change. The stylistic battles (which had included a 'Deconstruction' conversation that hardly touched UK practice) died overnight in the 1990-94 recessionary period, with architects now reoriented toward continental rather than American values.
***Grand Projets* and community**
• **1990 - now:** a period dominated by millennium *'grand projets'* such as Richard Rogers' Dome, Herzog & de Meuron's Tate Modern and by a proliferation of projects from Norman Foster's office, as well as some outstanding stations on the Jubilee Line and many new commercial buildings that, in effect, continued the boom years of 1970-90 (at an end again by 2003). Canary Wharf strode into a second phase, the City continued to change and sought tall symbols of its success, the masses finally discovered architects, designers and modernist tastes whilst larger apartment blocks went up all over London (especially in Docklands; good examples include Albion and Montevetro), and some new, socially-oriented architecture was built (e.g. Peckham Library, Stratford Circus, Plashet School bridge, and the Laban Centre).